WOMEN IN THE CHURCH I

Madonna Kolbenschlag, Editor

The Pastoral Press
Washington, DC

The addresses presented in this collection were given at the Women in the Church Conference, Washington, D.C., October 10–12, 1986. The Pastoral Press expresses thanks to Time Consultants for assistance in making this volume possible.

ISBN: 0-912405-39-2

The Pastoral Press
225 Sheridan Street, NW
Washington, D.C. 20011
(202) 723–1254

The Pastoral Press is the Publications Division of the National Association of Pastoral Musicians, a membership organization of musicians and clergy dedicated to fostering the art of musical liturgy.

Printed in the United States of America

Contents

Introduction

Fifteen years ago no one could have imagined 2500 women and men coming together for a conference on Women in the Catholic Church—at least not for the kind of conference that generated the essays in this volume. In short, these contributions represent the keynote ideas in what theologian Hans Küng once called the "New Reformation." Above all, they represent the fruition of the seeds of human liberation that were firmly acknowledged and planted in the church's self-understanding at Vatican II.

In many significant ways Jesus Christ and the early Christian church were ahead of their times in their estimation and treatment of women. Unfortunately the modern Catholic Church is considerably behind the times in this regard—indeed, lagging behind many other Christian churches. The women and men speaking in this volume are among the most outstanding voices calling the church to fulfill the charter announced in Galatians: that in Christ Jesus there shall be neither Jew nor Greek, slave nor free citizen, male nor female. These voices call the church to conversion, to evangelize itself by recognizing and empowering the full dignity of women, made also in the image of God.

The agenda for the next council could easily be gleaned from these pages: theological, scriptural and canonical foundations; a developing ecclesiology that includes women; the scandal of sexism in liturgy and ministry, as well as in marriage; the call to conversion from patriarchy and clerical culture; the legitimate self-determination of individual women and of women's communities; the empowerment of the laity; a spirituality and strategy for change.

As one witness to these testimonies remarked, "movement" is no longer an adequate word to describe the currents that are flowing in the contemporary church. "Force," "energy," a state of dynamism now characterizes the growing prophetic edge of the U.S. church. Women, and the issues affecting women most directly, are the core of that growing edge.

The reader will find this volume a reasoned as well as passionate, provocative, and faith-filled introduction to the subject that will explicitly and implicitly shape the theological, ethical, and ecclesial discussions of the church of the 1990s—women.

Madonna Kolbenschlag
August 6, 1987

THE TRADITION

1

Roles of Women in Scripture: A Perspective from the Church's Universal Mission

Donald Senior

HOW TO CONSIDER THE "ROLES OF WOMEN IN SCRIPTURE," A SUBJECT as broad as the scope of biblical history and as varied as the biblical literature itself? One could run through the dramatis personae of the biblical story: the earth mother Eve, Sarah who laughed at God, the fierce warrior judge Deborah, the sophisticated Judith, Ruth among the alien corn and her mentor Naomi, the unyielding revolutionary mother in the book of Maccabees, the barren Hannah grieving at Shiloh. And of course the New Testament examples abound: Mary, at once mother of Jesus and his disciple, Martha, Mary Magdalene, and all those anonymous but crucial characters: the Samaritan woman at Jacob's well, the widow hefting her two last coins at the mite box in the temple, another widow with her hand on the coffin of her only son, a Greek woman pressing the reluctant Jewish healer on behalf of her sick daughter, the woman caressing Jesus' feet with her hair, and another breaking nard and anointing his head, women as his disciples and friends, women weeping for him, and women charged with his mission. Or one could catalogue Paul's vast network of women collaborators: Phoebe, Priscilla, Junia, Apphia, Nympha, Mary, Julia, and several others that Paul mentions by name.

This lists some of the people, of course, but not necessarily the roles: how would one catalogue them all—earth mother, matriarch, rulers, warriers, revolutionaries, prophetess, wife, temptress, missionary, leader of prayer, apostle, friend, and so on.

Enumerating, analysing, and interrelating these myriad characters and roles would, no doubt, be a worthwhile enterprise. Despite the patriarchal ethos of the biblical world, there is a significant number of women who exercised important roles throughout the Scriptures and that fact should not be forgotten. But I am not sure it would help us understand a lot better our theme of women in the church, and in any case my catalogue will go no further.

Instead I would like to look at the roles of women in the Scripture from a single entry point, seeking a basic perspective that might take us deep within the biblical world and give us some wisdom for the experience of the church and of women and men in that church today. Bear with me as I try to elaborate.

IMPULSES FOR RENEWAL IN BIBLICAL HISTORY

When we survey the sweep of biblical and church history we find that the impulses for transformation and renewal came not so often from within but from outside the church. Usually it was not Israel or the church that dictated or initiated the agenda of change; very often it was forces within culture or geography or the vaster stretches of Middle Eastern or Mediterranean politics that left their indelible marks on the course of biblical history.

The same is true for much of *church* history, including that of the past century. The abolition of slavery, the death of colonialism, the civil rights movement, various peace movements, feminism, are all significant nineteenth and twentieth century movements whose ultimate origin was a not an explicit resolution of the Christian churches. No doubt the values of Christianity had a significant part to play and often religiously motivated people played some key roles, but these revolutionary brews were mixed in culture and history and splashed upon the church, sometimes with startling surprise. Even the Second Vatican Council and its agenda, which owed much of its inspiration to the warm genius of John XXIII, was also made inevitable by the worldwide political, social, and cultural upheavals that came in the wake of World War II.

If the thesis about change coming from the outside is debatable in the case of recent church history it is, I submit, clear-cut in the case of the Bible. General migrations of peoples throughout the Middle East in search of food and stability brought Abraham to the land of Canaan, just as the same search would drive a later generation of Jews into Egypt. Slavery and intolerable economic conditions in Egypt fueled the exodus. And the threat of the powerful indigenous peoples merged a rag tag assembly of desert refugees into an urbanized hill country people. Later, in the days of Saul and David, the need for internal cohesion and pressure from surrounding populations would lead Israel to adopt a monarchy. Later the excesses of monarchical structures would fuel the prophetic movement, and the empire building of the Assyrians and Babylonians would alter the map and the self-image of Judaism forever. The threat of assimilation by Greek and then by Roman would set up the divisions and factions in Judaism that Jesus would contend with. And one could quite surely assert that Titus' destruction of the Jerusalem temple in 70 A.D. and the resulting transformation of first century Judaism would be a decisive influence on the Gentile mission of early Christianity. Thus biblical peoples derived their language, their culture, their political structure, and even much of their theology from their surrounding environment.

In reciting this list of secular events I am not for a moment contending that the contours of biblical history have been shaped apart from the action of God's Spirit. Just the opposite: it is to remind us that the Spirit of God is not confined to an explicitly religious agenda nor is the Spirit locked into the vestibule of the church. The Spirit blows where she wills and, in the case of biblical history, the Spirit has roamed freely in the world and its turbulent events. From the pain and conflict of its history and its interaction with Egyptian, Canaanite, Assyrian, Babylonian, Greek and Roman cultures were forged the most fundamental symbols of the Bible: exodus, covenant, monarchy, exile, diaspora, return to the land.

Thus one of the fundamental lessons of the Bible is that sacred history is not a sectarian affair. The church is not a helpless victim of history. The faith of Israel and its traditions, the faith of the early church and its own vital impulses were an essential component in turning secular event into sacred revealing moment. Yet the basic contention is true: for most of history, even when they may have thought they were acting on their own, the biblical peoples and the church were the recipients of vital impulses rather than the creators of them.

A second operating principle of biblical history is worth noting. Without attempting to be grim, it is very often pain and conflict that were the catalysts for change, as the wedge of transformation sliced into the conciousness of the biblical peoples: torn away from home, exile, the desert wanderings, the violence of conquest, the clash with a dominant culture, the destruction of the temple, the conflict between Jew and Gentile—these were the searing touchpoints signaling new moments in the history of God's people. For Christian revelation the axiom that new life springs from conflict and suffering has been lifted up through the cross of Jesus to be the central revelatory experience, giving form and validation to all others. From these experiences of pain could—it was not guaranteed—spring new life.

There is a third and final operating principle in the biblical drama. Note that these transforming moments in the history of the biblical peoples almost always had to do with Israel's and the early church's self-understanding as a community. Were they to remain a submerged people in the nineteenth dynasty of Egypt? Or were they called to be a people with their own history and destiny. Were they to remain nomads on the fringes of the Judean desert or would they risk being a landed people in the midst of Canaanite culture? Would they survive exile and assimilation in Babylonia or try to reconstruct a new people and a renewed identity? Would they be a swirl in Alexander's dream of Hellenism or could they be Jewish in a Greek speaking world?

This biblical dynamic of defining oneself over against a wider cultural and historical milieu accelerated in the New Testament context. This was due, I believe, not only to the increasing pressures of the Roman world empire but also because at the center of the preaching and ministry of Jesus was the question of Israel's self-definition in relation to the world. So the early church had to struggle with the question of whether the community would remain a sect within Judaism or would find a new mode of existence within the cosmopolitan world of the Roman Empire. It was shaken with conflict over the inclusion of Gentiles in the community and on what terms. These were not simply questions of membership or even of cultural adaptation. At stake were even more fundamental questions about the meaning of salvation, the nature of the human person, and, further still, the mystery of God's identity. What would the inclusion of the Gentiles and their experience into the covenant circle of Israel mean for the destiny of God's people? One could make the case that all of the struggles of Israel—the forging of the covenant, the search for integrity within its own political and social structures, its purifying prophetic movements and its constant internal battle over cultural assimilation—all of these merged and came to a definitive expression in the early community's grappling with a universal mission incorporating Jew and Gentile.

And it is precisely here, from the vantage point of this struggle over the meaning of the Gospel call to a universal mission, that I would like to consider the roles of women in Scripture, particularly in the New Testament. I am convinced that there is much wisdom to be learned from the biblical materials on mission as well as from the mission experience of the church in our modern era.

THE STRUGGLE TO BE UNIVERSAL AND THE ROLES OF WOMEN

The struggle of the early church to come to terms with the Gentile question fills the pages of the New Testament: the letters of Paul, the Four Gospels, Acts, and other New Testament texts focus on this issue. I do not intend to cover all this ground, obviously, but to select some texts that have special significance for the question at hand.

Stories of Inclusion and Healing

In the Gospels there are stories of Jesus' direct encounters with Gentiles, but these are relatively rare: the Roman Centurion, the Gadarene demoniac, a deaf-mute, the Syro-Phoenician woman of Tyre, the hungry crowds of the Decapolis. Even though found in different settings and at the service of each evangelist's theology, there is a common thread in these stories. In each the note of alienation between Jew and Greek is stressed: the Roman Centurion is hesitant that Jesus should have to come to his Gentile quarters (Mt 8:5–13); the Gadarene is demented and threatening and bears the name "Legion," a name filled with dread for an occupied population (Mk 5:1–20); the Gentile deaf-mute on the eastern side of the lake and the crowds of the Decapolis are encountered during a long journey outside the confines of Israel (Mk 7:31–8:10); and in the case of the Syro-Phonecian woman, not only her Greek origins but Jesus' own hesitations stress the chasm between Jew and Greek (Mk 7:24–30).

And in each case the alienation is bridged through an aggressive cry of pain: the deferential but urgent plea of the Centurion on behalf of his dying servant, the mortal degradation of the Gadarene—alone in his city of the dead, the hunger of the crowds, the assertive, fierce loyalty of the Greek woman on behalf of her sick daughter. And, finally, Jesus the healer matching the initiative of those in need by reaching across the chasm of culture and alienation and pain and drawing these Gentiles into the circle of the community. In the case of the Centurion it is clear that the inclusion and acceptance of such outsiders is a forecast of profound changes in store for the community, too: "Many will come from East and West and eat at Abraham's table. . ." (Mt 8:11).

But it is not just through stories about Gentiles that the Gospels validate the universal mission of the church. Alienation and pain, conflict, healing and inclusion—these elements found in the Gentile stories spill over into other passages of the Gospels that, I believe, were used by the early community in its struggle with the question of self-identity. Here the list must include Jesus' encounters with tax collectors and sinners, with the sick and disabled, and not least, with women.

In each category vivid examples come to mind. The call of Levi (or Matthew) the tax collector is not only a startling discipleship story in which a social and religious outcast is drawn into the heart of Jesus' community, but it develops into a full-blown conflict story in which Jesus defends his table-fellowship with such sinners as essential to his ministry of proclaiming the merciful reign of God (Mk 2:13–17). The God who comes to rule and transform Israel is proclaimed by Jesus as a God with an eye for the stray and the excluded. A God whose advent will be Good News for the poor and the oppressed. In effect, Jesus redefines the boundaries of the sacred and thereby challenges Israel to a new self-understanding—a fact that Jesus' opponents, the religious leaders, have not missed.

The healing of the man with the withered hand in the synagogue of Capernaum is not only a story of mercy; the location of the story on the Sabbath, in a synagogue, in full view of the religious leadership, turns it into a conflict story where once again the inclusion of those perceived as unwhole, as marginal redefines the meaning of the community of Israel (Mk 3:1–6).

It is in this context that many of Jesus' encounters with women fit. The encounter with the woman in Simon the Pharisee's house and Jesus' unquestioning acceptance of her spectacular and scandalous public affection—drying perfume from his feet with her hair—is more than a story of forgiveness; in the face of opposition from Jesus' Pharisee host it redefines the nature of God's rule into an inclusive feast where those branded as public sinners have full access (Lk 7:36–50). Many issues are pressed into the Johannine story of the Samaritan woman at the well, but the text itself makes clear that the scandal of Jesus' inclusion of a woman and a Samaritan—and the resulting impact on the self-definition of Israel—are at the heart of it (Jn 4:1–42).

Many of Jesus' encounters with women are in healing stories. The woman bent double made straight in the synagogue on the Sabbath over the protests of the synagogue manager (Lk 13:10–17); the woman with an twelve year flow of blood who dares to touch the rabbis' tassels in public (Mk 5:25–34); the Syro-Phonecian demanding healing for her daughter (Mk 7:24–30); Simon's mother in law lifted from her cot and her fever and restored to active service (Mk 1:29–31); Jairus' daughter caught in death as she reaches the age of puberty brought back to life (Mk 5:35–43). As in the case of most of the Gospel healing stories, the issues go far beyond physical cure. Life threatening illness or visible disability involve much more than a biological condition. There are the dynamics of exclusion and taboo; the fear of contact; the struggle for rehabilitation into the community. Listen to the experience of the disabled as they struggle for access, both physical and attitudinal; listen to the experience of those who have gone through life-threatening illness; listen to the experience of those who have been freed from addiction and work for rehabilitation and serenity. Authentic healing involves a process of liberation and redefinition, not only for the person who has moved from health to illness and on to rehabilitation, but also for the community of the "healthy" from which the sick or disabled were taken and to whom they now return in a new mode of being.

These dynamics must be kept in mind when screening the

stories of the Gospel. There is a thin and very permeable line between stories that deal with Jesus' acceptance of Gentiles into the horizon of his mission or those that deal with the struggle of the sick and disabled to have access, on the one hand, and stories of Jesus' encounters with women pushed beyond the margins of propriety and acceptance, on the other. In each instance the struggle involves a profound realignment of the community and a challenging transformation of its understanding of God and salvation.

The New Family of Jesus

The issue of inclusion is also played out in other kinds of New Testament texts which were connected to the early community's struggle with its mission to the Gentiles. Particularly important is the tension between family ties and discipleship ties, an aspect of the New Testament material highlighted in feminist studies of the Scriptures.

There are several significant Gospel passages where the demands and authority structures of the patriarchal family are subordinated to the egalitarian structures of the discipleship community. Access to the community of Jesus is not based on familial relationships but is accessible to all through faith. When Jesus' blood family demands that he come outside, Jesus looks around at his disciples seated before him and declares: "Who are my mother and my brothers? Here are my mother and my brothers! Whoever does the will of God is my brother, and sister, and mother." (Mk 3:33–34). A woman from the crowd acclaims Jesus' mother: "Blessed is the womb that bore you and the breasts that nursed you!" But in Jesus' response, the bonds of the family are downplayed in favor of discipleship ties: "Blessed rather are those who hear the word of God and keep it." (Lk 11:27–28). A similar motif underlies the Cana story in John's Gospel: Mary's approach as the mother of Jesus seems to be deflected—"What is there between you and me, Woman?" (Jn 2:4). Only at the hour of the cross, when she is joined with the Beloved Disciple in the new community of Jesus, is her full relationship with Jesus as a disciple revealed.

The discipleship sayings about leaving property and family ties and the warning about divisions in the family for the sake of the Gospel, point in the same direction. Acceptance of the

Rule of God brings a new alignment, not based on the patriarchal family but on a relationship of learners, disciples bound together with their Lord. The rewards of discipleship, significantly, include *no fathers:* "Truly I say to you, there is no one who has left house or brothers or sisters or mother or father or children or lands, for my sake and for the gospel, who will not receive a hundredfold now in this time, houses and brothers and sisters and mothers and children and lands, with persecutions, and in the age to come eternal life." (Mk 10:29–3). The community of Jesus is not built on the family structure. This is clear in the startling text of Matthew 23 where three strong hierarchical relationships (including familial ones)—rabbi, father, master—are sharply devalued: ". . . you are not to be called rabbi, for you have one teacher, and you are all brothers and sisters. And call no man your father on earth, for you have one Father, who is in heaven. Neither be called masters, for you have one master, the Christ." (Mt 23:8–10).

I have no doubt that an important reason for the retention of these traditions in the early church was the struggle over the Gentile mission. If membership and position in the community were based on kinship ties, then only those with the bloodlines of Judaism needed to apply. But access to the community of Jesus was based on discipleship, not kinship. So it was equally accessible to believing Jew or believing Gentile. But once again the issue was not merely membership. Implicit here is a profound vision of a union of mind and heart that transcended cultural and historical barriers, a vision rooted in the God of Jesus whose love bounded across deep cut canyons of alienation and estrangment. These texts, which may have originated as a guarantee against an ethnocentric vision of the community, also point to a deeper reality of the universal Gospel itself and form the taproot of an inclusive New Testament ecclesiology.

So the evidence, I believe, is clear. A strong current of inclusion runs through the New Testament. It breaks the surface in stories of healing, in Jesus' encounters with Gentiles, and in many of the stories involving women. It is also seen stirring when the Gospel communities offer glimpses of their ecclesiology: a community structure based not on blood lines and familiar authority structures, but on discipleship. The early church and the authors of the New Testament themselves did not find this vision incompatible with the assignment of role and office within the community, but it was a vision with which every ecclesial structure would have to be reconciled.

I have concentrated on the Gospels but the traditions also sweep into the letters of Paul and other New Testament texts. The formula of Galatians 3:28 "There is neither Jew nor Greek, there is neither slave nor free, there is neither male nor female; for you are all one in Christ Jesus" is a resounding affirmation of this same inclusive vision, one cutting across the boundaries of race, economic class, and gender. What Paul expresses in a theological formula is the same perspective the Gospels illustrate in the healing narratives. There are many other things in Paul to indicate it was not an idle ideal. Paul's own fierce commitment to the Gentile mission is his badge of credibility: membership in the community was not to be based on blood lines. The faith experience of the Gentiles, as he insists in Galatians 3:2, is fully valid on its own terms because it originates in the Spirit of God. It need not be subordinated to or filtered through the experience of Judaism.

We might also mention Paul's remarkably collaborative ministry. In Romans 16 we get a glimpse of Paul's network: Phoebe, his "co-worker," Prisca and Aquila, the couple who had founded the church of Corinth with Paul and therefore the ones he names his "fellow workers" and ones to whom Paul and all the Gentile churches owe gratitude, Mary "who has worked hard among the Roman church," Andronicus and Junia, another couple, whom Paul calls his "kinspeople . . . my fellow prisoners . . . noted apostles . . . and people who came to Christ before Paul," the "workers in the Lord," Tryphaena and Tryphosa, Julia one of the "saints." While Paul has often been typecast as the "lone ranger" apostle and something of a chauvinist, evidence of his extensive collaboration with women and men as co-workers in the mission belies such an image. In so working Paul was embodying the very Gospel of inclusion that he preached.

There are other texts to be cited, although time permits only a quick reference: in the Acts of the Apostles Luke's masterful portrayal of the early community as it toils to work out in history the inclusive mission Jesus had initiated. The staggering surprises that befall the community and its leadership as Samaritans, Ethiopian eunuchs, Antiochian Greeks and a Centurion from Caesarea all crash in upon a group of Palestinian Jewish Christians who not only did not expect them but were shocked at their arrival. There is also the lofty ecclesial vision of Ephesians which sees the reconciliation of Jew and Gentile in the church as the paradigm of its cosmic mission, a mission of reconciliation that not only brings disparate peoples into communion but even touches the warring elements of the universe, melding all into a triumphant harmony before God.

The case can be made—in much more detail than I have—that at the heart of the New Testament is the issue of the inclusive nature of God's reign. But the New Testament not only proclaims the ideals and dreams of the Gospel, it also warns us of the cost. Some of the warnings are explicit: found in the conflicts that dog Jesus' inclusive healings; in the chorus of opposition which follows his outreach to Gentiles, tax collectors, and women; in his clear warnings about division in the household and persecution that allegiance to the Gospel can provoke.

But other warnings are more subtle and must be discerned by the reader. Such is the case where the perceptive reader can see, even within the span of the New Testament, the inclusive vision of the Gospel crashing upon the rock strewn shore of other deep seated social and cultural values. Paul's collaborative style and his vision of an inclusive community coexist with restrictive statements on the role of women in the assembly and a failure to deal directly with the issue of slavery. The cosmic unity trumpeted by Ephesians coexists with exhortations on marriage that put the woman in a subordinate role. The Greco-Roman world was a strongly patriarchal world; it permeated its political and social life on every level. While early Christianity made significant inroads in this system and retained, surely in its normative texts, a vision of equality, it is also clear that the early church struggled and compromised with that social setting. There should be no scandal in this. Vatican II's Dogmatic Constitution on Divine Revelation reminds us that the New Testament is not a bloodless charter of ideals dropped untouched from heaven. It is a text that exudes genuine human experience as the Spirit of God works and groans within the realities of history. So the Scriptures are not only the touchpoint for our ideals but we can also locate there the evidence of our failures.

SOME RAMIFICATIONS

Allow me to conclude by drawing from all this some reflections on the theme of Women in the Church.

My approach has been to draw an analogy between the early church's struggle with the Gentile mission—and the issues of inclusion it involved—and the question of the role of women within the church today. I am convinced that many of the New Testament texts that involve women were utilized by the biblical authors in the service of this issue.

The analogy to the global mission of the church offers some interesting perspectives, I believe, not only by considering the biblical roots of that mission but in being attentive to the arena of mission history. The current tension in the church over the role of women has instructive analogies with the church's struggle to be open to non-western cultures and experience. In the past century the church has crossed significant cultural boundaries and is undoubtedly more sensitive to non-western cultures now than it was in the recent past—even though the present record is far from perfect. Only now is the church beginning to fully realize the consequences of all this. Openness to non-western cultures means a lot more than representation on the hierarchy and adaptation of liturgy—although these are nothing to sneeze at either. As the church's case of nerves over liberation theology demonstrates, giving a place to the experience of these indigenous churches is the key. The most important consequence of crossing a cultural boundary and being open to another will come when the viewpoint and experience of the other is allowed to have an impact on me. Looking out from the windows of a tour bus or leafing through *National Geographic* is not enough. What is true of an individual is true of a community and is true of the church community. The faith experience of the churches of Africa, Latin America, and Asia is only beginning to have an impact on our understanding of salvation, of ecclesiology, of christology, and of theodicy. We are still to hear from one quarter of the human race—the people of China.

Moving away from the hegemony of western culture in the church and across cultural boundaries will lead us to frontiers of faith not yet imagined. As frightening as that might be for some (and perhaps they are the ones who sense what is at stake . . .), to be faithful to the Gospel of Jesus Christ those boundaries must be crossed. And is it not true that the gender boundary represents another boundary not yet fully discerned by many much less transcended? But does not the impulse of the Gospel compel us to risk crossing this frontier, too?

The analogy with cross-cultural mission leads to another reflection. Comparison with the early church's struggle over the Gentile mission should not lead us to think the situation is exactly the same today. The question for Peter and the Jerusalem leaders was whether Gentiles could come into the community and on what terms. In the case of many cultures today and surely in the case of women, it is not exactly an issue of membership. Many Latin Americans and Africans and Asians have been Christians for centuries; in some instances, such as Northern Africa and parts of Asia, they were Christian long before most of Western Europe had heard the Gospel. But, although insiders in one sense, their cultural values, their experience, and their voice were, for the most part, left outside. Their being, in its total mystery, was not allowed to be in communion with the rest of the church.

Women have been in the church for a long time! In this country at least, not only have they been "in" but they have been way in! According to the Notre Dame study of 1100 parishes in the U.S., women make up 55% of the membership lists, 61% of Sunday Mass attendance, 80% of daily Mass attendance, 60% of parish eucharistic ministers, 50% of the lectors, 85% of those active in programs for the poor, sick, grieving or handicapped, 80% of the CCD teachers and prayer group members, 75% of the Bible-study or discussion group leaders, 60% of those in recreational programs or youth ministries, 52% of the parish councils, and form 58% of those considered to be the parish's most influential leaders. That's what I call "in"! Reading those statistics gave me a wry thought; the topic of this conference should not be "Women in the Church" but "Men in the Church"! That would have a strong biblical precedent, too. If we take the Gospel tradition about the discovery of the empty tomb—as distinct from the list in 1 Corinthians 15—the first problem facing the Risen Christ was not the inclusion of women but the inclusion of men! The male apostles and disciples had fled and the women were sent to bring them back.

So what is the issue? As with the western church's dealings with non-western cultures it is not membership as such but the terms of the membership that is at stake. It means being open to the experience of women and allowing it to be publicly and pervasively let free in the church in theology, in its religious experience, in its leadership. Only then is full communion possible and only then will the universality of the Gospel be incarnate. This brings us once again to the nature of the Christian mission. Proclaiming the Gospel cannot be reduced to recruitment for membership but is the seeking of communion, in the name of the God of love, with the being of all persons and all cultures, and ultimately with creating itself, a communion that does not submerge or subordinate or violate but bonds in respectful nourishing love. Such love cannot be fully realized where there is oppression, exclusion, or neglect.

The Bible is our ally in all this. The theology of liberation and the oppressed churches from which it springs have taught us to read the Scriptures with new eyes, from the perspective and the experience of the oppressed. The sick and disabled can challenge us to read the healing stories from the vantage point of the unhealed. And the experience of women who have felt exclusion is also a revelatory moment for all of us, women and men. The experience of people in the church is a sacred guide for us. It is an opportunity to read the Scriptures and our sacred tradition with new eyes, to discover God's voice in a new way.

As strange as it might seem, the experience of pain and suffering is especially revealing. The most revealing moments of Jesus' ministry came when it intersected with suffering: exclusion, illness, possession, alienation, the cross. And the church, too, if it is to be attentive to God's voice should be most attentive to suffering within its own midst and in the world around it and reread its Scriptures and its tradition accordingly.

The church in the United States has already started down this path, though perhaps not always aware of where the Spirit may be leading it. The anxiety of the arms race and the oppression it spawns led the bishops to grapple with the barriers of hostility between nations and systems in its pastoral on peace. The exclusion of the jobless and homeless and economically deprived from the economic community led the bishops to speak on the United States economy and its global impact. And in this same context the bishops have reexamined the commitment of the church in the United States to global cross-cultural mission in their recent pastoral statement on world mission, "To the Ends of the Earth." Seen in this perspective at least, attention to sexism and the exclusion of women in the practical life of the church is a logical step. Attention to these issues is, in any case, no fad, no vapor from some alien spirit. Nor can it be considered the special interest of the right or the left. The question of inclusion has roots as deep as the Bible and a scope as wide as the mission of Jesus. It is a genuinely Catholic issue and Catholic Christians cannot ignore it and remain faithful to their biblical heritage.

As always the Bible is our common source of inspiration and unity. If used in the service of a one-sided ideology it can be a source of oppression; it was used this way to justify slavery, to bless warfare, and to condemn Jews. But the Bible is also our leaven. If read in concert with the church and with attention to the sufferings and hopes of God's people it can be our leaven. The dream is alive in the Scriptures: many peoples and many cultures and many histories but at the same time one body, one people, one faith. "Neither Jew nor Greek neither slave nor free, neither male nor female, all one in Christ Jesus"—so Paul wrote to the Galatians. If such a formula were composed today, without its biblical warrant, some might condemn it as radical and provocative. So it may be. But people of faith know that it springs from the heart of the Gospel and in the midst of our chronic weakness and fragile hopes remains with us as God's word.

2

An Ecclesiology for Women and Men

Richard P. McBrien

I AM HONORED TO BE PART OF THIS IMPORTANT CONFERENCE, AND to have an opportunity to make some small contribution to it.

The conference brochure advises you that "the major addresses will paint with the broadest brush, indicating the sweep of the questions and the challenges." You can tell that is the case by the topic I've been asked to address: "An Ecclesiology for Women and Men"—and all in a matter of forty-five minutes or less. I'll do my best, secure in the knowledge that the "breakout" sessions will fill in some of the gaps. There will be many—gaps, that is.

Let's begin with the title, "An Ecclesiology for Women and Men." I think we all know the meaning of the words "women" and "men." How they relate within the church is what this conference is all about. It's the term "ecclesiology" that has to be defined.

Ecclesiology is, literally, the study of the church. But it doesn't suffice to say that. Many disciplines other than ecclesiology *study* the church: sociology, psychology, political science, history, philosophy, economics, anthropology.

What is it that distinguishes the ecclesiological study of the church from studies conducted within those cognate disciplines?

Since ecclesiology is a specialization within theology, and since theology is "faith seeking understanding," the study of the church is ecclesiological only when it is done in faith.

And since the object of faith is God, and God alone, ecclesiology studies the church not simply as a religious organization, available to sociologist and theologian alike, but as a mystery or sacrament, as "a reality imbued with the hidden presence of God," to use the words of the late Pope Paul VI.

It is because the church is more than meets the eye that ecclesiology is possible. God is present and active in the church, sacramentally. To say, as we do in the Creed, "We believe in the church," is to say that we believe in the God who is present and active in the church. The church is an object of faith only because it is a sacrament of God.

Ecclesiology studies the church, but, unlike the sociology of religion, for example, ecclesiology studies the church as something more than a complex organization, more than a social movement, more than a hierarchically-structured institution. Ecclesiology is interested in more than the uses of pastoral authority, more than the distribution of canonical power, more than the analysis and resolution of organizational conflicts.

The church is a mystery, a sacrament, "a reality imbued with the hidden presence of God." This is what ecclesiology grasps in the first instance; this is what ecclesiology is essentially all about.

But it would be a serious theological mistake to set the institutional off against the charismatic, or the human against the divine. Precisely because the church is a sacrament, it is *both* human and divine.

It is both sign and cause of grace; it is both *body* of Christ and body of *Christ, people* of God and people of *God, temple* of the Holy Spirit and temple of the *Holy Spirit.*

However, in some of the discussions that took place prior to last year's Extraordinary Synod in Rome, one aspect of the church seemed to have been played off against the other, at least in the press if not also in the minds of some of the bishops themselves. It reached the point where you were considered a conservative if, in agreeing with Cardinal Ratzinger, you emphasized the mystery of the church, and you were considered a progressive if, in agreement, let us say, with liberation theology, you emphasized the social and political role of the church. It was either one or the other.

But in ecclesiology we rarely deal with either/ors. It's almost always a case of both/and. The church is *both* an institution *and* a community; it is *both* local *and* universal; it is *both* Catholic *and* ecumenical; it is called *both* to proclaim the word *and* celebrate the sacraments; and to work for justice *both* inside *and* outside the household of faith.

To view the church in any other way is to lapse into ecclesiological Nestorianism, on the left, and Monophysitism, on the right. Let me explain.

Nestorianism, out of a commendable motive to preserve the humanity of Christ, gave us *two* Christs: one a human person, the other a divine person. The Council of Ephesus, in the year 431, declared there to be only one person in Christ, and that a divine person.

Monophysitism, seeking to preserve the divinity, went to the opposite extreme. It affirmed the one Christ, but at the expense of his human nature. If he is only one divine *person,* the Monophysites concluded, then he possesses only one divine *nature.* The Council of Chalcedon, in the year 451, rejected Monophysitism. There *is* one Christ, but the one Christ is human as well as divine in nature.

Since the church is the Body of Christ, what is said of Christ can be said, for the most part, of the church as well. There are not two churches, but one. The human church is not separated from the divine. And that one church is not solely divine. It is at once *human* and divine.

The Church's greatest ecclesiologist, Father Yves Congar, expressed it this way in his excellent little book, *Christ, Our Lady and the Church,* published some thirty years ago: "The Church may not be 'divided' in a Nestorian sense any more than in a Monophysite one. This would be done by postulating a human element in it wholly separated from the divine, or by refusing to recognize in its human lineaments anything spiritually transcendent."

The Second Vatican Council said the same thing, but without explicit reference to these Christological heresies. "By her relationship with Christ," the Dogmatic Constitution on the Church declared in its first article, "the Church is a kind of sacrament of intimate union with God, and of the unity of all humankind, that is, [the Church] is a sign and an instrument of such union and unity." Indeed, the whole first chapter of *Lumen gentium* is entitled "The Mystery of the Church."

For the Council, the church is most fundamentally a mystery, or sacrament, just as Christ is a "profound" mystery (Eph 5:32; Col 4:3) and the primordial sacrament, that is, the sacrament which gives meaning and efficacy to all other sacraments.

It is precisely because ecclesiology studies the church as a mystery, or sacrament, that it does not focus only on the church's transcendental, other-worldly, spiritual, or heavenly dimensions. For the very same reason, ecclesiology does not focus only on the church's social, juridical, political, or organizational dimensions. Ecclesiology cannot treat the church as if it were only a creation of God, and neither can it treat the church as if it were only a human institution, subject to the same sociological and political vicissitudes as any other human institution.

Ecclesiology deals with the human and the divine alike: not separately (as the Nestorian would), and without denying the fully human character of the church (as the Monophysite would).

These tendencies, first, to separate the human from the divine (a tendency of the left), or, secondly, to exalt the divine at the expense of the human (a tendency of the right) continue to plague the life of the church today.

These tendencies have serious practical implications. They inhibit us from seeing the church as it is, and from dealing with it as it is; namely, as a reality which is at once human and divine, with the divine penetrating and informing the human and the human expressing and facilitating the divine.

I am reminded, in this connection, of one of the most important findings of the Study on Priestly Life and Ministry, commissioned more than fifteen years ago by the National Conference of Catholic Bishops. I should like to quote just a few lines from the report of the Subcommittee on Sociology, chaired at the time by Father Andrew Greeley:

> Does the dissatisfaction of the young with the distribution of power indicate trouble for the Church? It apparently does, precisely because the difference seems to be rooted in quite different values about the nature of the Church and the nature of Christianity. What we are witnessing today is not merely a disagreement between those who have power and those who do not, but a disagreement among those with opposing ideologies about the nature of the reality whose power structure is the subject of disagreement. Power conflicts that are rooted in ideological differences tend to be much more serious than power conflicts among those who share the same ideologies.

The use and abuse of power in the church, therefore, is not simply a political or a sociological question. It is a theological question, more precisely an ecclesiological question, because of the nature of the community in which that power is exercised.

If our power-conflicts in the church today are simply conflicts between the haves and the have-nots, such conflicts are unworthy of the church, which is the Body of Christ and the Temple of the Holy Spirit. Those who seek power without regard for its salvific, healing uses are not better than those who hold firm to power without regard for the same.

On the other hand, if our power-conflicts in the church do reflect fundamental differences about the meaning and purpose of the church itself, then the conflicts are actually much more serious than they might at first appear. To some extent, this is the case. And that is why it is so important to get our ecclesiological principles straight.

A year after the Greeley report was presented to the bishops, a canonical colloquium sponsored by what was then known as the *School* of Canon Law, at what was then known as The Catholic *University* of America, issued a consensus paper on the same topic. I should like to quote just one paragraph from that document:

> On the one hand, through Vatican II and the theological developments following it, the whole community is gradually appropriating a new vision of the Church and of its life, including priestly life and ministry. On the other hand, the present legal system of the Western Church dates back more than sixty years and originated in a significantly different understanding of the life of the Christian community. This growing discrepancy between vision and law gives rise to increasing tension. It creates a need for greater flexibility and instruments of harmony, since a community cannot long remain strong with a new understanding of its goals and an old set of norms to realize them.

Accordingly, canon law is never simply a matter for canon lawyers. It is a matter for theologians, and indeed for every member of the church. Laws exist to help the church *be* what it is called to be, and to *do* what it has been sent to do. Canon lawyers can't determine for us, on the basis of legal principles alone, the nature and mission of the church. What the church *is* and what the church has been sent to *do* are ecclesiological questions.

The ecclesiological Nestorian would make the church's legal system a purely human expression of a purely human organization. Consequently, for the Nestorian there is no limit to the challenges we might decide to mount against these laws. The ecclesiological Monophysite, on the other hand, regards the church's legal system for all practical purposes, as God-given. To challenge the law is to challenge God's plan, or, to use Raymond Brown's illuminating metaphor, Christ's "ecclesiological blueprint."

Both of these texts—the priesthood report of 1971 and the canon law symposium document of 1972—underscore, in very practical ways, the point I am trying to make; namely, that because the church is a mystery, or sacrament, its human and divine dimensions are inextricably linked one with the other.

But that point is even more general perhaps than this "general" address of mine is supposed to be. After all, this isn't just a conference on the church. It's a conference on *women* in the church.

I shall attempt now to connect what I have been saying with the specific concern of this assembly.

Are women discriminated against in the church? Are women excluded from significant ministries in the church? Are women alienated by the language of liturgy and by the manner of its celebration? Are the experiences of women inadequately expressed in contemporary spirituality?

These are the sorts of questions that have been addressed with increasing frequency and intensity in the church ever since the Council. Too often, however, some of the answers given on the left speak of the church as if it were a human institution alone, or a human institution divorced from any meaningful connection with God, the Holy Spirit, the supernatural, the sacred. They speak and write about the church as if it were an unreconstructed political party, or worse, the government of South Africa, with its own version of sexual apartheid. Ecclesiological Nestorianism.

The church about which we speak and write is, at the same time, a sacrament of God's saving presence in and for the world; it is "the fullness of [Christ] who fills all in all" (Eph. 1:23).

Some of the answers given on the right are also wide of the theological mark. They speak and write of the church as if it weren't really human, subject to many of the same social, political, economic, and cultural influences as other comparable communities, movements, and institutions. For the right, to criticize the church is somehow to criticize God. To seek to change anything in the church, like eligibility rules for presbyteral ordination, is somehow to second-guess Jesus Christ himself. They speak and write about the church as if it were already the kingdom of God on earth, and about the pope as if he were God's unchallengeable deputy within that kingdom. Ecclesiological Monophysitism.

The church about which we speak and write is, at the same time, a pilgrim people, a sinful people. Although the church is the Body of Christ, it is not similar to Christ in every respect. Because of his unique union with the Godhead, Christ is "holy, innocent, undefiled" (Heb 7:26). He knew nothing of sin (2 Cor 5:21). The church, on the other hand, embraces sinners in its bosom, to use the words of *Lumen gentium*. The church is "at the same time holy and always in need of being purified, and incessantly pursues the path of penance and renewal" (n. 8). Furthermore, the church is not yet the kingdom of God. At most it can be called, as the Council calls it, "the initial budding forth of that kingdom." In the meantime, the church "strains toward the consummation of the kingdom" (n. 5).

But still we've not yet focussed adequately on the subject of this conference, *women* in the church, or on the subject of this presentation, an ecclesiology *for women and men*. To do that, I shall now seek to apply to the subjects at hand both my point about the church's sacramentality, that is, about the union of the human and the divine in the one church, and also my words of caution about ecclesiological Nestorianism and ecclesiological Monophysitism.

To do so I shall change the key terms from human and divine to women and men. Or men and women, for that matter, because I intend no parallels certainly between the human and the male, or the female, and the divine and the male, or the female.

The church is composed of women and men alike. But our ecclesiological Nestorians always want to keep things separate that ought to be together. So we have a church of men, that is, the patriarchal church. That's bad. And we have a church of women, namely, women-church. And that's good?

No, that's bad, too. And we ought to be able to say so without having our feminist credentials revoked by some ersatz Sacred Congregation for the Doctrine of the Faith. No less a feminist theologian than Rosemary Radford Ruether makes this very point in a recent book review in *The Journal of the American Academy of Religion,* the spring 1986 issue. The book under review happens to be Elisabeth Schüssler Fiorenza's *Bread Not Stone: The Challenge of Feminist Biblical Interpretation.*

Ruether argues that "women-church, as a contemporary feminist translation of the New Testament discipleship of equals, cannot be the normative definition of church as the community of liberation of all women and men. Defined as 'self-identified women and women-identified men,' women-church reverses the androcentric definition of church as 'self-identified men and male-identified women.' This is necessary (I believe) as a transitional corrective both to a patriarchal Christianity and to a patriarchal society," Ruether continues. "But, as a normative concept, it threatens to become a gynecentric reversal of androcentric ecclesiology. Fiorenza fails to point beyond women-church to a further norm of both self and other-identified men and women in a mutual discipleship of equals."

I should say, parenthetically, that Elisabeth Schüssler Fiorenza insists that she does not advocate a separatist church of women.

In spite of the texts Rosemary Ruether cites in her review of *Bread Not Stone,* all three of us are in agreement, then: there are not two churches, one of men (the sinful church) and one of women (the righteous church). There is only one church, of women and men alike, in a community of disciples: equal in human dignity, equal in Christian dignity, equal in ecclesial ministry, equal in the sight of God, equal in final destiny.

Women-church, as a normative concept, is as distorting of the reality of church as men-church. We do not want to replace one form of Nestorianism with another. Or indeed one form of sexism with another.

On the other hand, ecclesiological Monophysitism, applied now to the question of women and men in the church, presumes to save the oneness of the church by absorbing women into men.

Women are present in the church, to be sure, but they are merely instruments of the ministries, authority and power reserved exclusively to men.

The only members of the church who really count are men: the pope, the bishops, the priests, alas, even the deacons. (Religious brothers, who never appear on such a list, ought to know better than most men what it feels like to be a woman in the church.)

On the matter of the relationship of women and men, we are still too much a Monophysite church. The female has been absorbed, or held in ecclesiastical escrow, by the male.

But the answer to Monophysitism isn't Nestorianism. That would be to replace one serious ecclesiological error with another. The answer is Chalcedonian orthodoxy, which teaches that there are two natures in Christ, "without confusion or change, without division or separation."

So, there are two sexes in the church, "without division or separation." We are a church of women and of men. What is said of the church theologically is said of the *whole* church, women as well as men, men as well as women.

The church is the people of God. Women are people. And so are men.

Fortunately, the official church has given evidence in recent decades of moving away from what I have somewhat loosely called its Monophysite view. Pope John XXIII began the process of revision with his widely-celebrated encyclical letter *Pacem in terris*, published in April 1963, even before Betty Friedan's groundbreaking *Feminine Mystique*. In that encyclical Pope John proposed that the present age has three distinctive characteristics: one concerns the working classes who refuse now to be treated "as if they were irrational objects without freedom, to be used at the arbitrary disposition of others"; a second characteristic pertains to the growing interdependence of nations in social and political life; and a third characteristic (which actually appeared second on Pope John's list) relates to women.

For Pope John it was "obvious to everyone that women are now taking a part in public life. This is happening more rapidly perhaps in nations of Christian civilization and, more slowly but broadly, among peoples who have inherited other traditions or cultures. Since women are becoming ever more conscious of their human dignity, they will not tolerate being treated as mere material instruments, but demand rights befitting a human person both in domestic and public life." Good Pope John!

As refreshingly broad as Pope John's vision was, he did not explicitly link this new consciousness of women in society with their place and role in the church itself. He spoke of "domestic and public life," not ecclesiastical life. It was left to Vatican II to add the ecclesiological dimension.

In the Decree on the Apostolate of the Laity, the Council declared: "Since in our times women have an ever more active share in the whole life of society, it is very important that they participate more widely also in the various fields of *the Church's apostolate*" (n. 9; emphasis mine).

There is one other conciliar text that is particularly relevant to the matter at hand. It's from the same Decree on the Laity: "As sharers in the role of Christ the Priest, the Prophet, and the King, the laity have an active part to play *in the life and activity of the Church*" (n. 10; emphasis mine).

I should suggest that the opponents of sexual equality in the church are not in the hierarchy or the clergy alone. They are also in the politically and theologically conservative laity. These lay persons, mostly in the middle-to-senior generations, and overwhelmingly male, hold fast to a pre-Vatican II notion of the so-called lay apostolate. Indeed, many of these lay persons were counted among the progressives of the pre-Vatican II period.

For them, there are two separate and distinct orders in the world: the sacred and the secular, the spiritual and the temporal, the ecclesiastical and the political. The sacred, the spiritual, and the ecclesiastical belong to the clergy; the secular, the temporal, and the political belong to the laity.

These laity make a great point of this hard-and-fast distinction between the two realms because many of them do not like the recent activist style of the U.S. Catholic bishops on such "secular" and "temporal" matters as nuclear deterrence and the U.S. economy. They want the bishops to stay out of areas they presumably don't understand and leave them to people who do; namely, lay Catholics. (These same lay Catholics, however, never explain why the bishops have any particular competence in matters of sexual ethics, especially in matters pertaining to marriage and homosexuality, for example.)

The fact of the matter is, as the Pastoral Constitution on the Church in the Modern World insisted, that all of these so-called temporal matters have a moral dimension. And insofar as they have a moral dimension, the hierarchy can and must appropriately address them.

"Secular duties and activities belong properly *although not exclusively* to lay persons," the Pastoral Constitution declared. Accordingly, bishops and priests must "so preach the message of Christ that all the earthly activities of the faithful will be bathed in the light of the gospel" (n. 43; emphasis mine).

On the other hand, we're all members of the church, laity, religious, and clergy alike. Therefore, the laity, including women, have as much interest in the inner life of the church as do the clergy and religious. To adopt the pre-conciliar lay apostolate theology of the neo-conservatives would be to exclude women—all women—from meaningful involvement in the governance of the church.

There is no impregnable wall between the sacred and the secular, the ecclesial and the temporal. "Therefore, let there be no false opposition between professional and social activities on the one part, and religious life on the other," the Council insisted.

Neither is there an impregnable wall between clergy and laity in the church. To posit one is to posit yet another form of ecclesiological Nestorianism: two churches, instead of one. There is only one church, of women and men alike, of laity, religious, and clergy alike.

All of us—women and men, clergy, religious, and laity—have a stake in the one church to which we belong. All of us—women and men, clergy, religious, and laity—have a moral obligation to use whatever resources we have to advance the mission of that one church. And all of us—women and men, clergy, religious, and laity—are called in principle to fulfill whatever ministries are required to advance that mission for the sake of God's kingdom.

The church to which we belong and the church that we serve is a mystery, or sacrament. It is at once the sign and instrument of our union with God and with one another in Christ. There are not two churches, one human and one divine, or one for women and one for men. Neither is the human absorbed into the divine, nor are women subordinated to men. It is a community of equal disciples, moving along a pilgrim path, seeking only to be faithful to God's call to be what all of us are called to be, and to do what all of us have been sent to do.

For that we need one another.

3

Human and Legal Rights of Women in the Church

James H. Provost

IT IS STRIKING TO NOTE TO WHAT EXTENT "RIGHTS" ARE A CONCERN of, by, and for women in our world today. Linda Brown wanted to go to a decent school in the 1950s; the educational and legal systems in the United States are still feeling the results of *Brown v. Board of Education.*[1] Rosa Parks' feet hurt, she wanted a seat on the bus, and she did not want to go to stand in the back of that bus; a whole chapter in civil rights in this country was the result. The grandmothers in Argentina demanded and demanded to know where their children and grandchildren were; these mothers of the disappeared, marching every week in the Plaza de Mayo, eventually led to the restoration of civil rights in that country.

Are these some of the "signs of our times," to which we in the church must attend? Conscious of their rights in everyday life, women object to being excluded from decision-making in the Catholic Church, where they are at least half the membership, where they often do significant ministry, and where they have a major contribution to make to church life. We hear our church accused of injustice and lack of fairness in reference to many aspects of internal church life.

Thus we have the topic of this study: the human and ecclesial rights of women in the church. Let me recognize from the beginning some limitations on what will be attempted.[2]

First, although this is clearly a timely topic it must not be considered something limited to this time, to the present moment. We must keep an historical perspective, and a view to the future. Talk about "rights" in the church may seem new to us, but it has a rich heritage. If rights in the church are based on the teaching of the ecclesiastical magisterium—as indeed they are—then they cannot be considered merely a passing fad.

Second, concern over rights—and rights of women in particular—arises from concrete experiences. But this presentation is designed to attempt a reflection on experience in light of the church's law; it cannot address, or redress, every individual experience.

Finally, the concern for rights of women in the church is not something limited to Roman Catholics. As a common Christian preoccupation, it has even served as the formal topic of multilateral dialogue with other churches.[3] Yet I will be addressing the topic primarily from a Roman Catholic perspective, given the perspective of this conference.

Within Roman Catholicism we are in a new situation, at least a new legal situation. The discrimination based on sex which was enshrined in the old code of canon law has been faced,[4] and in most respects is no longer evident in the church's law books. The distinctions today are between those in sacred ministry, and the rest of the Christian faithful—the *laos*—they serve. In addressing the rights of women, I do not mean to imply theirs are different from the rights of all the Christian faithful; indeed, the rights are the same. But it is also clear that the de facto condition of women in the church deserves specific attention; why else this gathering?

My reflections are organized into three sections: first, some introductory comments or warnings; then there will be a review of the rights of persons in the church; finally, I shall offer some reflections on the situation of women in the Catholic Church today.

INTRODUCTORY COMMENTS

Some Cautions

First, any discussion of "rights" is like peeling an onion. There are many different layers which do not seem to be closely interconnected—you can peel off one layer without disturbing the next. At times we can be tempted to slice through the whole thing, but then it falls apart. And no matter how hard we try not to, we're probably going to shed some tears in the process. Here are some examples of what I mean.[5]

Rights can be considered in light of one's geo-political setting. This is the outside skin of our onion. In the so-called "first world," major concern is shown for personal and civil liberties. In the so-called "second world," social and economic entitlements are the rights which are most addressed. In the so-called "third world" rights are discussed in terms of solidarity, and of liberation from all forms of external and internal oppression.[6] So depending on one's geo-political experience, to talk about "rights" can address quite different realities.

There is also the historical political setting. In an absolutist monarchy, rights were a concession from the monarch—the grant of royal favors and privileges. In a society structured according to various classes, with a distinct ruling class, rights were claimed as privileges pertaining to the class—determine one's class, and you automatically knew that person's rights. Today, rights are commonly held to be claims which arise from one's dignity as a human being—rooted in the person, rather than in the sovereign or in a social class.

A good illustration of this layer of the onion emerges from comparing the 1917 and 1983 codes of canon law. The 1917 code spoke of the *privileges,* rights and duties of the clergy—and by extension, of religious. This accurately reflected the monarchical, class-conscious character of that code and its times. The 1983 version drops "privileges" of clergy and begins with a whole section on the fundamental rights and obligations of all the Christian faithful, an accurate reflection of the personalism that marks Vatican II and some of the new code.

A third layer relates to the negative or positive approach to rights. The American "Declaration of Independence" or the French "Declaration of the Rights of Man and of the Citizen" focused on claims of personal spheres of liberty. They were negative claims—the government must stay out of certain aspects of life. Within the sphere of liberty, the individual was free to act or not. More recent declarations, such as the United Nations' 1969 "Universal Declaration of Human Rights," contain more positive statements. In light of an increased awareness of the injustice found in whole systems, these positive statements of the rights to food, clothing, and shelter, for example, are claims to entitlements: society must not only guarantee a certain sphere of personal liberty, but must also assure a certain minimum of human existence in order for the person to be able to exercise that liberty.

A fourth layer holds a number of distinctions. Sometimes "rights" are distinguished from "interests." In this light, "rights" are fundamental claims which must be recognized; there is no option. "Interests," on the other hand, are claims which one is free to pursue, but it is not guaranteed in principle that they will be realized.

"Rights" and "responsibilities" are often contrasted. Some see rights as liberties, something we are free to pursue or not; they recognize that we are responsible for what we finally decide to do. Others see things differently, and hold we are not free to decide whether to pursue a right; rights are seen as responsibilities which one must fulfill.

Here are some other ways of relating responsibilities and rights. If I have a responsibility to do something, an obligation that arises out of my situation in life, my Christian condition, or whatever, then I have the corresponding right to carry out that obligation, to fulfill my duty. On the other hand, if you have a responsibility to provide something for me—say, the word of God or the sacraments—then I have a corresponding right to receive them from you.

Finally, at the core of our rights onion, there are many reasons for talking about rights. Rights have been used as the means to critique another's system or way of acting. A second use has been to legitimate one's own system or way of acting—correctly, or perhaps as a "cover-up," the ideology of rights without the reality.

Most of the attention given to rights—whether in drawing up lists of rights, or in making claim to a particular right—has taken place in a situation of conflict. It is usually when someone denies me something, or tries to impose something on me, that I claim my rights. "Rights" talk is not generally carried on in great serenity.

So, a warning: beware of the complexity and difficulties in trying to talk about rights, especially in an international context such as the Roman Catholic Church.

Three Objections

There is another warning to be issued. There are some who claim we cannot even talk about rights within a church. There are three types of objections: one from a theology perspective, one from the critique of bourgeois ideology, and a third arising from the separation of church and state. We will look at each in turn.

1. Theological Objection

Here is the objection:

> The absolute Lordship of God does not admit of any claims "over against" God.
>
> The church is the community of the redeemed, wherein God dwells: we are the Body of Christ, a communion in the life of the Spirit.
>
> So, there can be no claims "over against" the church, such as "rights" would entail.

Here are my comments on this objection.

The church is a structured, orderly community of the redeemed. It has a visible form which makes visible its mysterious reality. Insofar as the church is visible and structured, it is possible to speak of law, rights, duties, and other elements of a human society.[7] It is possible to speak of rights within the church without thereby speaking of claims over against God.

2. The "Bourgeois" Objection

Here is the objection:

> Rights, as some claim them in the church, are nothing more than individualistic claims which do not recognize social obligations or the solidarity of the church as a communion.
>
> This is basically a "bourgeois" notion, and must be rejected.

Here are my comments on this objection.

Extreme individualism, as well as extreme collectivism, have no place in the church. Indeed, Catholic social teaching rejects both. But personalism—the dignity and importance of the human person, lived out in community—this is a genuine Christian teaching.[8] Insofar as rights are legitimate claims arising from the dignity of a human person, they apply within the church.

3. Separation of Church and State Objection

Here is the objection:

> Claims of personal rights and liberties are a secular, civil law reality.
>
> The church is not a state. It has its own theological reality, even as a visible and structured organization.
>
> Therefore, to talk about "rights" in the church is inappropriate, even though the church has the obligation to proclaim its social teaching about rights to the world.

Here are my comments on this objection.

There is a deep theological issue here: the relation of the church and the world. Are they two separate realities? Or, are they so intimately interrelated in virtue of God's irruption into history through the incarnation and paschal mystery, that we can speak of the church as distinct from the world only as a second moment, an abstraction? Such an issue is beyond the scope of our discussion here.[9]

But whatever side of the theological issue one may hold, the teaching authority of the Catholic Church has stated on several occasions that rights do apply within the church. For example, the Synod of Bishops in 1971,[10] the Synod of Bishops in 1974,[11] and the Pontifical Commission on Justice and Peace,[12] have all affirmed the church must practice what it preaches about rights if that preaching is to be credible. Moreover, Pope John Paul II has argued that concern for rights is among the major reasons for law in the church.[13]

Any discussion of rights in the church, therefore, has to take place with an awareness of the complexities involved in any discussion of rights, and of the theological realities involved—not as an individualistic claim, but respecting the dignity of the person, especially as that person is a new creation in Christ Jesus.

RIGHTS OF PERSONS IN THE CHURCH

The 1983 code of canon law is the first attempt to state in church law the fundamental rights and obligations of the Christian faithful. As mentioned earlier, the previous law did list privileges, rights and duties of clergy, and by association, of religious. Only one "right" was listed for lay persons—that of receiving the sacraments from the clergy.[14] At Vatican II, however, the official magisterium of the church listed a number of "rights" which pertain to all the Christian faithful, and the new code has collected most of these into an important statement or ecclesiastical "bill of rights."[15]

In approaching this list one must keep in mind that there are at least two systems for interpreting the meaning of a law. In the ancient Hebrew system, and in our own Anglo-American jurisprudence, the courts have the last word. Rights, for example, are often expressed very succinctly; court decisions work out the implications and limitations of the statement in the law.

In the continental system, the one used in canon law, it is the legislator who has the final say on the meaning of the law. This is done in several ways, ranging from legislating the principles for the interpretation of law [16] to phrases placed in the very text of the law itself to guide its proper interpretation. Thus a statement of a right may be couched in a number of cautionary phrases which are meant to help interpret its implications and limitations.

While we need to be aware of the differences in how laws are interpreted, and therefore how rights are expressed, we also must acknowledge the importance of the listing of rights in the new code. The International Theological Commission, addressing the dignity and rights of the human person, called for fundamental rights to be "written into the Constitution and everywhere given juridical sanction."[17] It viewed as significant the listing of rights in the new code.[18]

That same commission pointed to three constants found in every notable listing of rights: equality, freedom, and participation. The commission encouraged these to be seen as interactive—they must exist together, not as independent claims. Keeping this in mind, let us turn to the actual listing of rights in the church's law.

The list is like a good sandwich: hearty bread to begin and end, and substantial ingredients in between. For the sake of convenience, I will deal with the two foundational elements first—the bread—and then turn to the main categories of the ingredients.

Equality and Common Good

Equality, freedom, and participation are joined in the new code in the context of the church's social teaching on the common good. Here are the actual words of the law:

> Canon 208. In virtue of their rebirth in Christ there exists among all the Christian faithful a true equality with regard to dignity and the activity whereby all cooperate in the building up of the Body of Christ in accord with each one's own condition and function.

> Canon 223. §1. In exercising their rights the Christian faithful, both as individuals and when gathered in associations, must take account of the common good of the Church and of the rights of others as well as their own duties toward others.[19]

Note the sacramental basis for equality. Christ is the source of who we are in common, not some social compact or even the decree of a church official. This equality cannot be taken away, for it resides in Christ's sacramental act, transforming our human dignity into a renewed creation.

There are also existential differences—"condition and function." We are equal, but not the same. We are all responsible, but have different responsibilities as we participate in building up the Body of Christ.

The free exercise of rights is not without limits. Traditional Catholic social teaching has always placed the exercise of rights in the context of the common good; the law now does the same within the church. This is not just the common welfare, or good of the institution; more fundamentally, the common good refers to the sum of those conditions in the church by which persons can seek their perfection.[20]

The law goes on to recognize, with Vatican II from which this canon is taken, that the exercise of rights must always respect the rights of others, and one's duties toward others. Only in solidarity, respecting each other's rights and our respective responsibilities within the community, does a claim for rights make sense.

Turning to the substantial rights listed in the new code, I will organize them according to four general categories.

Communion

"The Christian faithful are bound by an obligation, even in their own patterns of activity, always to maintain communion with the Church" (c. 209, §1). If this is an obligation, it also is a statement of the fundamental reality of the church which is a communion.[21] As an obligation, it is also the basis for a right to communion. A Catholic cannot be denied the right to communion—and to the expression of it in eucharistic holy communion—without due process of law. All of Book VI of the code, on sanctions, and much of Book VII on procedures, are the fruit of the long tradition in church law protecting this right.

A Catholic is also called to live within the communion. This means obedience to the teaching and directives of church authorities, but also the right to petition to have one's needs addressed, and the right and at times the duty to express one's opinion in the church.

All of this is neatly packaged in a very interesting canon, canon 212. Permit me to spend a moment on some of the details of this canon, for it is a good example of a law written in the Continental or canonical system where the legislator, not the courts, provides the last word on what the law means.

Canon 212 opens by emphasizing the obligation to obey "what the sacred pastors, as representatives of Christ, declare as teachers of the faith or determine as leaders of the Church." Note the careful qualifiers. Not everything the pope or a bishop may say commands this obedience—only what they deliberately present in virtue of their specific role within the church, and this in the awareness that they do so not on their own but in the name of Christ. This is an awesome responsibility, not one to be taken lightly or exercised with caprice. By inserting the qualifiers, the legislator clarifies the limits beyond which Catholics are not bound by this obedience, as well as those within which such obedience is required for the common good.

The canon continues by affirming that the Christian faithful "are free to make known their needs, especially spiritual ones, and their desires to the pastors of the Church" (c. 212, §2). At least three consequences follow from this freedom. First, the sacred pastors have an obligation to be sensitive to the needs which the faithful present. The law calls on bishops to show this solicitude toward all (c. 383, §1), and to visit the parishes in the diocese regularly (c. 396)—a traditional means whereby the bishop is accessible to the faithful who have something to present to him. Other means of sounding out the needs of people are also encouraged in the law, including pastoral councils (cc. 511–514).

A second consequence of the freedom to petition is that I cannot be stopped from reasonably presenting a petition. An effort to gag the Christian faithful when they responsibly seek to present their needs is totally contrary to the law.

A final consequence is that the law does not limit petitions to purely spiritual matters. While these are especially obvious topics for petition, other matters—such as material, social, or institutional needs—would also be legitimate topics for petition.

Canon 212 also contains a section on public opinion. Much as the freedom of speech, protected in our own constitutional system by the First Amendment, is nevertheless limited by laws against libel, pornography, and the common good—you cannot cry "fire" in a crowded theater—so in the canon law system the exercise of the right to express one's opinion in the church has its limitations. The canon calls for such opinion to be expressed first to those who can do something about the matter, the church authorities responsible. But it also recognizes the right, within obvious limits, to express this opinion to others in the church as well.[22]

There are other rights and responsibilities related to the communion of the church. For example, the freedom of scholarly research and publication in the sacred sciences, with due regard for the church's magisterium; the opening of many church positions to any qualified Catholic, even while continuing to restrict other offices to clergy;[23] the availability of various liturgical ministries to all Catholics (c. 230);[24] and of course the obligation to contribute to the support of the church (c. 222, §1).

This latter obligation is interesting in that the three traditional reasons for the church having money—support of sacred worship, care of the poor and needy, and support of ministry—are not limited to the support of the clergy. Canon 231, §2 calls for a just family wage and appropriate benefits to be paid to lay persons involved in ministry, and canon 1286 requires the same for church employees or laborers. The right to a just family wage and the attendant benefits which the church has been preaching to society since the time of Leo XIII is clearly a requirement within the church in virtue of its own law, as well as in keeping with its teaching.

Holiness of Life

Equality, freedom and participation are applied not only to the communion of the church, but also to another cluster of rights and obligations which center on one's holiness of life. "All the Christian faithful must make an effort, in accord with their own condition, to live a holy life and to promote the growth of the Church and its continual sanctification" (c. 210). This general statement is buttressed by various other declarations of rights.

As in the previous code, all have "the right to receive spiritual assistance from the sacred pastors out of the spiritual goods of the Church, especially the word of God and the sacraments" (c. 213). Sacred ministers cannot deny the sacraments to those who reasonably seek them, are properly disposed, and are not impeded by law from receiving them (c. 843, §1). In other words, people have a right to be given adequate preparation for the sacraments and to have them provided on a timely and reasonable basis.

Catholics have the right to have the word of God preached to them. The law calls for preaching which is adapted to the hearers and the needs of the times (c. 769), and which expounds the mystery of Christ (c. 760). Only time will tell whether these canons provide the basis for Catholics to bring a suit in church court, claiming their rights have been violated by those whose preaching fails to measure up to even these minimal legal standards.

Holiness of life also implies other rights: to worship according to one's own ritual church, and in keeping with the rites of that church (c. 214); to follow one's own spirituality, consonant with church teaching (c. 214); and to receive a Christian education which will develop human maturity and introduce one to the mysteries of salvation (c. 217). Parenthetically, could there be here the legal basis for efforts to develop a feminine spirituality?

Missionary Responsibilities

A third cluster of rights and duties can be grouped around the concept of mission. All Catholics "have the duty and the right to work so that the divine message of salvation may increasingly reach the whole of humankind in every age and in every land" (c. 211). Equality, freedom and participation apply to the very core of what the church is about, the continuation of the mission begun in God, revealed in Christ, and continued in time through the action of the Spirit.

The canons on the teaching function in the church spell out the responsibilities of bishops, priests, religious, and lay persons in the ministry of the word (cc. 756–759). But even before such distinctions, there is the common responsibility we share in virtue of baptism, a responsibility which is emphasized again for lay persons in a statement on their rights and duties to spread the Gospel (c. 225).

There are related rights as well: the right to form associations (c. 215);[25] the right to assemble or hold meetings (c. 215); the right to initiate and to participate in works of the apostolate (c. 216); and the right to an adequate theological formation for all.[26]

The law emphasizes the practical application of this missionary responsibility in an option for the poor: Catholics are "obliged to promote social justice and, mindful of the precept of the Lord, to assist the poor from their own resources" (c. 222, §2). Note this obligation applies to all Catholics personally, of whatever sex or status in the church.

Human and Civil Rights

Finally, the code emphasizes certain human and civil rights which are to be given special recognition within the church. Each of us is to be "free from any kind of coercion in choosing a state in life" (c. 219)—that is, the choice cannot be forced upon a person. The law considers the person's choice to be a personal interest, but guarantees a right that this interest not be forced upon the person.

Other human rights guaranteed by the new code include the protection of one's good name (c. 220), and the right to one's own privacy (c.220). The rights of married persons and of the family are given special recognition in several places in the new code.[27]

The civil liberties of lay persons are guaranteed, but with some cautions appropriate to a legal system in which the legislator determines the final meaning of the law:

> Canon 227. Lay Christian faithful have the right to have recognized that freedom in the affairs of the earthly city which belongs to all citizens; when they exercise such freedom, however, they are to take care that their actions are imbued with the spirit of the gospel and take into account the doctrine set forth by the magisterium of the Church; but they are to avoid proposing their own opinion as the teaching of the Church in questions which are open to various opinions.

Clergy and religious are restricted in the exercise of some of their civil rights—are not to hold public office, or engage in various kinds of business activities, for example, without permission. But this is similar to the restrictions which apply to civil servants, who cannot participate in partisan politics, or to elected officials who must give up various business involvements.

SITUATION OF WOMEN IN THE CHURCH

Equality, freedom and participation—three interrelated values which the International Theological Commission presents as the basis for a common interpretation of human rights. But do these three values apply to all in the church? This brings us to the third and last major section of these reflections, namely the situation of women in the church. Three issues can be touched on only briefly here.

Discrimination on the Basis of Sex

As mentioned earlier, the 1917 code reflected the times and attitudes in which it was written, and was obviously discriminatory on the basis of sex. But at Vatican II the official magisterium of the Church declared, "every type of discrimination, whether social or cultural, whether based on sex, race, color, social condition, language or religion, is to be overcome and eradicated as contrary to God's interest" (*Gaudium et spes,* 29).

So in drafting the new code there was a deliberate effort to eliminate discrimination on the basis of sex. To a remarkable degree, the code succeeded. The main distinctions in this code are on the basis of ordination, rather than sex. Regrettably, a few isolated examples of sex-based distinction remain.

Papal cloister applies only to nuns, that is, contemplative women; it does not apply to contemplative men. Only a man can abduct a woman and have it to be an impediment to marriage; if a woman abducts a man, it does not affect the validity of marriage. Only lay males can be installed permanently in lay liturgical ministries of lector and acolyte, a throwback to when these were "minor orders" and were merely steps to becoming a priest.

These few examples aside, whatever rights apply to lay men in the church apply, at least in law, equally to lay women. However, lay men and all women remain excluded from various responsibilities in the church, since these are restricted to the ordained, even in situations when the power of orders is not required for the position in question. Must this be so?

Let me address that question in two stages. The first concerns the exclusion of women from ordination; the second considers expanding roles of responsibility for all Catholics in the church.

Exclusion of Women from Orders

For valid ordination in the Roman Catholic Church, the person being ordained must be a baptized male (c. 1025). For the ordination to be lawful, at least to the priesthood and episcopate, the man must also be celibate (c. 1042, 1°), although this can be dispensed) (c. 1047, §2, 3°).

The restriction of ordination to males is not considered a merely disciplinary question in the Roman Church; it is a doctrinal issue.[28] The Roman authorities recognize the crucial role which women have played in the history of the church and continue to exercise in special ways today. They also acknowledge the ecumenical significance of the issue, the studies of Scripture scholars and theologians. You are all familiar, I am sure, with the arguments presented in the document from the Congregation for the Doctrine of the Faith, so I need not review them here. However, let me offer three observations on this topic.

First, this is a very complicated factor for a world church such as the Roman Catholic communion, and one which is engaged in ecumenical dialogue. The roles of men and women vary in diverse cultures; what may be felt as a right in one cultural setting may not be seen this way at all in another. In this context we can learn from the experience of our Anglican and Protestant sisters and brothers. On the other hand, the Roman Church will always be sensitive to the tradition and attitude of the Orthodox, for in one sense they are our history, just as we are the history of the churches issued from the Sixteenth Century Reform. It seems to me that only a renewed anthropology will provide a means to cope with such a complex situation.

Second, we are not dealing here with a purely intellectual issue; it has deep roots in the human psyche. Indeed, the relationship of male and female in many ways touches the level of archtypes, of the kind of "myths" that hold worldviews together. The church has had experience recently in reaching down into that symbolic level, and we are still reverberating from the effects of liturgical change. Again, a renewed anthropology may enable us to approach this deeper level.

Finally, there is the question of rights. Is there a right to be ordained? The Vatican declaration clearly denies such a claim.[29] The petition for ordination is at most an "interest."

Others point to the statement of Vatican II that charisms give rise to rights and obligations in the church (*Apostolicam actuositatem,* 3), and claim a right to be ordained because of the charism they have received. What can be said of this?

It is true the church can require various charisms as a prerequisite for various offices, and even for ordination. For example, currently the church requires the charisms of celibacy and preaching for those to be ordained priests.[30] Moreover, church authorities can decline to formalize various charisms without thereby extinguishing the Spirit (ibid.). So the reception of a charism, while it does give rise to rights and duties in the church, does not necessarily give rise to a specific right to ordination.

From another perspective, the right to minister is distinct from ordination. Ministry is a broad concept, even in Roman documents; Pope John Paul II has referred to parents as exercising a "ministry" in a true and proper sense of this term.[31] So not all ministry requires an office in the church. Moreover, not all official ministry is ordained ministry; lay persons can be named to various church offices (c. 228). And we must admit that not all official ministers or ordained ministers are necessarily engaged in active ministry.

All this being said, however, there remains the impression which others have of the Catholic Church as perpetuating a system of injustice by in principle excluding women from positions of responsibility in the church, since these positions are restricted to the ordained. Let us turn to this concern.

Roles of Responsibility

While equality may not give rise to a right to ordination,[32] it is inextricably bound up with the value of participation. The argument is made that when a whole class of persons are excluded from participation, what can be said of their equality? So it is important to address the participation of all Catholics in various aspects of the life of the Church.

1. Certain offices and activities are restricted by law to clerics. For example, only clerics can be given offices for whose exercise is required the power of governance (c. 274, §1); only clerics can preach the homily (c. 767, §1). If we just stop there, then there does appear to be significant exclusion of lay persons from participating in the life of the church. But the law does not just stop there.

For example, the law itself wavers in the application of the restriction of the power of governance to clergy; lay people can "cooperate" in it (c. 129, §2), and "cooperate" is a term deliberately left flexible so its meaning can develop through practical experience.[33] While homilies are restricted to clergy, lay people can be authorized to preach in church; when a homily cannot be given, there is a distinct possibility of competent lay persons being authorized to preach instead.[34]

2. Law in most instances follows life. What has become law on the books frequently begins in the practices of the community, and from these customs there develop binding norms of action. Such customs can even be contrary to disciplinary law (cc. 23–28). There is also the legal dictum that no one is held to the impossible; where observing the law is impossible, some other way must be found to serve the needs of the church.

On the other hand, restrictions on full participation by non-ordained in activities which do not require the power of orders are frequently the result of attitudes rather than law. Some seem to feel that if it is not expressly permitted in the law, something cannot be done. Yet what is not prohibited is not prohibited—a wide area for creative development exists in the church.

3. Let me suggest that to achieve realistic equality, freedom and participation in the church, we need to apply our secular experience to the human limitations that exist within the church. In the United States, this secular experience includes the civil rights experience of recent decades.

I am not advocating vigilante action, taking the law into one's own hands. That leads to anarchy and disaster. But I do advocate developing a working consensus on what are the key interests of God's people. Such a consensus cannot be found on peripheral issues, but only on the central issues of what it takes to proclaim and live the gospel today.[35]

We also need perspective. Rosa Parks was not the first person to be arrested for refusing to go to the back of the bus. But her arrest happened to catalyze a whole movement of men and women because the consensus had been developing. Linda Brown did receive her schooling, but her struggle was not over. Today as a grandmother she has returned to court to continue the struggle for equality, freedom, and participation. Can we expect the road to be easier for any of us in dealing with the human elements in the church?

The civil rights experience may teach us one final key lesson in the promotion and protection of the rights of women—and of all Christians—in the church. Hold the church accountable for its own teachings. Do not let anyone get by with mouthing platitudes, or denying in practice what is preached in theory. The rights set forth in the new code will only be dead letters until God's people put some life into them.

Notes

1. *Brown v. Board of Education*, 347 U.S. 483 (1954), 349 U.S. 294 (1955).

2. The literature on the topic of rights in the church is too vast even to attempt a summary here. For a reasonably balanced overview of major themes, see Alois Mueller and Norbert Greinacher, *The Church and the Rights of Man*, Concilium 124 (New York: Seabury Press, 1979). See also the commentary on the 1983 Code of Canon Law's canons on fundamental rights in *The Code of Canon Law: A Text and Commentary*, ed. James A. Coriden et al. (New York/Mahwah: Paulist, 1985), 134–173, with bibliography.

With reference to the rights of women in the church, see among other writings, the results of the Canon Law Society of America Symposium, *Sexism & Church Law: Equal Rights and Affirmative Action*, ed. James A. Coriden (New York: Paulist, 1977), and the collection of studies, *Women and Religion: A Reader for the Clergy*, ed. Regina Coll (New York: Paulist, 1982).

3. See, for example, *Women in the Church*, A Statement by the Worship and Mission Section of the Roman Catholic/Presbyterian—Reformed Consultation, Richmond, Virginia, October 30, 1971. See also the study on the ideas of John Calvin, *Women, Freedom & Calvin*, by Jane Dempsey Douglass (Philadelphia: Westminster Press, 1985).

4. For an analysis of the approximately 150 differentiations found in the 1917 code based on sex as such, rather than on clerical status or other conditions of life, see the appendix to Anthony J. Bevilacqua, *The ERA in Debate: What Can it Mean for Church Law?* (Toledo, OH: CLSA, 1978).

5. For a more detailed treatment of what follows, see the various studies in Mueller and Greinacher; see also James H. Provost, "Ecclesial Rights," *CLSA Proceedings* 44 (1982) 41–62.

6. See Krzysztof Drzewicki, "The Rights of Solidarity—The Third Revolution of Human Rights," *Nordisk Tidsskrift for International Ret* 53/3–4 (1984) 26–46.

7. See John Paul II, apostolic constitution *Sacrae disciplinae leges*, January 25, 1983: *AAS* 75/2 (1983).

8. The dignity of the human person is the foundation for the right to religious liberty (see Vatican II, *Dignitatis humanae*, 1) and has been developed by papal social teaching since Leo XIII, and strongly reaffirmed by John Paul II on several occasions.

9. For a discussion of this issue, see Joseph A. Komonchak, "Clergy, Laity, and the Church's Mission in the World," *The Jurist* 41 (1981) 422–447.

10. 1971 Synod of Bishops, *Justice in the World* (Washington: NCCB, 1971) 44.

11. 1974 Synod of Bishops, *Human Rights and Reconciliation*, *Origins* 4:20 (1974) 319.

12. Pontifical Commission on Justice and Peace, working paper *The Church and Human Rights* (Vatican: Pont. Comm. "Justitia et Pax," 1975).

13. John Paul II, *Sacrae disciplinae leges*.

14. 1917 code, c. 682: "Laici ius habent recipiendi a clero, ad normam ecclesiasticae disciplinae, spiritualia bona et potissimum adiumenta ad salutem

necessaria." In his study of rights of Christians in the 1917 code, Robert Kennedy discerns a variety of rights flowing from this key provision. See Robert T. Kennedy, "Canonical Tradition and Christian Rights," in *The Case For Freedom: Human Rights in the Church*, ed. James A. Coriden (Washington: Corpus, 1969) 91–106.

15. See 1983 code, cc. 208–223; a special list for lay persons follows immediately, cc. 224–231.

16. Many of the norms in Book One of the new code are examples of this.

17. International Theological Commission, *Propositions on the Dignity and Rights of the Human Person*, October 6, 1984 (Washington: USCC Publications, 1986) 16.

18. Ibid. 4.

19. This and subsequent translations of canons from the 1983 code are taken from *The Code of Canon Law, Latin-English Edition* (Washington: CLSA, 1983).

20. See discussion on the various meanings of common good, and an argument for the interpretation presented here, in the commentary on canon 223 in *The Code of Canon Law: A Text and Commentary* 158.

21. See the emphasis on this point by the 1985 Extraordinary Synod of Bishops, "The Final Report," *Origins* 15/27 (December 19, 1985) 448.

22. Can. 212, §3: "In accord with the knowledge, competence and preeminence which they possess, they have the right and even at times a duty to manifest to the sacred pastors their opinion on matters which pertain to the good of the Church, and they have a right to make their opinion known to the other Christian faithful, with due regard for the integrity of faith and morals and reverence toward their pastors, and with consideration for the common good and the dignity of persons."

23. In virtue of c. 228 lay persons can be named to church offices, yet c. 274, §1 limits certain offices to clergy. See Julian Herranz, "Le statut juridique des laics: l'apport des documents conciliares et du Code de droit canonique de 1983," *Studia Canonica* 19 (1985) 229–257.

24. Yet see below on the sexual discrimination retained in c. 230, §1, permitting only lay males to be installed in a permanent basis as lectors or acolytes—a provision which seems to be turning these "lay" ministries back into being merely steps for those preparing for sacred orders.

25. See also the entirely reformed law dealing with associations in the church, cc. 298–329.

26. This is applied specifically to the laity in c. 229; it is required for clergy and religious in other sections of the law.

27. In addition to c. 226, see a variety of rights assured to parents in regard to the education of their children (Book III on the church's teaching function), and in preparing them for various sacraments (Book IV on the church's sanctifying function). For an overview, see *The Code of Canon Law: A Text and Commentary* 162–163.

28. Congregation for the Doctrine of the Faith, *Declaration on the Question of Admission of Women to the Ministerial Priesthood*, October 15, 1976 (Washington: USCC, 1977).

29. Ibid. 15–16.

30. See *Presbyterorum ordinis,* 4 and 16.

31. See John Paul II, apostolic exhortation *Familiaris consortio,* November 22, 1981: *Origins* 11/28–29 (December 24, 1981) 445.

32. See Declaration on the Question of the Admission of Women to the Ministerial Priesthood 15–16.

33. For further development on these possibilities, see Herranz, cited above at n. 20; for a review of various positions see James H. Provost, "The Participation of the Laity in the Governance of the Church," *Studia Canonica* 17 (1983) 417–448.

34. See James H. Provost, "Lay Preaching and Canon Law in a Time of Transition," in *Preaching and the Non-Ordained,* ed. Nadine Foley (Collegeville: Liturgical Press, 1983) 134–158.

35. An example of one such effort to develop a consensus within the church are the statements issued by the Roman Catholic Bishops of Minnesota in 1979, together with an action plan developed for the Archdiocese of St. Paul and Minneapolis. See texts in *Origins* 8/45 (April 26, 1979) 709, 711–721.

4

The Refusal of Women in Clerical Circles

Mary Collins

IMAGINE A CLERICAL CIRCLE. SOME WILL SAY IT CAN'T BE DONE; CLERICS group in pyramids, not circles. Circles are a feminine shape, and clerical bodies have masculine shapes. Or circles are the shape of groups of friends, the shape of a collaborative enterprise, the shape of relationships of mutuality. A circle is what you might get if the pyramid gymnasts climbed down off each others shoulders and made contact by joining hands. Imagine a clerical circle? Oxymoron is the grammatical name for such a contradiction of terms—like "booming silence" or "happy fault," as in *O felix culpa!* Or perhaps clerical circle is a Zen koan—a riddle like "the sound of one hand clapping."

Try again. Imagine a clerical circle. Imagine the gathering in the parish house when the bishop comes for confirmation. What do you see, if not a clerical circle? Imagine the 1987 Roman synod on the laity. What comes into view but a clerical circle? Imagine a pope taking counsel on women's place in the church. Again, the mind's eye sees a clerical circle. The kind of circle my title refers to is the circle formed by a select group with common interests which they celebrate, protect, and promote.

Refusal of women is a constitutive mark of the clerical circle, one of the ways clerics define themselves over against other baptized Christians and other human beings. It is essential to the self-definition of clerics that they name maleness as a primary qualification for incorporation into their circle, that they pledge themselves to restrict their associations with women, that they never marry one, and that they understand themselves, in any necessary relations with women, to be superior to them. If a quasi-authoritative article in the *New Catholic Encyclopedia* of the 1960s is to be trusted, associations with women are perceived to be high risk situations because of the consequences of loss of sexual control. That clerical writer notes that sins against the chastity of a cleric have the quality of sacrilege—the profaning of the holy, the desecration of the sacred.

I invite you to call that clerical construction of human society reality curious. I invite you to risk the anathema pronounced at the Council of Trent against anyone who dared to question whether that construction of reality is God given. I invite you to be as adventuresome as Alice the morning she followed the rabbit down the hole, as daring as Dorothy when she and Toto set out on the yellow brick road, all of them attracted by and put off by the oddness of what they were seeing. When the guardians of the clerical construction of reality erect warnings that divine law has decreed the clerical world with its refusal of women, allow yourself to be astonished. Like Miss Piggy, utter your disarming "*Moi?* Inferior?" and refuse the refusal. Then wonder how the teachers know what they claim to know. Be amazed at all the emotional and intellectual energy clerics are willing to spend to argue women's human and ecclesiastical inferiority. Dare to consider the clerical construction of reality *cosmic wrongheadedness*.

In issuing you these invitations to you I am presuming a viewpoint different from the clerical world view. I would like to do three things: first, to discuss viewpoints in general; second, to enter briefly on a walking tour of the clerical world in order to understand it; and third, to move back to a viewpoint from which we can critique some of the assumptions that hold the clerical world together. Why bother to try to understand a viewpoint which refuses me? Why not ignore it? Put directly, the church is being held in bondage by this unexamined construct. In New Testament language, the clerical viewpoint is one of the "principalities" or "powers of this world" insofar as it is impeding the spread of the Gospel of freedom and salvation in Christ.

Viewpoints and Blindspots

Human beings operate with a common sense approach to reality. "Whatever is is right" was the way a nineteenth century poet put it. The world as we are born into it carries its own authority. Our early socialization and education is aimed at getting us to adjust to this reality. We learn to adopt the viewpoint of our culture, to find it eminently plausible, to appreciate the wisdom of its arrangements for good order, and to accept the consequences of our deviance from common sense.

Common sense is normally full of blind spots, however. These blind spots interfere with our ability to see everything that is worth seeing. Matters of significance escape our vision. The late Bernard Lonergan taught us much about viewpoints and blindspots, and some of it is worth considering here.

It is a simple fact of being human that our psyches cannot respond to all the stimuli that bombard us at every moment. The human psyche is protected by a censorship function, which generally serves a constructive purpose—namely, sorting out and presenting to our consciousness matters of significance. But the psychic censorship process of sorting and presenting images to consciousness can malfunction. Psychic blocking can occur; then the consciousness refuses a significant image and it is repressed.

Why does this happen? Lonergan recalls psychotherapy's answer that the human consciousness often refuses images because images are keys to insight, and in many cases the insights are unwanted. They lead to further questions and they demand changes of us, in response to them, which may be both painful and overwhelming.

With additional images and new insights we see things connected to one another in new ways. Lonergan suggests that the impact of admitting new data into our inner vision of reality is comparable to the impact on us of turning again and again to see the countryside as we climb a hillside. With each changed viewpoint we see familiar things in new relationships and we see things we had not noticed before. Reality changes when we turn.

Malfunctioning psyches which love blind spots and refuse insight in order to avoid change result in inevitable distortions in our lives. Lonergan names the resultant distortion dramatic bias; in essence, it sets the stage and provides the script from which we operate. Psychotherapists devote their lives to assisting people to discover blind spots, to recover long-blocked images, to welcome long-refused insights, and to make changes in their behavior.

Just as there is an individual bias, Lonergan invites us to attend to our experience of two similar phenomena: group bias and general bias. General bias refers to a situation in which a whole culture refuses insight by blocking significant experience and banishing unwanted images. Just as the individual psyche represses what it does not want to deal with consciously, so in similar fashion a society can design its social institutions so as to keep from view what is painful or threatening.

In the 1960s for example, social analysists began to look at the way American society as a death-denying culture dealt with its unwanted elderly and engaged the elderly themselves in this complicity to deny death. Most recently, feminist scholars among us have worked to expose to consciousness the many ways western society has resisted attending to the reality of women's personhood. Western civilization has so effectively maintained this general bias that both women and men have learned to exalt men, to promote their interests, to protect their egos, while diminishing women, banishing them from society, and negating or concealing their fully human identity.

Group bias, in Lonergan's analysis of insight and the failure to achieve, designates the distorted common sense viewpoint of a smaller segment within a larger society. Groups, too, can refuse to admit to consciousness data that might yield unwanted insight, raising questions and demanding changes too painful or too overwhelming to face. *Blessed Assurance,* the recently published study of the people of Amarillo, Texas, might be viewed as a study of group bias. It documents how decent people with common sense have come to terms with making their livings by assembling nuclear weapons that may destroy the planet. Outsiders who do not participate fully in the group's viewpoint and have no commitment to their blindspots might wonder at that group's inability to grasp more of reality. It is nevertheless possible to find the intelligiblity of an alien viewpoint.

Individual human beings, groups, and whole civilizations can and do ignore significant realities like human mortality, the human personhood of women, and the nuclear danger. We live daily with the consequences of our massive denials of the givenness of our human mortality and our human sexuality. Within this large problem of human perception, the human desire for and avoidance of truth, we are concerned with the clerical refusal of women in the Roman Catholic Church. Women, the visible, historical, and personal manifestations of the fact of human sexuality, the fact which is being refused in the clerical bias, must refuse the refusal. Accepting ourselves with gratitude for our female humanness, we must nevertheless be curious about the blind spot in the clerical construction of reality. It is to this that we now direct our attention, trying to understand an alien viewpoint.

The Emergence of the Clerical Viewpoint

The clerical class within the church come into being as an event of history. There was a time when it was not. The assertion of the Council of Trent that the clerical state differs essentially from the lay state *ius divinum*, by divine right or by divine law, appears to the ordinary twentieth century Catholic, lay or cleric, and also to some members of the theological community, to make a transcendent claim. Years ago Karl Rahner handled the question of a similar tension between historical information about the origins of the sacraments of the anointing of the sick and marriage and the dogmatic claim that all sacraments had been instituted by Christ with the broad affirmation that in constituting the church Christ had implicitly instituted whatever was necessary for the church's being and well-being. Some similar assertion may be more that we want to make here in any effort to reconcile historical information and apparently conflicting dogmatic assertions as these pertain to the clerical class. It is not clearly the case that the historical emergence and persistence of a clerical class has worked to the well-being of the church. The loss of all women's gifts and the gifts of lay men for 1700 years has been a high price to pay for organizational efficiency.

Imperial Rome's sense of social ordering and the Hellenistic culture of the Mediterranean world in the centuries immediately surrounding the birth of Christ each made their contributions to the emergence of a special class of ordained males who were named clerics. It is possible, from our viewpoint, to look at the ecclesiastical world constructed by the contributions from these cultural achievements as manifestations of general bias and group bias. This is not a grandiose judgment. All cultures, including our own, are partial achievements of human insight; all cultures also manage to conceal matters that are repressed rather than integrated adequately into the socio-cultural design.

Cultural historians of our era have begun to take note of the curious flight from human sexuality that characterized the Hellenistic culture of the whole Mediterranean basin from at least two hundred years before the birth of Christ well into the formative period of the Christian church. None of the historians have been able to give wholly adequate accounts of the pervasive antisexual bias undergirding the Hellenistic cultural ethos. However, expressions of the bias are found in the prevailing philosophical dualism, with its split between body and soul, matter and spirit, good and evil, things carnal and things spiritual, and the reductionist identification of the polarities with female and male human being. It expressed itself also in ascetic social movements which were characterized by repudiation of marriage, the denial of sexual existence, and the cultivation of the virginal life for both men and women. The origins of Christian monasticism, of the Christian institution of the order of virgins, and of the church's growing preference for celibate ministers are all grounded in the psychic and social dynamics of this period. The vilification of women found in the writings of the bishops and teachers of the early church is the rhetorical expression of the general bias of the times.

The Hellenistic cultural bias also expressed itself in a perception of hierarchies among beings. Hellenism was a relentless binary system factoring all relationships among things in terms of higher and lower. The resultant hierarchical ordering of the world of everyday experience was judged to have cosmic significance. In the words of a fifth century churchman of Hellenistic mystical bent summarizing the insight of his culture, earthly hierarchies were manifestations of heavenly hierarchies.

From another viewpoint, we can and must ask the question whether what he and his contemporaries knew to be true is indeed the case, that all reality exists in binary relationships of higher and lower, and that the resultant hierarchy of relationships is part of the immutable transcendent design for the universe. At least since Einstein's theory of relativity began to have its impact on our culture, most of us have been able to entertain an alternate viewpoint from that of the Hellenistic world. We can imagine that all things are indeed in relationship but that those relationships are mutable and are themselves related to human perceptions of them. We will return to some further consideration of that alternate viewpoint shortly. Now we need to look at least briefly at the contribution of the Roman imperial social design on the construction of the clerical viewpoint.

One of the great achievements of imperial Rome, the birthplace of the clerical class, was the development of a social design that expressed itself in terms of imperial orders. These orders performed distinct and distinguishing public services. Members of the senatorial, equestrian, and priestly orders, for example, filled all the offices and performed all the duties—but only those office and duties—assigned to their order. The Roman social design did not allow for lateral mobility. The orders were literally to mind their own business. Upward mobility was part of the social design, however. The offices of each order were ranked and graded. Young men advanced from lower to higher ranks within their orders according to their aptitude and their connections. Women had no place in the civil service of the empire, although other public roles existed for women.

Roman imperial order was a practical cultural achievement for administering a large empire. Pragmatic in its orientations, it made no claims to cosmic significance. Imperial religion, particularly, was politically pragmatic. The priestly ordo had collapsed in pre-Christian times when the various oriental cults alive in the provincial corners of the empire made their way to the great city and captivated the religious sensibilities of the Roman people. Rather than outlawing the cults, Roman pragmatism chose to regulate and to domesticate them. In a later era, the emperor Augustus, son of Julius Caesar, reestablished the defunct priestly ordo for political purposes, and recruited young men to its ranks. Priestly duties were once again understood to be services performed by officers of the empire for the public good. Always pragmatic, the later emperors Constantine and Theodosius were able to replace the pagan imperial priesthood with Christian ministers when they judged that the older order no longer served the public interest.

The fourth century suppression of pagan priesthood did not create a vacuum. The bishop of Rome and his presbyters and deacons, and his brother bishops in the provinces of the empire, already constituted a network of new religious leadership. All that was lacking was public recognition. Theodosius made Christianity the official religion of the empire. And it was Theodosius who provided the imperial legislation that declared the church's ministers to constitute a new ordo in the empire, insofar as they were the agents of the new cult. By this imperial act, bishops, priests, and deacons, and their lesser associates became the ranked members and office holders in the public order of clerics.

Imperial Rome did not require a celibate priesthood. However, the Roman sense of imperial order did require that only males would hold public offices in the clerical or any other social order. Imperial Rome also bequeathed some of the organizational language left over from the pagan priesthood. The bishop of Rome became the new Supreme Pontiff, presiding now as did his pagan predecessor, over a "college" of official collaborators. The church even adopted the imperial Latin tag *ius divinum,* by divine right or divine law, as the formula for stabilizing and protecting the Roman regulation of public cult everywhere in the empire. The church also inherited the pagan concern that its male priests at least protect themselves from sexual "pollution" immediately prior to their performance of sacred rites.

If the priestly tradition of imperial Rome did not require celibacy of its new clerical ordo, other cultural forces made celibacy seem the only plausible development for spiritual leaders. Clerics began to require celibacy of themselves in their own synods. Why? Perhaps because as participants in the Hellenistic culture they shared uncritically in the widespread common sense viewpoint that human potential for nearness to God was able to be measured by distance from involvement with the pollution of sexuality. Women, even their own wives, were almost hopelessly mired in their sexual condition. As clerics themselves aspired to the ideal of celibacy to protect their sense of their own holiness, they begin to define their own reality and to discipline their own kind. Men who consorted with women were de facto excluded from the clerical ordo. The acts took on the force of public law.

Two systems, one pragmatic and the other cosmological, met to create a new thing for the service of the Gospel in the empire:

the male, celibate, hierarchically ordered clerical class in the Roman Church. Christian communities in the provinces of the empire were more conservative than the church in the imperial city, and they resisted the novelty. We have ample historical documentation of popular resistance to the suppression of women's ministries and the imposition of clerical celibacy in the name of the new Roman ordo.

Persistence of the Clerical Viewpoint

The emergence of the clerical viewpoint is understandable as an event of human history, even if it is based on a cosmological bias which invites cross-examination in the interests of achieving greater truth. How does the clerical world persist, and why? We cannot underestimate the role the institutions and rituals of the clerical ordo have played in the maintenance of the clerical world-view for clerics. The Roman Catholic seminary is one such institution which successfully inculcates this world view; as such, it is a carefully protected institution. Young men predisposed to the clerical viewpoint for whatever reason are inducted into the church's clerical ordo step and step and taught its ways. No curriculum attends to the matter explicitly, but the patterns of seminary life include overt and covert lessons on a necessary suspicion of women as sexual beings and of male superiority to them. Sometimes lessons in contempt have been taught.

Rites of ordination celebrate hierarchical relationships of higher and lower status, inferior and superior rank, and proclaim that all this is God's design. The consecratory prayer for the ordination of deacons declares: "Almight God . . . you are the giver of preferments, the assigner of roles, the one who arranges official appointments . . ." Those who gather in solemn liturgical assembly for the ordination of presbyters hear it said of God: "[you are] the source of preferments, the one who assigns all ranks, the one through whom the whole world advances and everything is made secure . . ."

Regular clerical convocations provide periodic reinforcement of the self-understanding learned in the Roman seminary and celebrated in the liturgies of ordination. Bishops and priests gather for retreats, synods, and study days and reflect together on the dignity of their clerical status, their responsibilities to one another and to the maintaining of good order, and the indignities to which they are inevitably subjected by those who do not share their viewpoint. At the high point of such clergy gatherings, clerics concelebrate the eucharist, pulling themselves together into a self-contained, hierarchically-ordered circle. The unexamined dogmatic assertion that this world exists *ius divinum* insures the commitment of clerics to the clerical viewpoint. Only the boldest ever dare to submit the clerical construct to examination in the light of available human experiences that defy explanation on clerical terms. Even the bold can be controlled. Tragically, clerics themselves can be counted on to humiliate and to shun members of the clerical ordo who, for whatever reason, call into question any part of the clerical construction of reality.

The Sunday eucharistic assembly has for centuries provided the ritual setting in which all lay Catholics learned that they were not clerics, learned the consequences of their lesser status, and learned about women's special deficiencies based on their sexual identity. Ritual learning is pre-conscious, not conscious, learning. The overt content the eucharist celebrates is the mystery of Christ. Yet through the centuries the whole church learned through the restrictions placed on women's liturgical participation that baptized women were still unfit for singing at worship, for reading the Scripture, for preaching the word, for approaching the altar, and for leading public prayer. Because these restrictions occurred in a setting whose origins were said to be *ius divinum,* few wondered that the mystery of Christ made such distinctions between men and women and between men who consorted with women and those who avoided them.

The Roman church, presided over by a Supreme Pontiff and a male, celibate hierarchically-ordered clerical class since the fourth century, has deliberately even if unconsciously denied itself access to the experience of women's spiritual gifts. By banishing women from leadership roles and by controlling women's access to religious knowledge, the clerically defined church concealed women, making women invisible even to themselves. Through the strategy of concealment the clerically-dominated church has blinded itself to images of spiritually gifted women. In doing so, it has successfully avoided unwelcome insights. Following Lonergan, we assume the insights are unwelcome because they would lead to meaningful questions and to an inner mandate for change. I, for one, do not doubt that changes in self-understanding could be painful, even overwhelming, for most clerics. Fifteen years ago I had a newly ordained priest cry out in anguish in a university classroom, "If I am not superior to the rest of the church, I'm wasting my life!" Ten years ago I was amazed to read a popular article by an eminent priest theologian in which he fell back to unfathomable divine design as his final reason for maintaining celibate male priesthood after he had conceded intellectually that there was no sound traditional, theological, or anthropological reason for refusing to admit women to orders. Perhaps he was responding finally and intuitively to the logical inconsistency of admitting women to a state which defines itself by its refusal of women.

Refusing the Refusal Intellectually and Pastorally

Can we refuse the clerical refusal of women; and if so, on what grounds? I think we have no choice but to refuse it, and to refuse it both on the basis of our scientific knowledge of the Gospel and on the basis of our own ecclesial experience.

Let us consider briefly the discrepancies between the Gospel viewpoint and the clerical one on two points. The clerical worldview attends selectively to some but not all of the data available to us from the apostolic church. It regards as authoritative texts reflecting the early emergence of ecclesial order. In fact, the clerical viewpoint over-identifies in inappropriate ways with much of what the New Testament says about bishops and presbyters and deacons, presuming that there is some exact correlation between the New Testament use of those words and what the words finally came to signify in the clerical ordo as it developed under Hellenistic and imperial influence. The clerical viewpoint welcomes whatever New Testament language and imagery bolsters clerical authority over the community of believers. On the other hand, the clerical worldview suppresses the witness of the apostolic church to Jesus's welcoming of women. It rejects as insignificant those memories of the first Christians about women's participation in the life and ministry of Jesus and in the life and ministry of the church in its early days.

If, as many before me have argued, the origins of clerical consciousness can be traced to the general cultural bias of an earlier era, the maintenance of this viewpoint—in the face of reliable information to the contrary about the apostolic tradition and about the historical origins of the clerical ordo—needs some explanation. The persistence of the viewpoint is comprehensible to me, but only as an expression of group bias, the refusal of unwanted insight. Insofar as I accept the reliable interpretations of historians and biblical scholars, I must refuse the clerical refusal of insight. I must take an alternate viewpoint on intellectual grounds.

But I must also take an alternate viewpoint on the grounds of my own ecclesial experience. The clerical construction of reality denies my experience of my own life in the church. Despite the rhetoric of clerical consciousness, shaped by the dualistic bias and exclusively male administration of an ancient world, I know that I am neither essentially passive as a human being nor mentally enfeebled; I am not in need of male authority. As I human person, I am sexual and mortal; limited, but not defective. Furthermore, I know I am not an exceptional woman; other women here and everywhere know the same things about themselves.

The clerical construction of reality with its refusal of women also denies my lifelong experience of women's demonstrated leadership in the church and women's spiritual giftedness. I honestly do not know what it is that women cannot do in the service of the Gospel. My hunch is that there is not a churchman in this country—deacon, priest, or bishop—who does not have access to the same data. Contemporary ecclesial experience contradicts the clerical worldview.

I am less confident about what churchmen will do with the data they have. Public policy and social institutions in the United States assure the continuation of the general western cultural bias against women. This general bias will provide a protective canopy, within which the personal bias of individual clerics and the group bias of the clerical ordo can be sustained, and the insights available from the Gospel and significant ecclesial experience can be refused.

Refusal of insight carries with it the risk of bad faith and great inner stress, both for the church and for each of us who are its members. Acceptance of insight will set us all off in a new direction, as insight always does. A new order will have to be achieved, with new patterns of authority, decision-making, and administration. We can be confident that these, too, will be human and fallible, despite our best efforts to be faithful to the

Gospel of Jesus and the mysteries of creation and redemption in which we participate. Our cultural biases will weaken our achievement, but our insights will give the global church new vitality. Great stress will inevitably accompany individual and group efforts to make the turn in consciousness and to change our behaviors accordingly. Catholic women are special witnesses to the stress that accompanies living as a Roman Catholic with new found conviction, first, that women, who are sexual, are also saved and sent to preach the Gospel, and second, that this reality, not the clerical world view, is *ius divinum,* the will of God.

As I completed this presentation, I read in the press a report that Pope John Paul had recently addressed the theological faculty at the University of Lyons. He exhorted theologians to "faith" and warned them against "intellectual temptations" which would "destroy the church." I was momentarily tempted to a little guilt; it is emotionally intimidating to be charged with contributing to the destruction of the church. Then I recognized it is because of faith in Jesus Christ that we must also refuse to be intimidated.

5

Women Preaching the Gospel

Mary Catherine Hilkert

RESURRECTION PREACHERS

WOMEN CALLED TO PROCLAIM THE GOSPEL IN TODAY'S WORLD AND church find their contemporary situations not unlike those of the first preachers entrusted with the Good News of the resurrection. Mark's Gospel describes the response of Mary Magdalene, Mary, the mother of James, and Salome, who had come to the tomb to anoint Jesus. Arriving and finding the stone rolled back, they are told by a man in white that Jesus who was crucified has been raised. The women are then sent to share the Good News: "Go and tell the disciples and Peter that he is going ahead of you to Galilee" (16:7). The earliest version of this Gospel concludes, however, with these words:

> They made their way out and fled from the tomb bewildered and trembling: and because of their great fear, they said nothing to anyone (16:8).

The longer ending of Mark says that the risen Jesus

> . . . first appeared to Mary Magdalene out of whom he had cast seven demons. She went to announce the good news to his fol-

> lowers, who were now grieving and weeping. But when they heard that he was alive and had been seen by her, they refused to believe it (16:9–11).

According to Matthew's Gospel, after the Sabbath, as the first day of the week was dawning, Mary Magdalene came with the other Mary to inspect the tomb. Suddenly there was a mighty earthquake as an angel descended from heaven (Mt 28:1f). Again the women are told:

> Do not be frightened. I know you are looking for Jesus the crucified, but he is not here. He has been raised, exactly as he promised. Come and see the place where he was laid, then go quickly and tell the disciples . . . They hurried away from the tomb, half-overjoyed, half-fearful, and ran to carry the good news to his disciples (28:5–7).

In the midst of their mission they experienced Jesus' word of "Peace" and his own commission: "Go and carry the news to my brothers" (28:10).

In Luke's version the women arrive at the tomb, find the stone rolled back, enter, but cannot find Jesus. They are, as Luke says, "still at a loss over what to think of this" (24:4), and are terrified by the presence of two men in dazzling garments who confront them with the question: "Why do you search for the Living One among the dead?" (24:5). It is precisely in remembering the words of Jesus that the Son of Man would be crucified and rise again that they are empowered to return from the tomb and tell the disciples. However, Luke notes, "The story seemed liked nonsense and they refused to believe them" (24:11).

In John 20 we have the story of the woman who would in later tradition be called "the apostle to the apostles."[1] Mary Magdalene stood weeping beside the tomb, "but even as she wept she stooped to peer inside" (2:11). The focal question of the passage repeated first by the angels and later by Jesus is: "Woman, why are you weeping?" (20:13). Mary's response is: "Because the Lord has been taken away, and I do not know where they have put him" (20:13). It is in her very loss, confusion, and pain that she "catches sight of Jesus" (20:14). Her greatest hope had been to find the dead body of the one she loved. Instead, that hope is broken open beyond all expectation, and she experiences the mystery and power of the resurrection in the calling of her own name: Mary. In John's version, when Jesus commissions Mary to tell his brothers, she goes immediately and announces what she has experienced: "I have seen the Lord" (20:18).

"Different Voices"

These biblical accounts describe the experience of women called to proclaim the Good News in our time as well. Many women disciples are seeking God but meeting confusion, even empty tombs. At the same time, however, we are discovering the power of the resurrection. Many of us are experiencing a real call and empowerment to preach the Good News even when our message and experience are rejected. The "experience of women," however, while shared in many ways, still remains diverse and unique. As preachers, women speak (and hear) not only, to borrow a phrase from Carol Gilligan, "in a different voice," but also in different voic*es*. There are women in our tradition who came "to anoint Jesus," who came for ministry, came in love, but who have now "made their way out, fled from the tomb, bewildered and trembling." Some, "because of great fear, say nothing."

Others among us have faced their demons—the demons of fear and rejection as well as those of sinfulness and personal limitations. Having experienced a power beyond themselves, the power of God casting out those demons, they find ways to announce the Good News to others—to those who are grieving and weeping.

Still others grapple with where "Good News" is to be found, where life is to be found among all the dying; those who are still at a loss over what to think of all that is happening to the Body of Christ. Some ask themselves: "Why search for the living one among the dead?" But as Luke's Gospel suggests, it is in remembering Jesus' words, the words of the Gospel, that transformation and empowerment happen. The Gospel now takes on a whole new meaning and power, though as women speak new words the story still "seems like nonsense" and others "refuse to believe."

There are, too, those who experience more of the joy of the commission and vocation to preach and who, "half-overjoyed, half-fearful" (not a bad posture for any preacher!) *run* to carry the Good News.

Finally, there are those who identify with the witness of the woman who is consistently included among the witnesses to the resurrection—Mary Magdalene, who moved beyond her own grief, loss, and confusion to speak in the power of the Risen Christ. Like Mary, they announce the truth of their experience with conviction: "I have seen the Lord!" All effective preaching of the Gospel comes ultimately from that kind of deep human experience in faith. The history of most women as disciples and as preachers is some combination of each of these responses.

All Christian preaching ultimately centers around the proclamation that the one who was crucified has been raised and lives among us. Preaching is a matter of announcing the power of the resurrection, the power of the Spirit active here and now in human history. But there is a unique way in which the reality of women preaching the Gospel shares in the very mystery of the resurrection. In the resurrection the impossible has happened. God has broken into human history in a radically new way and reversed all ordinary human expectations. The resurrection is the ultimate surprise and overthrow of former categories and limitations. Further, we claim that the proclamation of the word is an event in which the Gospel happens again, here and now. We are confronted with the new possibilities of the reign of God once again in such a way that a response is demanded. The Gospel "catches us up short"—God's ways are not our ways. For many in our churches, hearing the word of God proclaimed by women is just such a parable experience. Their categories and expectations are shattered as God once again proves to be "doing a new thing" (Is 43:19).

WOMEN: PREACHING AND PROHIBITED FROM PREACHING

The "new thing" the Spirit is doing today among women who are preachers of the Gospel is not entirely new, however. The Christian tradition—specifically the Catholic tradition—includes a history of women preaching, interlaced with a history of the prohibition of women from the public proclamation of the Gospel in the name of the church. We stand at a new moment within that tradition, nonetheless claiming to be faithful to the living

Christian and Catholic tradition. Thus it is important for us to re-read the history of that tradition with a critical hermeneutic in order to identify the forgotten history of women commissioned to preach the Gospel, and to uncover and analyze the reasons given (or the presumptions surrounding) the restrictions on women's proclamation of the Gospel in the name of the church.

New Testament

The New Testament offers clear evidence of women as preachers of the Gospel, yet at the same time it contains the classic texts used repeatedly in the tradition to restrict women from public preaching. It is significant to note that the passages which attest to women as the first witnesses to the resurrection are not debated in the later tradition. Rather, the distinction is made between "unofficial" and "official" witnesses—women being the former; men, the latter. Thus, even the 1976 Declaration on the Question of the Admission of Women to the Ministerial Priesthood, for example, states:

> Contrary to the Jewish mentality, which did not accord great value to the testimony of women, as Jewish law attests, it was nevertheless women who were the first to have the privilege of seeing the risen Lord, as it was they who were charged by Jesus to take the first paschal message to the apostles themselves . . ."[3]

But then the document adds: *in order to prepare the latter to become the official witnesses to the resurrection.*[4] Note the reasoning here. Although women were clearly the first witnesses to the resurrection and were commissioned by Jesus to proclaim the Good News, they cannot have been official witnesses because of the restrictions of the Jewish tradition of the time. Is it not possible that the charging of women as the first official witnesses, the first preachers of the Gospel, is actually part of the great surprise of the resurrection? Is it not commissioning by the risen Jesus, rather than cultural or religious limitations of the time, which determines who are Christianity's official witnesses?

In terms of specific ministries, it is important to recall that ministry, as described in the New Testament, is largely charismatic and diverse. The Spirit bestows different gifts on various members of the community for the common good, distributing to each as the Spirit wills. Numerous authors have noted that there is no evidence that women were excluded from any of the ministries in the earliest Christian communities.[5] In terms of preaching, there is, on the contrary, clear evidence that women were so gifted and did exercise ministries of preaching, prophesying, and teaching. Women exercised significant leadership roles in the early Christian communities, founding and maintaining house churches. Women's role as prophet is attested to in 1 Corinthians 11:2–16, the very passage used later in the tradition to argue that women are subordinate to men according to the order of creation, and even to argue that women do not image God as fully as men.

In the often-cited passage Paul writes:

> I want you to know that the head of every man is Christ: the head of a woman is her husband; and the head of Christ is the Father. Any man who prays or prophesies with his head covered brings shame upon his head. Similarly, any woman who prays or prophesies with her head uncovered brings shame upon her head . . . she ought to wear a veil. (1 Cor 11:3–6).

This very text, however, gives evidence of women praying and prophesying in the context of public worship. Paul's argument is not that the practice should stop, but that when women do exercise this authority in the community they should have their hair covered or bound up. Detailed exegetical debates concerning this custom and its symbolic value are available elsewhere.[6] The point here is simply to establish that women did in fact preach publicly in worship in the early Christian communities.

With respect to teachers in the early church, Prisca (or Priscilla) is mentioned specifically, along with her husband Aquila, as having instructed Apollos in the Christian faith (Acts 18:26). She is mentioned again in the final chapter of Romans as one of Paul's co-workers in the service of Jesus Christ:

> . . . not only I but all the churches of the Gentiles are grateful to them [Prisca and Aquila]. Remember me also to the congregation that meets in their house (16:5).

In the same chapter Junias is described as an outstanding apostle

(16:7). While the name is a well-known one for women at that time, exegetes, until recent challenges from feminist scholars, have commonly interpreted it as the shortened form of the male name Junianus. Once again the operative assumption is that a woman could not have been an apostle: hence, the name must have been either incorrect or abbreviated.

Another woman, Phoebe, is named *diakonos* of the church at Cenchreae (Rom 16:1). Applied to men, the term is translated missionary, minister, servant, or deacon and indicates an itinerant missionary, the leader of a local congregation, involved in preaching and teaching.[7] Again, however, in the case of the woman Phoebe, exegetes and translators have traditionally translated the term "deaconness" and have argued that her role was not parallel to the male deacons.

We have been searching for historical clues of women in preaching roles in the New Testament. If we were to approach the biblical texts on the level of literary text, rather than from an historical-critical perspective, we might also include the following: the four daughters of Philip, gifted as prophets (Acts 21:9); Anna and Mary, who function as prophets in the infancy narratives (Lk 2); Mary of Bethany, who is the exemplary disciple listening to the word (Lk 10); and the role of witness attributed to women, including the Samaritan woman, in John's Gospel.[8] One cannot, however, leave the New Testament simply on this note of good news. The New Testament also contains the classic texts prohibiting women's preaching in the Christian tradition:

> According to the rule observed in all the assemblies of believers, women should keep silent in such gatherings. They may not speak. Rather as the law states, submissiveness is indicated for them. If they want to learn anything they should ask their husbands at home. It is a disgrace when a woman speaks in the assembly (1 Cor 14:33a–35).

> A woman must listen in silence and be completely submissive. I do not permit a woman to act as teacher or in any way have authority over a man, she must be quiet. For Adam was created first, Eve afterward; moreover, it was not Adam who was deceived, but the woman. It was she who was led astray and fell into sin. She will be saved through childbearing, provided she continues in faith and love and holiness—her chastity being taken for granted (1 Tim 2:11–15).

In addition to the fact that 1 Corinthians 14:33a–35 occurs in the same letter in which Paul refers to women praying and prophesying publicly without criticizing the practice, biblical scholars have noted that the verb in 1 Corinthians 14 is "to speak" (*lalein*) and that the reference is not to the official function of teaching or preaching.[9] The passage from 1 Timothy, a later pastoral epistle, which does admonish women not to teach (*didaskein*) but to be submissive and silent, is clearly a later development in conflict with the earlier Pauline evidence that women not only prayed and prophesied at worship (1 Cor 11:5) but also exercised the ministry of teaching (Acts 18:26).

Critical exegesis reveals that the above texts are pastoral injunctions in light of specific historical-cultural circumstances (including clear patriarchal bias) in diverse communities—not texts which were intended to be applied universally or handed down as "the Christian tradition." The cultural conditioning and patriarchal bias of the texts may seem evident in an age of critical biblical interpretation, but it is important to realize that these texts, taken as authoritative and inspired, functioned to prohibit women from preaching in the majority of Christian churches until well into the nineteenth century.[10]

Early Church

The gradual hierarchical structuring of the church and accompanying clericalization of ministry have been described in detail elsewhere.[11] What is significant to note here is that preaching became connected with the church's teaching office; hence, it became the prerogative of the bishop as guardian of the authentic faith tradition.

There is evidence of officially authorized lay preaching by Origen in the third century, but by that time women were clearly excluded from preaching. The *Didascalia Apostolorum* specifically stated:

> It is neither right nor necessary therefore that women should be teachers and especially concerning the name of Christ and the redemption of his passion. For you have not been appointed to this, O Women . . . For He, the Lord God, Jesus Christ, our teacher, sent us, the Twelve, to instruct the people and the gentiles; and there were with us no women disciples . . . but he did not send them to instruct the people with us (III,6).[12]

The *Didascalia*'s prohibition of women's teaching was repeated in the *Apostolic Constitutions* (fourth century), although it was clear that lay*men* could be teachers if properly trained:

> He who teaches, even if he is a layman, let him teach as a skillful person properly equipped in word and deed, for they shall all be taught of God.[13]

There is also evidence that women preached and presided earlier in the Montanist sect (second century), but the condemnation of Montanism as heretical only further reinforced the suspicion that the practice of women preaching endangered orthodoxy.

The case of Origen is significant, however, because it reveals that at least in some local churches in the third century public preaching was not yet identified with ordination or office, but was based on charism and training. Some local churches preserved the synagogue practice of allowing any man gifted with the Spirit to address the congregation. (This was precisely the setting of Jesus' preaching in Lk 4. As a layman Jesus read from the Isaiah scroll: "The Spirit of the Lord is upon me . . ." [4:18] and then proclaimed "today this passage is fulfilled in your hearing" [4:21].) As the head of the catechetical school in Alexandria, Origen was invited by the bishops of Jerusalem and Caesarea "to preach and expound the scriptures publicly, although he had not been ordained a presbyter."[14] when Demetrius, Origen's local bishop, called him home for what he regarded as a breach of discipline, the bishops of Jerusalem and Caesarea took issue with their brother bishop:

> He has stated in his letter that such a thing was never heard of before, neither has hitherto taken place, that laymen should preach in the presence of bishops. I know not how he comes to say what is completely untrue. For whenever persons able to instruct the brethren are found, they are exhorted by the holy bishops to preach to the people.[15]

Evidence of officially authorized public lay preaching is not available again until the Middle Ages. While the concern for the church's authentic tradition was the motivation behind Pope Leo V's fifth century censure of dissident monks whose preaching was not faithful to the Council of Chalcedon, his statement which restricted preaching according to state of life rather than orthodoxy was quoted frequently in the later tradition:

> Apart from those who are priests of the Lord, no one may dare to claim for himself the right to teach or preach, whether he be monk or layman and one who boasts a reputation for some learning. For although it is desirable for all the church's sons to be learned in what is right and holy, no one outside the priestly order is to assume for himself the rank of preacher. For it is necessary that all things be ordered in God's church; that is in the one body of Christ, the superior members are to carry out their office, and the inferior members are not to resist superior ones.[16]

As the Council of Trullo later would ask:

> Why dost thou make thyself a shepherd when thou art a sheep? Why become a head when thou art a foot? Why dost thou try to become a commander when thou art enrolled in the number of soldiers?[17]

With the compiling of the *Statuta Ecclesiae Antiqua,* a reform work which originated in France (fifth-sixth centuries), there was something of a retrieval of the possibility for authorized lay preaching. Canon 38 reads: "Laity should not dare to teach in the presence of the clergy." The compiler, however, added: *unless the clergy approve.*[18] While this provided some basis for authorized lay preaching, women were still completely forbidden from preaching. The prohibition was based on the authority of St. Paul and the *Apostolic Constitutions:* "A woman, no matter how learned and holy, should not dare to teach men in assembly" (Canon 37).[19] The issue here was clearly not one of charism, authentic doctrine or training, but merely gender in a patriarchal system which subordinated women to men. Further, it was not until the sixth century that even the priest was given explicit permission to assume the preaching office along with the bishop. Deacons at that time were permitted only to read the writings of another—usually one of the Church Fathers who were considered recognized authorities in the community. In the seventh century even the bishops were exhorted to

> gather out of holy scriptures meditations and determinations of truth, not going beyond the tradition of the God-bearing Fathers

> . . . and not composing things out of their own heads, lest through their lack of skill they may have departed from what is fitting.[20]

There was no question of the authorization of women preaching publicly in the name of the church in a hierarchical system which defined women as subordinate to men, laity to clergy, and priest to bishop. Where the practice of lay preaching continued, it was condemned on the grounds that subordinates were usurping the rank of their superiors.

Middle Ages

Although by the Middle Ages the church's hierarchical character and the strong distinction between clergy and laity had developed significantly, traces of the earlier approach to preaching based on charism remain. These traces are found particularly in the lay preaching bands which were given temporary papal authorization and encouragement. Further, it is significant to note that even where preaching was based on rank it was not yet clearly linked to ordination, nor was it always assumed that the woman was subordinate. Consequently, an abbess, because she was the superior of the community—even of joint monasteries of women and men—had the right to preach to her "subjects."

Hildegard of Bingen, a twelfth century Benedictine nun, is said to have preached to clergy, laity, monks, nuns, and ecclesiastical officials—preaching even to bishops and clergy during their synods.[21]

What is perhaps of greatest interest to us in the present day, however, is the rise of itinerant preaching bands composed of lay men and women who, in a period of evangelical renewal in the church, felt called to live the *vita apostolica,* that is, to imitate Jesus and the apostles through lives of voluntary poverty and the preaching of penance and reform.[22] While the issue of heresy emerged eventually with regard to several of these groups (Cathari, Humiliati, Waldensians), it is significant to note that the medieval notion of heresy comprised not only incorrect doctrine but also departure from the church's disciplinary norms.[23] The Waldensians, who were originally authorized by Pope Alexander III to preach with the permission of their parish priests, later departed from church discipline by preaching without permission and eventually were condemned for doctrinal heresy as well. The Humiliati, who had similarly been excommunicated for preaching without permission, were later officially authorized by Innocent III to preach words of exhortation (*verbum exhortationis*) but not doctrine concerning faith and the sacrament (*articuli fidei et sacramenta*) since doctrinal preaching required a solid knowledge of Scripture and theology.

A final example of papally authorized lay preaching is found in the Franciscan Order. Founded as a lay movement dedicated to the imitation of Christ and the apostolate of preaching, the Franciscans were given permission by Innocent III to preach penance everywhere, provided they received the approval of Francis. Franciscan historians note that to "any of the brethren, layman or cleric, that had the Spirit of God, he gave the permission to preach," and that this permission included both liturgical preaching and the exhortative sermon.[24] Early on, however, the Franciscan Order became clericalized (though not without challenge nor without "qualms of conscience for Brother Francis").[25] With the Fourth Lateran Council (1215), lay preaching was definitively prohibited as the unauthorized usurpation of the clerical office.

What is fascinating in the various medieval disputes about the right to preach—between monks and secular clergy, mendicants and the local bishops, lay preachers and local clergy—is the shift in claims about the source of authority to preach. The lay preaching bands grounded their authority to preach in the living of the Gospel life which impelled them to preach the Good News. In other words, they claimed a charismatic authority. In other cases, permission or authorization became the basis of the claim to authority: the permission of Francis, of the local priest, of the bishop, or, as was the case in the Dominican Order, of the pope (whose authority superseded that of the authority of local bishops who were resisting both reform and this new "order" of preachers"). Rank or office provided the justification for the preaching of the medieval abbesses but also constituted grounds for the eventual prohibition of all lay preaching by the Fourth Lateran Council. Finally, in the disputes between monks and diocesan clergy, the sacrament of ordination, rather than jurisdiction or permission, was offered as the basis for the authority to proclaim the Gospel in the name of the church.

The practice of lay preaching continued to be an issue in the thirteenth and fourteenth centuries (John Wycliffe and the Lollards, Jan Hus), but the interrogations of suspected followers of Wycliffe and Hus at the Council of Constance reveal that by the fifteenth century lay preaching was clearly considered heretical. Two of the questions used to determine heresy were: 1) Does the person believe it is permissible for people of either sex, men as well as women, to preach freely the word of God? and 2) Does the person believe the priest should preach, even if not sent?[26] By the time of the Council of Trent preaching was clearly connected with office in the official tradition of the church.

Before leaving the medieval period it is important to consider not only juridical legislation but also theological reflection on the question of lay preaching and specifically women's preaching during this period. Because the writings of Thomas of Aquinas have been used repeatedly in the tradition to argue for the natural (and divinely intended) subordination of women to men, his treatment of the question of whether women are granted the charism to preach is particularly significant.

In the *Summa Theologicae* (II–II, q.177) Aquinas describes what he calls a "charism of speaking," that is, a grace given for the profit of others to instruct them, to move their affections to hear God's word and to desire to fulfill it and to sway the hearers of the word that they may love what is signified by the word and desire to fulfill it. In other words, Aquinas discusses what we identify as a charism or gift for preaching. In the second article of the question Aquinas notes that this charism clearly belongs to women since women can teach as a mother teaches her children.[27] Furthermore, says Aquinas, the grace of prophecy, which is an even greater gift of speech, was given to such women as Deborah, Huldah, and the four daughters of Philip. And St. Paul himself, Aquinas observes, referred to women prophesying and praying in the community. Finally, Aquinas notes that a responsibility derives from being gifted with a charism:

> It is said in 1 Peter: As each has received a gift, employ it for one another. But certain women receive the grace of wisdom and knowledge, which they cannot administer to others except by the grace of speech.[28]

Aquinas' only opposing argument are the two biblical passages cited earlier:

> On the other hand, St. Paul says that women should keep silence in the Churches, and I permit no woman to teach or to have authority over men.[29]

Aquinas' reconciliation of the conflicting evidence is the familiar one of making a distinction: Women do have the charism, but they should exercise it privately rather than by publicly addressing themselves to the whole church. The legitimation he offers for this conclusion reflects clearly the patriarchal and hierarchical bias of the world-view of the time, combined with a literal interpretation of Scripture. Aquinas' argument that women should not address the whole church is based on three elements: 1) Principally, this is fitting because of the condition of the female sex which according to Gn 3:16 must be subject to men. To teach and persuade publicly in the church is not the task of subjects but of prelates. Men, when commissioned, can far better do this work because their subjection is not from nature and sex, as is the case with women. 2) Lest men's minds be enticed to lust. "Many have been misled by a woman's beauty. By it passion is kindled like a fire" (Eccl 9:8). 3) Because, generally speaking, women are not perfected in wisdom so as to be fit to be entrusted with public teaching.[30]

In spite of the androcentric bias of the medieval world-view evident in Aquinas' argument, it is clear that he did at least recognize the central issue: women *are* gifted with the charism to preach and have a responsibility to exercise that gift.

Vatican II and Canon Law Revision

It was not until Vatican II that preaching was again approached on the basis of charism. The 1917 code of canon law, citing Pope Leo's prohibition against lay preaching, reaffirmed the connection between preaching and office which had existed since the time of the Councils of Constance and Trent. Canon 1342 stated:

> the faculty to preach is given only to priests and deacons . . . and preaching in the church is forbidden to all the laity, even religious.

With Vatican II, however, came a fundamental shift in the Roman Catholic understanding of church and ministry. Conciliar developments which have particular significance with regard to the question of women preaching (and lay preaching in general) include: the return to the biblical images of church as people of God and Body of Christ; the emphasis on the universal call to holiness and the universal priesthood of all the baptized; the role of the laity in the priestly, prophetic, and kingly mission of Christ; the recognition of the variety of gifts or charisms given in the Body of Christ for the sake of the common good and the church's mission; and the responsibility of the entire church to preserve the word of God and to pass on the Christian faith.

Further, when discussing contemporary legislation on the question of lay preaching (and thus, all preaching by women in the Roman Catholic context), it is important to remember that church law comprises the documents of Vatican II, post-conciliar decrees implementing the Council and renewal, liturgical law, particular law, special indults and permissions, and customs of church people, as well as the code of canon law.[31] Vatican II and the new code espouse a renewed vision of church as the community of the baptized, equal in dignity by virtue of baptism. Ministerial roles are not determined by the status of "superiors" and "inferiors" in the one Body of Christ. Rather, it is baptism which gives every member in the body a basic participation in Christ's mission, though members exercise different functions in the community deriving from the different gifts received from the Spirit.

At several places in the new code the baptized are not only encouraged to proclaim the Gospel but told that it is their responsibility to do so (c. 225). Further, canon 213 puts the discussion in focus when it says that one of the rights of the Christian faithful is "a right to the word of God and the sacraments." According to canon 759:

> in virtue of their baptism and confirmation lay members of the Christian faithful are witnesses to the gospel message by word and by example of a Christian life (c. 759).

Lay persons can exercise the ministry of the word and function as lectors (c. 230), although patriarchal bias remains in that even today only lay men can be installed officially as lectors. A significant reversal of the 1917 code is found in canon 766 which states that lay persons can preach in a church or oratory if it is necessary in certain circumstances, or if it is useful in particular cases according to the prescriptions of the conference of bishops and with due regard for canon 767, paragraph 1. That canon deals with the problematic area of preaching at the eucharist:

> Among the forms of preaching the homily is preeminent; it is part of the liturgy itself and is reserved to a priest or deacon.

The purpose of this article is not to focus entirely on canon law and its proper interpretation and implementation in the area of preaching. However, since canon law is usually cited as the primary contemporary restriction of lay persons—therefore of all women—from preaching at the eucharist, it may be valuable to review two relatively recent official authorizations for lay preaching at the eucharist and highlight the reasons given in both cases.

The 1973 Directory for Masses with Children, published by the Congregation for Divine Worship, indicates that

> one of the adults may speak to the children after the gospel, especially if the priest finds it hard to adapt himself to the mentality of children.[32]

Note the principle here: Who can best communicate God's word in this congregation here and now? For pastoral reasons it may be that someone other than the presider may be the more effective preacher. The concern is that God's word be proclaimed—and heard.

Perhaps the most notable authorization of lay preaching at eucharist is found in a precedent in particular law in West Germany. In 1973 the West German Bishops' Synod requested permission for authorized lay preaching at eucharist. The Congregation for the Clergy granted permission for four years, and in 1977 extended that permission for another four years. In their request the bishops alluded to the shortage of clergy, the number of well-educated, theologically literate lay persons in Germany and, finally, their basic concern: more effective preaching. They recognized the primary liturgical reservation with respect to lay preaching at eucharist: the unity of word and sacrament, but did not stop there. Rather, the bishops claimed:

> Because of the close relationship between the liturgy of the word and liturgy of eucharist, it is suitable that the preacher and presider of the eucharist be one and the same person, but this is not absolutely necessary. Moreover since the church teaches that the entire community preaches the gospel and celebrates the liturgy, the responsibility for maintaining the office of preaching should not be given to the priest alone. Finally, lay preaching is a way of making visible the different charisms, services, and offices which exist in the Christian community without detracting from the unity of its mission.[33]

Summary

Several basic conclusions emerge from this rereading of the Christian (and specifically Catholic) tradition on preaching:

1. Regardless of the reasons given for the authorization of preaching, the charism to preach is grounded in baptism and confirmation—source of all ministry.

2. There is in the tradition a history of authorized and official lay preaching, even at eucharist.

3. The restrictions on women from preaching publicly in the name of the church have stemmed from a) inadequate interpretations of 1 Corinthians 14 and 1 Timothy; b) a hierarchical model of ministry which subordinated women to men; c) the lack of theological training which would ensure that the church's authentic doctrine would be preserved or d) the connection of liturgical preaching with ordination. Points a, b, and c above are no longer valid criteria in the post-Vatican II church. Point d does represent a valid concern for the unity of word and sacrament, but not the only possible model of liturgical presidency.

WOMEN NAMING GRACE

A final significant source for theological reflection on women's charism and commission to preach the Gospel is to be found precisely in the contemporary experience of both preacher and community as women exercise this ministry. What deeper aspects of the mystery of preaching emerge as women "name grace"?[34] Ultimately, that's what preaching is all about: handing on the Christian story in such a way that the experience of grace—God's presence in ordinary human life—is communicated. The retelling of the Good News becomes an invitation of discipleship to others: an invitation to "come and see," to "go and do likewise." Preachers do not simply retell a story from the past—not even the story of Jesus being raised from the dead. Rather, preachers point to the power of the resurrection here and now in new and concrete life situations. That is true of all Christian preaching; however, the very experience of women preaching the Gospel brings new dimensions to, and initiates deeper questions about, both the ministry of preaching and the meaning of the Gospel. Here we will consider briefly five fundamental questions which emerge: 1) What constitutes the preaching of the church? 2) Who should preach in the liturgical, and specifically the eucharistic, context? 3) Where is the source of the authority to preach located? 4) What are the connections between human experience and preaching? 5) What is the Gospel that we preach?

1. *What constitutes the preaching of the church?* Women do preach the Gospel as they have done so from the beginnings of Christianity. Without dismissing the fundamental importance of explicit liturgical proclamation by women, we need to claim the broader ways in which women (and men) preach the Gospel today. The preaching of Jesus is the paradigm for all Christian proclamation, and Jesus announced God's reign in his person and actions as well as in his words. He proclaimed God's compassion not only in words of forgiveness, but by sharing meals with sinners. He preached God's healing mercy when he touched lepers. He challenged social structures that fell short of the promise of God's reign by healing on the Sabbath and relating freely to women and the outcast. Jesus announced God's reign (which is what preaching is all about) not only in preaching and teaching events—and rarely in a liturgical setting.

So, too, we need to claim the experience of women active on behalf of God's reign as "the preaching of the church." Preaching the Good News of salvation requires that the Christian community make the experience of salvation more of a concrete reality in our world. Equally important is naming the power and source of that experience of salvation—the power of God. Women disciples are actively involved in both forms of the proclamation of the Gospel—word and deed.

Women in prison ministries, women ministering to other women (the battered, the homeless, the grieving and the sick), women involved in legal advocacy or political lobbying on behalf of the poor, are participating in the "action on behalf of justice" which the 1971 Bishops' Synod statement, Justice in the World, says is a "constitutive part of preaching the gospel."[35] But women are also involved int he explicit naming of the power of salvation in our world. In a variety of ministries of the word (spiritual direction, teaching, theologizing, pastoral counseling, church leadership), women are involved in discerning and naming the experience of God in the midst of human struggle. Further, an increasing number of Catholic women from a variety of age groups, backgrounds, and styles of life are now involved in ministries most explicitly identified as preaching or announcing the Gospel: full-time missionaries, members of itinerant preaching teams, pastoral associates, leaders of Scripture-sharing groups, and the like. Women are also preaching in a number of prayer contexts: directing retreats and days of recollection, preaching at morning and evening prayer and at services of the word, forming the faith of the church as catechists in the revised rites of Christian initiation, and preaching in a variety of forms of worship, including eucharist, in both Catholic and ecumenical contexts.

As women embrace the commission to "spread the Good News" and engage more fully in processes of creative imagination, other possible avenues and modes of preaching the Gospel will emerge. There is a real danger in restricting our understanding of preaching to the pulpit or the liturgical context. Most of the people in our world who hunger for the Good News of salvation or liberation are not to be found in our churches. If preaching is a matter of making connections between concrete human experience and God's word, enabling people to hear the Gospel as Good News *for them,* then the Gospel and its preachers have to meet people where they are.

2. *Who should preach in liturgical, specifically eucharistic, contexts?* On the other hand, this is not to relegate the preaching of women only to the broader spheres of evangelization, much less to legitimize the exclusion of women from the public proclamation in

what we claim is the "fullest word" of the church—the eucharist.[36] On the contrary, it is precisely our experience of women preaching in the broader ministries of the word that raises the question of who should preach in liturgical contexts, and specifically in the context of the eucharist.

Liturgical ministries are profoundly connected with the reality of ministry or service in the daily life of the community.[37] It is here that we find the theological-liturgical reason which underlies a frequent pastoral experience today. More and more often someone who has exercised a clear ministry of the word in the broader life of the community is requested to preach the homily in the context of a liturgical service or at eucharist: for example, a marriage, funeral liturgy, jubilee celebration, or final vow ceremony.

However, the recovery of the ancient liturgical homily at the time of Vatican II, and specifically that emphasis that the homily is "part of the liturgy itself," has led to the restriction in canon law that the homily is reserved to the ordained priest or deacon.[39] A number of theologians would concur that lay preaching "breaks the intrinsic bonds between word, sacrament, and community leadership."[39] This does not mean, however, that these theologians necessarily oppose women preaching at the eucharist. On the contrary, they argue that to have a layperson exercise this leadership role is in practice to suggest that the discipline of ordination be reconsidered. William Skudlarek, for example, has written:

> the link between preaching and the sacraments, especially the Eucharist, is a close one. We need to consider it carefully, not so much to limit who may preach, but to widen our understanding of who may rightfully lead a community in its sacramental response.[40]

The question of women preaching—or married persons preaching—does raise further questions about the charism of leadership, including liturgical leadership in the Christian community. However, even given the ordination of women and married persons, as is already the case in other Christian churches, the question of the appropriateness of lay preaching at eucharist remains.

Here I agree with Mary Collins who has suggested that we need new models of presidency over the word which would include the possibility of another believer sharing the ministry of the word without disrupting the presidency of the assembly or breaking the unity of word and sacrament. Collins states that:

> If Eucharist is the act of the whole church, and if the ordained is someone who presides within, not over, the community of believers, then it seems possible and necessary to seek new models for understanding sacramentality in relationship to liturgical presidency. Ecclesial experience confirms that it is possible for the one who presides within the liturgical assembly to engage another believer to lead them all together into deeper communion with the mystery of Christ by the power of the word, and this collaborative ordering does not fracture the sacrament of unity.[41]

The case of the West German bishops and even present liturgical law indicate that someone other than the presider may preach the homily. The Introduction to the Lectionary cites specifically the deacon or one of the concelebrants.[42] In the case of permanent deacons, who often have considerably less theological training and preparation for preaching than many women in the community, the restriction of women from preaching the homily at eucharist becomes even more incomprehensible.

Pastoral practice in this area seems most clear where a foreign language is the issue. In numerous Spanish-speaking parishes, or at Vietnamese Masses, for example, frequently non-ordained members of parish teams who speak the language have been formally authorized to preach at eucharist. Again I would emphasize that the pastoral principle needs to be extended to other contexts: Who can most effectively proclaim God's word in this situation here and now?

3. *The source of authority to preach.* At least implicitly, any preacher of the Gospel speaks in the name of the church, interprets the heart of the Christian tradition, and exercises the charism of prophecy in the sense of naming where God is active here and now in human history and experience. What is the source of that authority?

Ultimately, both the ability and the call to preach come from the source of all real power in the Christian community—the

Holy Spirit. But we have always insisted that the power and presence of the Holy Spirit is mediated in and through the church. That is also true for women who feel called and empowered to preach the Gospel, but with a new emphasis. Frequently women describe the source of authority or empowerment to preach as a combination of an inner desire to preach and the invitation and confirmation of local communities of believers. Women's experience of the vocation of preacher comes through the people who are the church and through the Holy Spirit who is active in the depths of all the baptized. Learning to trust one's own deep and mysterious experience of the Spirit of God and a real relationship with the community to whom one preaches is essential to the preaching ministry and the vocation of the preacher.

Even when the individual's charism has been recognized and affirmed by the official community leadership, specifically by the bishop who is responsible for ordering the public exercise of the ministries of the word within the local church, that recognition and commissioning is not the ultimate source of the ability or authority to preach. The grounding of all ministries—including the ordained ministry—is to be found in baptism and confirmation.

4. *Preaching and life experience.* The human experience of the preacher is central both in terms of how one understands the Gospel and how one touches the human experience of others, that is, how one communicates the mystery of salvation as a living reality. Attempts to name what distinguishes women's experience from that of men often fall into stereotyped categories: women are more compassionate, intuitive, sensitive, relational; men are more logical, assertive, objective, and the like. Similarly, the claim is made that women's preaching—or at least feminist preaching—is more relational, more rooted in experience, more in a narrative style, more collaborative, and so on than is the preaching of men. I think that is simply not always the case.

However, it is true that women's experience of sexuality and life, the relation of woman to body, nature, the childbearing and nurturing processes and the *historical* experience of marginalization, exclusion and subordination within society and the church, constitute a different framework for perceiving reality from that of men. Without being able to spell out the dimensions of gender differences, I would still claim that women bring a different experience of life to the hearing and preaching of the Gospel. What is most basic here is that because women both hear and speak the Gospel "in a different voice" the whole community is impoverished if we hear the word of God only as interpreted in and through the male, and primarily celibate, experience of life. The story of Jesus, which we believe is the story of God, is inexhaustible. The richness of the mystery which we proclaim is diminished and distorted when we fail to hear the Good News as reflected through women's stories.[43]

Restriction of the public proclamation of the Gospel in the name of the church at the key moment of the community's celebration and identity—the eucharist—suggests implicitly that men have a privileged hearing of the Gospel whether by divine plan or by church discipline. On the other hand, the very reality of a woman preaching, particularly in the liturgical context, shatters traditional stereotypes and suggests a new vision of church and ministry, a new vision of humanity—female as well as male—as imaging God, a new vision of the image of Christ as located in baptism, and ultimately a new vision of God. Here it is not simply a question of inclusive language and richer imaging of God,[44] though that too is fundamental, but of the depths of women's experience of God which we have in many ways just begun to explore. As preachers women are called to give birth in new ways to God's word and wisdom.

5. *What is the Gospel we preach?* All preachers wrestle with the word of God they are called to proclaim, but women wrestle for a blessing in a particular way because the biblical texts themselves include a patriarchal bias (for example, the classic texts from 1 Cor and 1 Tim). Not everything in the Scriptures is "good news" for women. Thus, the challenge of all preachers to find the Good News of salvation in a particular text requires a critical hermeneutic which can distinguish historical-cultural conditioning and patriarchal bias from the word of God.

But as women we continue to wrestle with and to preach this word precisely because we believe that a blessing is to be found there for all humanity. Beneath the words the word of life is to be found. The Gospel we preach is ultimately the same Good News which Jesus preached. It is the vision of God's reign in which the blind see, the lame walk, the captives go free, and the poor hear good news. The mystery of salvation also includes the liberation and wholeness of women as well as men; a new relationship, not only between women and men, but among all peoples and nations. The time of salvation promises a time of peace, a time when the only ruling power will be the rule of God which is a rule of love.

As preachers, women share in the experience of the prophet Ezekiel. Before we can preach we must eat the scroll, sweet and sour, and find a life-giving and truthful word to speak (Ez 3:1–3). Only if we have struggled ourselves with how this Gospel is a source of freedom for us, can we then speak a word of hope to others. Post-Christian feminists, among others, raise the question of why we continue to preach the Gospel of Jesus crucified and risen, rather than other stories more compatible with our experience as women. Others within the church question why women feel so strongly the desire to preach and to hear the word preached—to have it enfleshed—by other women. For many of us the response to both groups is the same:

> We speak because we have believed. This is what we proclaim . . . What we have heard, what we have seen with our own eyes, what we have looked upon and our hands have touched.—We speak the word of life. (1 Jn 1:1).

Notes

1. Bernard of Clairvaux, *Sermones in Cantica,* Serm. 78, 8 (PL 183, 1148).

2. Carol Gilligan, *In a Different Voice* (Cambridge: Harvard University Press, 1982).

3. Congregation for the Doctrine of the Faith, *Declaration on the Question of the Admission of Women to the Ministerial Priesthood, Origins* 6 (Feb. 3, 1977) 520.

4. Ibid.

5. "Women and Priestly Ministry: The New Testament Evidence: A Report by the Task Force on the Role of Women in Early Christianity," *Catholic Biblical Quarterly* 41 (Oct. 1979) 610. Cf. Elisabeth Schüssler Fiorenza, *In Memory of Her* (New York: Crossroad, 1983). Regarding the specific ministry of preaching, see Sandra Schneiders, "New Testament Foundations for Preaching by the Non-Ordained," in *Preaching and the Non-Ordained,* ed. Nadine Foley (Collegeville: Liturgical Press, 1983) 60–90.

6. See, for example, Elisabeth Schüssler Fiorenza, *In Memory of Her* 226–30;

and Jerome Murphy-O'Connor, *I Corinthians* (Wilmington: Michael Glazier Press, 1979) 104–09. (Murphy-O'Connor observes that this form of praying and prophesying is a "ministry of the word deriving from a profound knowledge of the mysteries of God based on the Scriptures. It would be very difficult to justify a distinction between prophecy in this sense and our contemporary liturgical homily" [p. 105].)

7. Elisabeth Schüssler Fiorenza, "Word, Spirit, and Power: Women in Early Christian Communities," in *Women of Spirit: Female Leadership in the Jewish and Christian Traditions,* eds. Rosemary Ruether and Eleanor McLaughlin (New York: Simon and Schuster, 1979) 35–36. Cf. K.H. Schelkle, "Ministry and Ministers in the New Testament Church," *Concilium* XI (1969) 5–11 and A. Lemaire, "From Services to Ministries: Diakonia in the First Two Centuries," *Concilium* XIV (1972) 35–49.

8. See Sandra Schneiders, "Women in the Fourth Gospel and the Role of Women in the Contemporary Church," *Biblical Theology Bulletin* 12 (1982) 35–45. Cf. Raymond E. Brown, "Roles of Women in the Fourth Gospel," *Theological Studies* 36 (1975) 688–99.

9. Robert J. Karris, "Women in the Pauline Assembly: To Prophecy but Not to Speak?" in *Women Priests: A Catholic Commentary on the Vatican Declaration,* eds. Arlene and Leonard Swindler (New York: Paulist, 1977), 205–08.

10. See Barbara Brown Zikmund, "The Struggle for the Right to Preach," in *Women and Religion in America,* Vol. 1, ed. Rosemary Radford Ruether and Rosemary Skinner Keller (New York: Harper and Row, 1981) 193–205.

11. See Yves Congar, *Lay People in the Church* (Westminster, Md: Christian Classics, Inc., 1985) and "My Path-Findings in the Theology of Laity and Ministries," *The Jurist* 32 (1972) 169–88; Edward Schillebeeckx, *Ministry: Leadership in the Community of Jesus Christ* (New York: Crossroad, 1981) and *The Church with a Human Face* (New York: Crossroad, 1985); David Power, *Gifts That Differ: Lay Ministries Established and Unestablished* (New York: Pueblo, 1980) 59–87; Mary Collins, "The Public Language of Ministry," in *Official Ministry in a New Age,* ed. James H. Provost (Washington, D.C.: Canon Law Society of America Permanent Seminar Studies, No. 3, 1981) 7–40, and "The Refusal of Women in Clerical Circles," Paper presented at Time Consultants Conference "Facing Issues on Women in the Church," Washington, D.C., October 11, 1986, and reprinted in this volume; Bernard Cooke, *Ministry to Word and Sacraments* (Philadelphia: Fortress, 1976); Thomas F. O'Meara, *Theology of Ministry* (New York: Paulist, 1983) 95–133, 161–67; "In Solidarity and Service: Reflections on the Problem of Clericalism in the Church," CMSM *Documentation,* April 8, 1983). For specific discussion of the shift of the preaching ministry from various charismatic ministries to the official ministry of *episkopos* and later of *presbyter,* see Thomas K. Carroll, *Preaching the Word* (Wilmington: Michael Glazier, 1984); Edward P. Echlin, *The Priest As Preacher Past and Future* (Notre Dame: Fides Publishers, 1973); Mary Collins, "Baptismal Roots of the Preaching Ministry," in *Preaching and the Non-Ordained,* ed. Nadine Foley, 111–33.

12. *Didascalia Apostolorum* III, 6, trans. R. Hugh Connolly (Oxford: Clarendon Press, 1929) 133. For a well-documented study of the historical development of lay preaching and its prohibition with particular attention to canonical issues

and developments, see Elissa Rinere, "Authorization for Lay Preaching in the Church," (J.C.L. dissertation, The Catholic University of America, 1981). For a critical theological analysis of the question see Edward Schillebeeckx, "The Right of Every Christian to Speak in Light of Evangelical Experience 'In the Midst of Brothers and Sisters'," in *Preaching and the Non-Ordained* 11–39. Cf. *The Church with a Human Face* 174–89. See also Yves Congar, *Lay People in the Church* 271–323.

13. Translation by Rinere, 21. Cf. F.X. Funk, *Didascalia et Constitutiones Apostolorum* (Paderborn: Ferdinandi Schoeningh, 1905) 539.

14. *The Church History of Eusebius*, VI, 19, 16, trans. Arthur Cushmann McGiffert in *The Nicene and Post-Nicene Fathers*, ed. Philip Schaff and Henry Wace (Grand Rapids: Wm. B. Eerdmans Co., 1952) 267.

15. *The Church History of Eusebius* VI, 19, 18.

16. *St. Leo the Great: Letters*, number 119, translated by Edmund Hunt (New York: Fathers of the Church, Inc., 1957) 207–08.

17. Council of Trullo, canon LXIV, trans. by Henry Percival in *The Seven Ecumenical Councils* (New York: Charles Scribner's Sons, 1905) 394.

18. Translation by Rinere, *Les Statuta Ecclesiae Antiqua, Edition-Etudes Critique*, Charles Munier, ed. (Paris: Presses Universitaires de France, 1960) 86.

19. Ibid.

20. Council of Trullo, canon XIX in Percival, 374.

21. Peter Dronke, *Women Writers of the Middle Ages* (New York: Cambridge University Press, 1984) 149.

22. See Congar, *Lay People in the Church*, 300–02. For fuller discussion of the controversy surrounding lay preaching in the Middle Ages, see William Skudlarek, *Assertion without Knowledge? The Lay Preaching Controversy of the High Middle Ages*," (Ph.D. dissertation, Princeton, 1979) and Rolf Zerfass, *Der Streit und die Laienpredigt* (Freiburg: Herder, 1974).

23. Janet Nelson, "Society, Theodicy, and the Origins of Medieval Heresy," in *Studies in Church History*, ed. Derek Baker, vol 9, *Heresy and Religious Protest* (Cambridge: University Press, 1972) 74.

24. *Legenda trium sociorum* (*Acta Sanctorum*, October, II, 737–38), as quoted by M-D Chenu in *Nature, Man and Society in the Twelfth Century* (Chicago: University of Chicago Press, 1968) 261. Cf. Anscar Zawart, O.F.M. Cap., *The History of Franciscan Preaching and Franciscan Preachers, 1209–1927*, no. 7, *Franciscan Studies* (New York: J. Wagner, Inc., 1928) 262.

25. Chenu, *Nature, Man and Society in the Twelfth Century*, 260. Cf. Lawrence Landini, *Causes of the Clericalization of the Order of Friars Minor, 1209–1260 in the Light of Early Franciscan Sources* (Chicago, 1968).

26. DS 1277. Translation from Rinere, 101.

27. Thomas Aquinas, *Summa Theologicae* II–II, 177, 2, 1 and ad. I, trans. Roland Potter, Blackfriars, vol. 45 (New York: McGraw-Hill, 1970).

28. *Sum. Theol.*, II–II, 177, 2, 2, 3.

29. *Sum. Theol.*, II–II, 177, 2, contra.

30. *Sum. Theol.*, II–II, 177, 2, reply.

31. James H. Provost, "Lay Preaching and Canon Law in a Time of Transition," in *Preaching and the Non-Ordained* 134–58.

32. Directory for Masses with Children, #24, ICEL translation in *Documents on the Liturgy 1963–1979* (Collegeville: Liturgical Press, 1982) 682.

33. "Die Beteiligung der Laien an der Verkundigung," 2.33, trans. William Skudlarek, Appendix III in *Assertion without Knowledge?*

34. See Mary Catherine Hilkert, "Naming Grace: A Theology of Proclamation," *Worship* 60 (Sept. 1986) 434–449.

35. Justice in the World. Statement of the 1979 Synod of Bishops (Washington, D.C.: United States Catholic Conference, 1972) 34.

36. For fuller development of the theology of the eucharist as the fullest word of the church, see Karl Rahner, "The Word and the Eucharist," *Theological Investigations* Vol. IV (Baltimore: Helicon Press, 1966) 253–86.

37. See David Power, *Gifts That Differ* 13–15.

38. For fuller canonical discussion of the possibility of lay preaching at the eucharist, see Provost, note 31 above.

39. Joseph Komonchak, " 'Non-Ordained' and 'Ordained' Ministries in the Local Church," *The Right of a Community to a Priest,* Concilium, vol. 133, eds. Edward Schillebeeckx and J.B. Metz (New York: Seabury, 1980) 47–48. Cf. Skudlarek and Power, note 40 below.

40. William Skudlarek, "A Response (to Edward Schillebeeckx)," in *Preaching and the Non-Ordained,* 59. Cf. David Power, *Gifts That Differ* 155.

41. Mary Collins, "Baptismal Roots of the Preaching Ministry," in *Preaching and the Non-Ordained* 130.

42. The Introduction to the Lectionary #24, #50. (Washington, D.C., United States Catholic Conference, 1982). Cf. William Skudlarek, "Lay Preaching and Liturgy," *Worship* 58 (1984) 500–06.

43. See Elizabeth Schüssler Fiorenza, "A Response (to Walter Burghardt)," in *A New Look at Preaching,* ed. John Burke: Wilmington: Michael Glazier, 1983) 43–55.

44. See Elizabeth Johnson, "The Incomprehensibility of God and the Image of God, Male and Female," *Theological Studies* 45 (1984) 411–65.

THE PRACTICE

6

Zeal for Your House Consumes Me: Dealing with Anger As a Woman in the Church

Fran Ferder

WHENEVER I HAVE SPOKEN TO EAST COAST CONFERENCES, I HAVE found a wonderful enthusiasm and real zeal for God's house among the participants. Those experiences made this invitation to speak again exciting in itself. The topic was even more exciting: it is one that has been very close to me for years. However, I did have one small concern. Given the topic that I was asked to address—anger and how to deal with it in the church today—I was concerned that I was not currently angry. However, I had been living in Seattle for about six months—history intervened! I now stand before you with enough experiences of the church in western Washington to have at least some energy around this topic again.

ANGER AS GIFT

What I would like to do is to take a deep look at that simple, emotional reaction of anger: what it really means, where it comes from, and what happens to our bodies, to our sacred flesh, when we experience the passion of anger. In the process I want to look at some of the situations in the church today which continue to generate that emotion, that energy, in the lives of many women and men who are committed to tending the Gospel.

I will be looking at anger primarily in its psychological meaning. When I use the word "psychological," I am not referring to aspects of us that are somehow apart from the holy. That is a misunderstanding perpetrated by many people who are critical of psychological intervention, as though persons who are pursuing the Gospel could live apart from their psychological reality.

Let me give you an example. I was talking with someone not long ago who was very critical of a sociological-psychological analysis of the conflicts with Rome these days. That person said to me, "The church is not simply a democracy. It's more than that. And you can't apply human psychological principles to something like the church." When I hear that kind of fragmentation, I respond this way: if you do not apply these principles, you are going to be in big trouble, because human beings do not cease to operate apart from psychological realities just because they are part of the church. This premise is equally true of leaders in the church. People who are attempting to lead also have a psychological reality. I think it would be fair to say that the leadership in the church today is not operating out of pure, unadulterated, raw holiness. There are some strong psychological realities that are impinging on and influencing the style of leadership that we are seeing in the church, particularly in the institutional church. That leadership style has nothing to do with the Gospel of Jesus, but it has a lot to do with persons' interior psychological pathology.

None of us can live outside of our psychological and sociological reality, no matter who we are. We can avoid looking at it; we can refuse to name it; we can be critical of it; but we cannot take it away. We are fooling ourselves if we say that psychology has nothing to do with real religious faith. It has a lot to do with it. When I am angry as a Christian person who follows the Gospel of Jesus of Nazareth, I do not react to that anger apart from my psychological reality. We are psychological, social, emotional persons in the midst of our religious experience and along with it, and we have to understand the implications of those realities. That is why we are going to look at anger.

Anger has been a somewhat confusing emotion in the history of the church. We have been warned about it and encouraged not to experience it. It is even listed as one of the seven Capital Sins. People have a great deal of resistance and guilt about naming that simple emotional experience when it occurs in their lives.

Sometimes I find that even among healthy people, who understand that anger is a normal, neutral emotion and a wonderous source of fire and passion, there is a fear of anger, and a hesitation to admit angry feelings.

I would like to look at anger briefly from a strictly physiological sense and then move on from there. Before anger is anything else, before it is even a cognitive awareness, anger is a physiological reaction. It is simply part of our flesh, part of our bodies. As such it was purposefully and lovingly created and shaped by God as a source of energy, as a source of fire. The only aspect of anger about which we have choices is how we let it move us. We do not have choices about whether or not we will experience it, unless we choose to cut off a very significant dimension of God's life in us.

Anger, in addition to being a physiological reaction that has vascular, muscular-skeletal and respiratory changes (fig. 1), is a sign of divine revelation in our lives. When we experience the rapid heart, the flushing, the warmth, the energy that surges up inside of us when we are angry, that is God gaining our attention through our flesh. That is part of being a person who is walking in God's presence. Noticing the physiological reactions that go with anger, then, is critical to responding with holiness to the call of the Gospel today.

When we turn to the psychological meaning of anger, we find a number of studies which tell us that anger is one of the primary emotions. The specific purpose of anger is to mobilize us to remove barriers to important needs. Knowing that, we can find it easier to appreciate several things about God's design in creating anger and giving it to us as a powerful gift. We know that we all have needs. We also know that different people, even holy people, can create barriers to our meeting those needs and responding to them appropriately. It is the emotional-physiological response of anger that provides the energy in us to strike down, take away, remove barriers to important needs.

ANGER AND BASIC NEEDS

Many people find the psychological model of Abraham Maslow helpful in the understanding basic human needs. As you can see from the chart (fig. 2) Maslow arranges these needs in

Diagram of the Anger Response

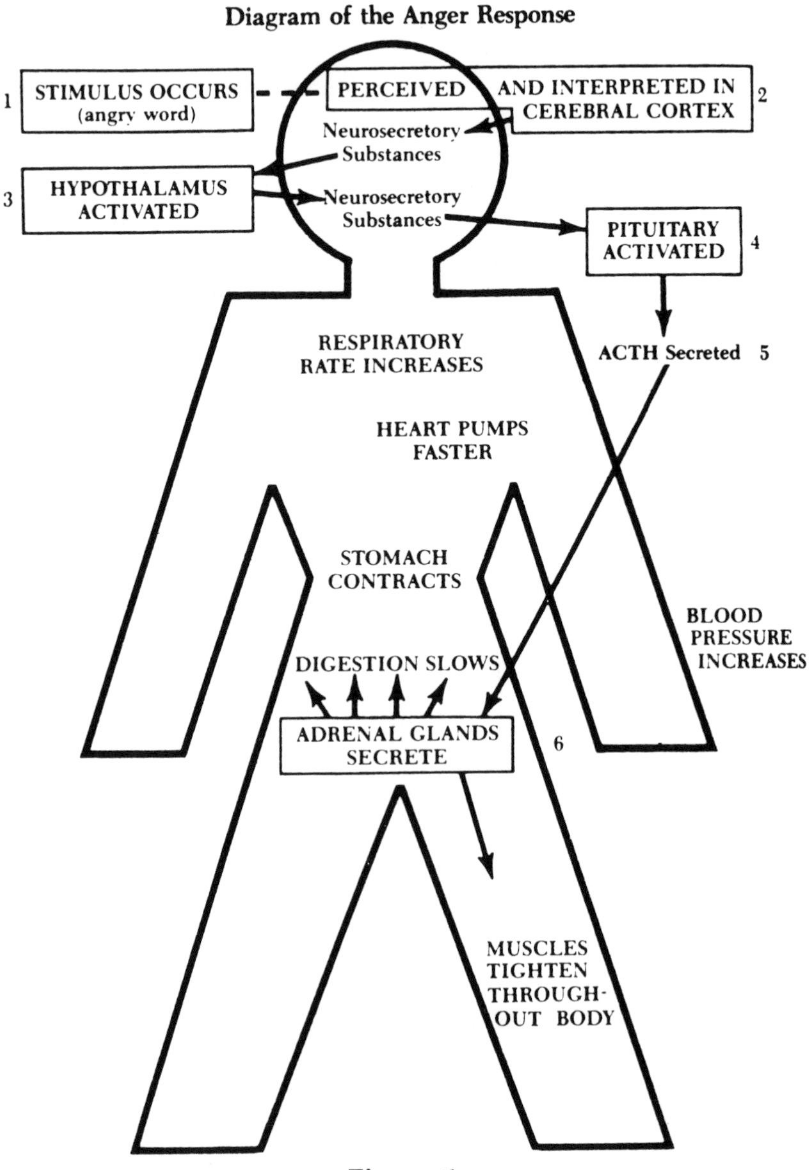

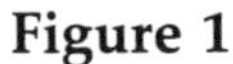

Figure 1

an ascending order. It seems to me that hierarchical leadership, or institutional leadership, is attacking human needs today at very basic levels. Sometimes it is esteem which is threatened, sometimes it is acceptance, and sometimes the more fundamental area of safety.

Maslow's theory maintains that one cannot really meet higher needs on the scale if more basic needs are in jeopardy. Let us begin then by looking at the most basic of the three needs identified, the need for safety. All of us, every single person in this room, has the need to feel safe, not just physically, but safe in the sense that it is really acceptable to say what we think and what we feel in an appropriate way, in an appropriate time and place without having to be afraid of losing our job, of having our professional advancement cut off, of being hurt, shunned, neglected. There are many ways to make people feel unsafe.

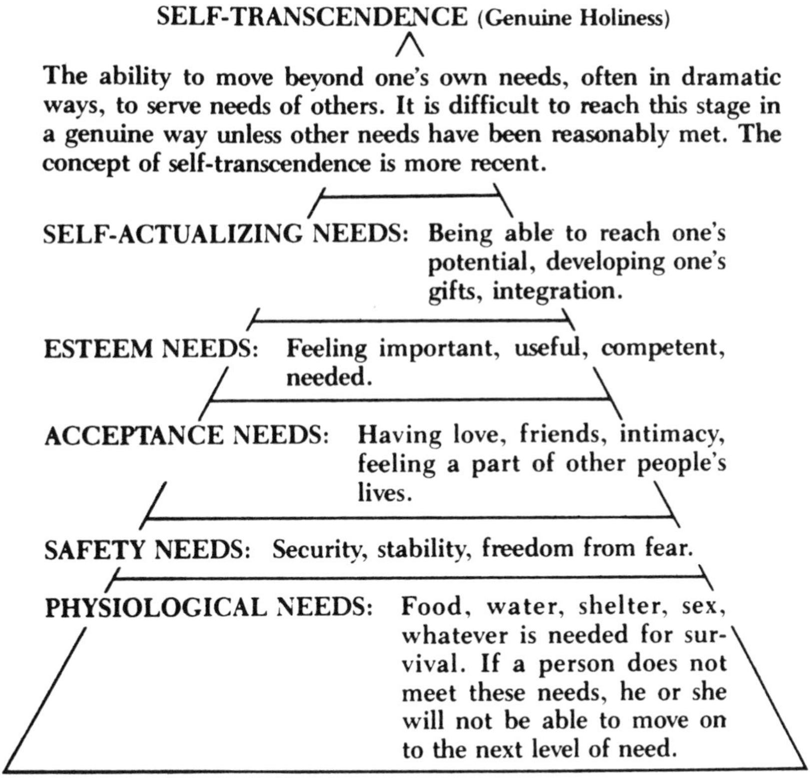

SELF-TRANSCENDENCE **(Genuine Holiness)**

The ability to move beyond one's own needs, often in dramatic ways, to serve needs of others. It is difficult to reach this stage in a genuine way unless other needs have been reasonably met. The concept of self-transcendence is more recent.

SELF-ACTUALIZING NEEDS: **Being able to reach one's potential, developing one's gifts, integration.**

ESTEEM NEEDS: **Feeling important, useful, competent, needed.**

ACCEPTANCE NEEDS: **Having love, friends, intimacy, feeling a part of other people's lives.**

SAFETY NEEDS: **Security, stability, freedom from fear.**

PHYSIOLOGICAL NEEDS: **Food, water, shelter, sex, whatever is needed for survival. If a person does not meet these needs, he or she will not be able to move on to the next level of need.**

Figure 2

Unfortunately, some parts of the institutional church have been good at using them and we need to name that.

A friend of mine, in responding to Charles Curran's situation, decided to write a letter to Rome in protest, simply to say what he was experiencing. This friend holds a fairly high position in a men's religious community. He told me, "As I dropped the letter in the mailbox, I had a quivering sensation that this could be very dangerous for me and for my community. There could be retaliation that would be so subtle and so difficult to target that I would never be able to name its source." He added, "Further, it occurred to me that last year, when I mailed a similar letter to President Reagan protesting aid to the Contras, I was angry, but I didn't fear for my life." What does that say about some of the kinds of methods that are bubbling under the surface in our church today? It does not speak to me about psychological health or holiness. People have the need and the right to feel safe. You have the need and the right to experience that you can be vital witnesses to the Gospel, and whatever stance you take, be it liberal or conservative, you will be safe.

At the next level, that of acceptance, you have a need and a right to feel that whatever your position is, wherever the Gospel walk takes you, you will be accepted in the community with which you have affiliated yourself, namely, the institutional church. Whether you are a woman or a man in the church, you are able to arrive at your own conclusions. You need, then, a basic acceptance of your ability to think, to make decisions, to choose, to disagree.

Again, we all have a right and a need to feel valued. I think this area of basic esteem is also one that evokes anger in the church today. Fundamental to feeling valued or esteemed is having the experience that the folks you are dealing with are being honest and upfront with you, insofar as they can. When I sense that someone is being deceitful or evasive, saying one thing to me but something else at a meeting behind closed doors, that does not honor my esteem. When that kind of deception happens, it evokes anger. It is tough to name and get at the source of that anger because if you do not know the truth, you do not know what you are missing. It is a subtle sort of thing that you can just sense. When we get angry in this kind of

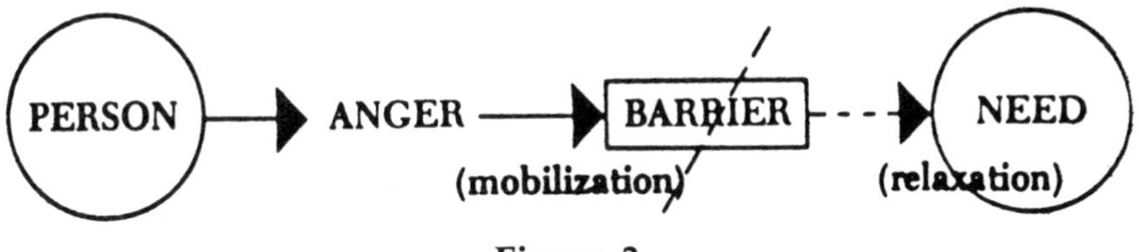

Figure 3

situation we do not know exactly at what, we kind of know at whom. But how do we get at that? It is very nebulous.

We all have basic needs, then, for safety, for acceptance, for esteem. When these get violated, what happens? God's wonderful gift bursts forth in us. That is how I think we must view it. It is a protective gift and an energizing gift. It gives us energy to fight—F*I*G*H*T.

How we fight—that is really critical. If the other folks fight dirty, that does not mean that it is all right for us to retaliate. One of the most helpful ways we can deal with our anger in the church is to look carefully at what is happening when this passion is evoked. The simple diagram (fig. 3) may help you to clarify the situation in which you find yourself. As you can see, anger is evoked when there is a barrier. The barrier could be a thing, a person, an event, but whatever it is, it stands in the way of our meeting a basic need. For example, as a woman in the church today, I experience the institutional church as a barrier to my sense of being fully accepted as an intelligent and gifted woman. Perhaps you are in a parish and you have a need to be part of program development. There is a pastor who is autocratic and authoritarian, who does not even have meetings at which policies can be discussed. Perhaps you work in a situation where there is another person, perhaps your supervisor, who is in real conflict with you. Each one of you can probably supply your own concrete details to make the diagram come alive.

The first thing to do when you experience anger is to look around your life for a basic need that is being violated. You must name that need and recognize the barrier. You may want to address the other person in terms of that. "Mrs. Smith, Mr. Jones, when you do this, I really feel duped. I feel that my self-esteem is lowered when you tell me half of what is going on but not all of it."

RESPONSES TO THE BARRIER

Once you have named the barrier you can look at what it is that you need to do to get rid of it. That is what our anger is for. Ultimately when we are angry, our bodies are mobilized to get rid of the barrier. Now if I really knew how to do that, the walls would come tumbling down. I do not know how you effectively and non-violently remove the many barriers that the institutional church has erected between good people on the side of the Gospel and the need that those people have to live the truth of that Gospel. I have some ideas, however, that might help us to work together in the same direction. And I would encourage all of you to rack your brains and bodies and hearts and to figure out effective ways to remove the barriers.

We need to be aware that there are a number of ways to address those barriers. Some ways are healthy; some are healthier than others; some not only are unhealthy, but do not work. I can accept the barrier and deal with it. I can avoid it. I can even abuse the barrier. I have to admit, and I suspect maybe some of you would too, that many times that last one is my first choice. I feel like destroying barriers.

Whether we act on that feeling can make the difference between being a person who tends the Gospel and follows it and being a person who just mouths the words. People who are filled with a tremendous amount of energy to bring about the Basileia vision that Elizabeth Fiorenza talks about (the reign of God or the kingdom), people who are really filled with zeal for God's house, have two things. They have sustained anger out of which their energy comes and they also have at least one eye on the Gospel, and it is from the Gospel they draw a sense of direction. They are very careful that the methods and the tactics that they use to break down barriers have threads of connection with the Gospel that they say they are fighting for. When that connection is not there, we are not filled with zeal for God's house. People who do not have that zeal have only one thing: raw passion. That is not bad, but it is not going to bring about the reign of God.

Destroying barriers is ultimately a way of retaliating, of "getting even." Any time you or I calculate to hurt someone because they have hurt us, we are using retaliation. It is psychologically unhealthy, and it is grossly unchristian. It does not fit with the Gospel. That does not mean we might not feel like retaliating. If you do feel this way, talk about it with someone who will understand your feelings. But do not do it. It does not work. It is not Christian. Ultimately, it does not bring about the Basileia vision.

However, too many people act as if the way to keep from retaliating is to deny the barrier altogether. Avoidance is not a healthy choice. I would like us to look a little more closely at ways people avoid anger, avoiding the barrier. One way is through what I call the "Nutra-Sweet Syndrome." This is different from what we used to refer to as the Sacherine Personality. You can't miss the Sacherine Personality because he or she is so drippy-sweet that it just sort of oozes out of their pores. The Nutra-Sweet Syndrome is a little more subtle. This kind of person holds a fundamental belief that anyone who is in a position of leadership which should be characterized by holiness is fundamentally incapable of doing evil. Anyone who says, "The pope, the cardinals, the bishop, ourselves (because we say we are on the side of the Gospel), really aren't capable of doing evil", fits that category. It is naive. Whether we are skid-row alcoholics or pope we are capable of doing evil. We just use different means.

The Nutra-Sweet person can be recognized by the way he or she responds to oppression. When somebody in authority, and supposedly holy, does something oppressive or hurtful, the Nutra-Sweet person says, "But I'm sure he or she didn't have all the information." Or, "I know that he didn't mean it," or "I'm sure he or she is acting in the best interest of the whole."

There is another whole group of people that are part of what I would call the "Sunglasses Syndrome." These are people who walk around as if there is a film over their eyes. They will leave the room, physically absent themselves, or psychologically do something so as not to hear, feel, touch, or see oppression when it exists on the part of hierarchical leaders. The Sunglasses person also will often give excuses for people who are responsible when there is real oppression going on.

There are many other ways to deny anger. One of the easiest is for people simply to lose themselves in their work. People who avoid anger, however, may actually turn it against themselves or just hold it in so tightly that they get sick. I would wager that there were a lot of aspirins or muscle relaxants sold in Seattle in the last several months. Many people get headaches, or gastro-intestinal difficulties. Real diagnostic diseases can occur simply because a person is too angry for too long, and does not acknowledge it. I am somewhat embarrassed to reveal this, but a recent study showed that Catholic sisters have a higher preponderance than women in general for obscure complaints for which no diagnosis is found. Someone speculated in a discussion of the study that many of these women were very angry and had just never been given permission, either by themselves or someone else, to deal with that up front. So they turned it inside. It really happens.

If you have chronic physical problems perhaps you should look for anger that you are not expressing adequately. And if you are in a situation where you are expressing it adequately, but it keeps getting generated all the time, you may be facing a decision between your stomach and, for example, your job. The choice is yours. Sometimes it is that fundamental. Am I going to reverence my flesh, which is a primary responsibility that all of us have, or am I going to see this thing through because I am not a quitter?

Unfortunately, acknowledging the barrier and choosing not to demolish it violently do not exhaust all the unhealthy ways of addressing the barrier. You can for example, kick and scream, pout and cry. In fact, occasionally some of these may not be fully unhealthy. At our therapy center, we just finished lowering the ceiling and carpeting some walls in a room. We are calling it "Rag Room II" (Rag Room I is in Spokane at a personal growth center). It is a place where people can go to release anger and grief—that is where "rag" comes from. There are times when it is appropriate to kick and scream, pout and cry, but you do it at an appropriate time and place, hopefully with someone who can support that process. If they are your only response, however, and if they are a frequent response, you are usually caught in a cycle that leaves the barrier intact but you demolished.

Inadequate ways of dealing with the barrier are particularly harmful when they are rooted in genuine abuse. I ask you to keep this in mind: If you are a person who comes from a home where either or both of your parents abused alcohol while you were growing up, you qualify for being an adult child of an alcoholic—A.C.O.A. We increasingly recognize that such children learn ineffective coping patterns that affect them as adults. You need to get treatment, therapy, for that. If you grew up in a home where there was alcohol abuse, if you yourselves were physically, sexually, or emotionally abused as a child, you are automatically going to have a lot of difficulty in the area of anger and conflict.

One of the things that can happen is that I can find myself today in a situation which repeats the experience of abuse. Let's say I am Mrs. Mary Smith. I work in a diocesan office and there is a lot of little stuff that just eats at me. I feel that everything I do gets reworked by Father Jones. I do not get invited to any of the meetings that the clergy attend, and so on. At some level of my consciousness I will recognize the same pattern of abuse I knew as a child, even though the outward particulars are different.

I will deal with the situation, then, with some baggage from my past. Feelings and ways of coping with abuse from the past will influence my response in the present. This is very important to realize. If any of you, if any of us, carry baggage from the past, we have to make sure that we look at that first because it will interfere with the tremendous amount of baggage that is going around at present. Make sure that you are clear and straight in responding to the oppressions of today and not responding today with leftover anger from the oppressions of your past. I cannot emphasize that enough.

The other side of this reality is that many of the most oppressive people today, oppressive pastors for example, are people who were in fact oppressed themselves as children—children who were abused or who grew up in alcoholic homes. Know the background of the person you are having trouble with. That will give you some clues as to why they might be behaving the way they are. If Father Johnson is giving you grief, and you find out that he grew up in a home where his father was alcoholic from the time he was three, that is a major presence in his life to be aware of, to deal with, even to address with him if you can.

INSTINCT AND AGGRESSION

One other thing I want to mention is that women and men are slightly different in how they instinctively deal with anger. It has been shown consistently that the one trait on which males and females differ practically from birth, is the dimension of aggression—physical aggression. Unlike other traits, such as nurturing, which depend heavily on conditioning, this one seems much more biologically based. From infancy, males have a greater propensity toward physical aggressiveness than females.

One theory which attempts to account for this is "Androgen Bath." This theory hypothesizes that in the x-y chromosome pairing which occurs at the conception of male children, the presence of the y chromosome produces the almost immediate presence of the male hormone androgen. This hormone has been associated with active and agressive behaviors. The theory further hypothesizes that the brains of developing males get more or less deluged in the androgen—thus the term "androgen bath." While this does not determine male behavior, it creates a tendency toward aggressive, quick responses on the part of males. Stated simply, what this means is that every man in this room had his brain bathed in androgen when he was being formed, and you had better watch out!

Culture and environment also have a great influence. Our culture tends to strengthen the biological differences in aggression. For example, we give little boys much tougher toys to play with than we give little girls. The results of all these factors can be seen early on in children's responses. Studies show that when female children are hurt, crossed, or faced with a barrier, they are much more apt to cry or withdraw than to hit. A male child is much more apt to hit.

If we observe what is happening in the church today we can see how these habits continue to operate. When women are told by church officials, "No, you can't do that," we find a lot of women quitting the church. Many, many women are leaving the church today. They are withdrawing, they are backing away. They are saying, "I am not going to be part of this." This saddens me, but I recognize some people may need to make that choice.

There is something, however, which is important to keep in

mind concerning the decision to quit or to stay. It struck me again recently while I was reading a statement by a Seattle women who was quoted in the *National Catholic Reporter*. She said something like, "With the way things are going in the church today, I sometimes wonder if I can stay a member of the institutional church without being hypocritical." That seemed to me to identify church with people—specifically men—who lead it, and not with the Gospel of Jesus. There is a big, big difference. When I fuse leadership in the church with the church, and the leadership is oppressive, I have no choice but to leave. But if I fuse the institutional church with the following of the Gospel of Jesus of Nazareth, and consider the leadership part of the trappings of that in history, then I do not have to leave it if the trappings abuse it.

It is important for us to make a constant and conscious effort to remember that the institutional church is not synonomous with the institutional leaders. The institutional church is about the Gospel. A friend of mine says, "The kingdom is not the church." That is true; the basileia is not the church. The Gospel of Jesus is bigger than the church. When the Gospel of Jesus, a message of love and fidelity and compassion, is contradicted or is not supported by the institution that claims to uphold it, my loyalties must fall on the side of the Gospel. The Gospel came first. I do not have to disengage myself from the church, but I might have to disengage myself from the leadership of the church. We are talking about a very critical distinction!

In the meantime, there will be things—perhaps styles of leadership in particular—which evoke anger in us. I cannot claim to have an inside track on God's mind, but I believe strongly that the purpose of that rage is to give us energy to remove barriers to our needs in appropriate and non-hurtful ways. It prepares us to fight. When we do fight, blood pressure goes down, heart rate goes down, breathing slows down, muscles relax, adrenaline stops getting pumped out—all kinds of comforting things occur in the body. The parasympathetic nervous system takes over again and soothes us and relaxes us. It is so complicated an electro-chemical process that nobody but God could have thought of it. It did not happen because some little particles happened to slide together. This works for a purpose. Keeping this in mind can help us be friends with our anger rather than being fearful or guilty about it.

PSYCHOLOGICAL VIGILANCE

There will be times, however, when you cannot fight or when fighting does not work. This is the dilemma in which we women often find ourselves. What frequently occurs is that we enter into a state of psychological vigilance. This state has definite physiological consequences. In other words, my blood pressure stays up just enough, my pulse rate is slightly speeded up, and the blood is diverted from my gastro-intestinal system to my muscles and limbs. This condition of vigilance keeps me poised to fight. Because of the pumped up respiration, blood pressure, and so on, I end up with a constant feeling of being slightly "reved up" to go. I feel that it would take next to nothing to set me off. The explosive potential is high. Suspicion levels are high. If someone comes to me and says, "The meeting next week with the priests in Detroit was canceled," I shout, "What!" It is an instantaneous "How dare they do this to me!" reaction.

Psychological vigilance keeps us a little tired all the time. Even eight hours of sleep does not quite do it. It would be safe to say that we are in a situation today where a large percentage of women and men in the church are in the state of psychological vigilance. Interpreted, this means that more and more of these people are ready to fight. The more the fight gets stopped, thwarted, ignored, disattended, the more the vigilance goes on. I think this is the psychological reality we are in today, and I do not know where it is going. I do know enough about adrenaline to know it does not just go away. Sometimes this reality moves into apathy, but it does not just disappear. There does not come a day, a year, five years, ten years from now, when everybody says, "Oh well, let's not fight it anymore. Rome must be right." That is not going to happen. Our bodies do not work that way. Divine Revelation, that is, God's Divine Intention, did not prepare us to be victims. When we adopt a victim's stance, instead of a sacred reverence stance toward ourselves and each other, we are subverting God's creative act.

If you are in a state of psychological vigilance, there are things you can do to help yourself. Number One—name it and talk about it. Talk about it with people who understand it. Do not talk about it so much that you hyper it up even more. You probably do not need much more adrenaline than you have here today. The amount of energy that is tangible in this room today will do just fine. It is fully adequate for what lies ahead. We do not want to squander it by pumping ourselves up so much that we are exhausted before we are done. Sustain it to a certain level by talking about it; keep in mind that through talking our bodies are more able to manage it. That is important. Otherwise we become so reved up that we, symbolically, go out and throw bombs at someone. That is a nuclear mentality, not a Christian mentality, and there is a big difference.

Number Two. If you are in a situation that is keeping you vigilant, and your body is saying (accurately), "Wait a minute, I have had enough of this. I was not designed for this", know when to call it quits. Know when to back out for a while. Know when to quit a job, change parishes, stay home for a while and not go to church. Whenever you make such decisions in order to tend yourself, however, make sure others know your intention.

Number Three. Let people know what you are experiencing and why you are choosing what you are choosing. You do not want to generate more suspicion and animosity in the situation than is already there. Let me share an example of one of my clients. She is in a position of leadership in a large parish. Her pastor recently called her in and said, "I notice that you don't go to daily Mass." Now this had nothing to do with her job. At the time she was so upset she could not respond. When we talked about it, I suggested we do some role-playing. Then she went back and said to him, "I want you to know why I have chosen not to go to daily Mass here, or daily Mass period." She explained to him in a very low-key and articulate manner why she had made that choice, and what she was doing for herself in the process of making it. He ended up by simply saying, "Well, I don't agree with you, but I guess you have to do what you have to do." She said, "Yes, I do."

If you really want your actions to be part of the process of working for change, you have to make sure you communicate what you mean. Don't just walk out with your mouth shut. That does not help. (Of course, the other person has a choice: he or she can choose to listen to you or ignore you.)

THE ANTI-SOCIAL TYPE

There is one particular type of person who tends to generates the most anger in us. This is the anti-social personality. It has some very identifiable characteristics. It was once called the sociopathic personality. The term has been changed to sound nicer; the person is just as ill. Know when you are dealing with such a person. Anti-social personalities are often very bright, articulate, charming individuals who set out to create the kind of impression of themselves that they want others to have. They are very difficult to recognize.

Characteristics of the anti-social personality include charm, evasiveness and lying, guiltlessness, loner behavior, limelight behavior, and divisiveness. They are very charming. They are also extremely evasive. They distort the truth, they manipulate what they want you to know, and they will not tell you everything. They are guiltless. Unlike most of us, they do not feel guilty when they know they have hurt people. One of the things you do not want to do with this person is tell them how bad you feel. It does not matter to them. Do not tell them you are hurting; they may use that against you.

Anti-social personalities vacillate between being loners and being in the limelight. In their personal lives, they are loners. You would have to look long and hard to find a close friend who has stuck with them through the years. They tend to have multiple superficial friends, but they do not have consistent relationships in their lives. However, they do very well on a stage with a microphone and spotlights. They like being in the limelight and often seek it out. Because they are intelligent as well, these people are often found in positions of leadership—even in the church. When this is the case, the last characteristic I listed—divisiveness—shows up about six months after this person has arrived on the scene, in the parish, chancery, school, and the like. Six months after they have arrived, people are divided for or against them. Anti-social personalities do best in transient situations because, over the long haul, as soon as people begin working with them, divisiveness becomes one of the dynamics of the setting.

There are a few other traits which are fairly typical. Anti-social personalities fail to learn from the past. They tend to make the same interpersonal mistakes repeatedly. If I am this type of person and have treated two DREs so badly that parishioners organized petitions against me, I will not learn from the mess I created. I will make the same mistake next year.

Anti-social personalities have a strong need to control people and maintain power. They are the types who will issue statements that stress characteristics such as obedience, orthodoxy, and faithfulness (These are not personal judgments, I am reading material copied from a psychology textbook!). Another critical trait is a high tolerance for pain. They can stand tension and interpersonal pressure. It just does not get under their skin. Most of the time they can outlast us. Finally, it is critical to be aware of what occurs when these people feel betrayed. Their primary tactic is retaliation. They will get back at you sooner or later. They might sit down and, eyeball to eyeball, nose to nose, lip to lip, earlobe to earlobe, tell you how grateful they are that you confronted them. Six months later you will be searching through the Help Wanted section of the newspaper.

These are the personalities who tend to generate the highest levels of anger in us because they are so difficult to reach. The big word here is "subtle." It is very subtle. You can say to someone, "You know you lied to me. This is what you said. This is what the situation was about." You think that, finally, this person will have to deal with the situation out in the open. But the anti-social person will find a way to get out of it.

There are specific ways to handle these people. Do not go to them one-on-one. Always talk to them with at least one other person present. If this person is your group leader, meet with the group and identify by behaviors what it is that you are experiencing, for example, "We are experiencing being lied to. We are experiencing abusive power and these are the examples." Be very specific. Find someone who understands this personality type to work with the group. Maintain a united front. It is the only thing that unhinges them; they are terrified of unity, particularly if the unity disagrees with them. They usually back down and frequently simply go into hiding.

CONCLUSION

One of the things that we do not want to do in the church today is to turn potentially explosive situations into explosions. One of the key dimensions of accomplishing this is to be tough enough to know and to name what it is that what we are dealing with. We cannot be naive. We cannot be duped into believing or assuming that someone in authority in an organization which values holiness is automatically holy. When you are making judgments on how to respond, you need to look at the behavior of the person, not the office. When you look at the behavior ask yourself several questions: How do these people treat folks? What are they doing? Are they being open? Are they being honest? Do they tell the truth? Do they dialogue when there is conflict? If you see things like distortion, deceitfulness, refusal to dialogue, power positioning, then you are dealing with pathology, not behavior which flows from the Gospel. We have to know this. We have to to name it or we will be victims, and that is not what Christianity is all about. Christianity is about making lovers, not victims. Victims do not make good lovers.

There is a story about Jesus going to the temple from which I drew the title for this talk. I would like to end with it. As the story is recounted in the Gospel of John, Jesus goes into the temple, takes up a whip and you know the rest. Why did he act this way? The background of the story is this: Jews had a practice of making pilgrimages to the temple and part of that pilgrimage required the offering of sacrifices. Those coming from a long distance found it easier to purchase the animals for sacrifice in the porch of the temple. Because the Tyrian half-schekel was the only coinage allowed in the temple, people from other areas had to change their local currency into the schekel. They could then purchase the animal for sacrifice.

In John's Gospel, it is not the commercialism or dishonest business transactions that disturb Jesus. Rather, he feels that the temple is being destroyed. The temple he is referring to is not the building. If we look at this story in the context of Jesus' own life, we come to realize he is referring to the temple of every woman or man who came up to present themselves to God. What Jesus is attacking is the religious system: a system requiring buying and bartering of something tangible in order to be worthy of offering sacrifice. Jesus attacks the oppressive structure which denies the reality that pilgrimage people are good enough without goats, pigeons, or lambs. Their inherent goodness stands on its own merits.

The story offers several points for our reflection. First, we are that good too. We are good enough without needing additional genitals of a particular type. We are good enough without the addition of particular educational degrees or characteristic office titles. We are good enough to go as far up in the temple of worship as we want to go. Any institutional structure that says we have to have this, and this, and this, before we get there is oppressive. Jesus stood over and against that.

It is important also to look at how Jesus did what he did. It was not very pretty. He said what he felt and he acted very physically there in the porch of the temple. Sometimes this is called for. We also know from his life that he was a reflector. Jesus never reacted haphazardly with violence. This is important to remember today when you and I live in a church which feels oppressive to us. We live in a church which feels oppressive to us. We live in a church which has in fact attempted in many ways to destroy something sacred: people. We need to fight that. God has given us a tool—it is called anger—to fight that oppression. We must never use our anger without reflection. We must always let it operate from out of our solid center rather than out of raw adrenaline.

Sometimes there is no visible difference between someone just being physically violent and someone operating out of a choice. The one who is acting is the only one who knows the difference. In my life when I choose to say a particular thing, to undertake a particular action, I am the only one who knows if that action is coming out of retaliation, out of a secret place of residual anger inside me or genuinely out of a mobilization of everything in me, out of zeal to bring about the reign of God. To give me that zeal, to give me the ability to act which is fueled by zeal, God has given me the gift of anger. I need to welcome it as a gift and learn to use it well in order that I contribute to the purpose for which all gifts are given: the Basileia vision of the Gospel.

7

Sexism in Marriage

Kathleen Fischer and Thomas Hart

WE BELIEVE THAT A NEW VISION OF CHRISTIAN MARRIAGE IS EMERGING. It is not being shaped primarily by theologians, although their input is influencing it. Rather, it is growing out of the lived experience of married couples themselves as they respond to changing social forces and new ideas, and struggle with what it means to live an intimate relationship in light of the Gospel. Because married couples themselves are primary in shaping this new way of life, we will be relying on evidence we have heard from them, as we have known them in our counseling, teaching, and marriage workshops. From this experience we will treat three topics: 1) Sexist models of marriage, specifically hierarchy and complementarity; 2) The meaning of mutuality in marriage and efforts of couples to live out of this model; and, finally, 3) Suggestions for how the church can work against sexism in marriage.

A CRITIQUE OF SEXISM IN MARRIAGE: HIERARCHY AND COMPLEMENTARITY

For centuries, patterns of relating and role expectations in marriage have been carefully prescribed. Two models have prevailed: hierarchy and complementarity. These two models have intersected and overlapped in various ways, their impact on marital relations being much the same. Hierarchy says that the husband is superior to the wife, and that she should be subject to him. Complementarity assigns certain characteristics to husbands and wives: husbands are active, aggressive, rational, and material providers; wives are passive, emotional, nurturing, and altruistic. Incomplete in themselves, women and men come together in the heterosexual union of marriage to find their completion in their relationship to one another. In the complementarity model, male qualities are more highly valued than female. And so the hierarchical and the complementarity models come out in the same place: male superiority/dominance and female inferiority/submission.

Translated into role relationships in marriage this schema leads to clear expectations of wife and husband. The husband is to hold an outside job and support the family financially. The wife is to raise the children and maintain a well-ordered home to which a husband can return from work to meet his practical and emotional needs. Parenting is equated with mothering. The wife's contributions are relegated to the "domestic sphere," and it is assumed that she is primarily responsible for the success of the marriage. Other conclusions follow: marriage is held up to women as the supreme goal and source of their highest happiness and fulfillment—they are to find their meaning and completeness in a man; the single life style represents a failure to reach one's fulfillment. For many women the situation is made worse by their status as part of a minority. In writing about Hispanic women, for example, Guadalupe Gibson says that they have been conditioned both as women and as members of a minority group to believe that they are inept, incapable, and that they should limit their aspirations.[1]

Many of the married couples with whom we have worked retain the traditional roles and attempt to live them out with love and care for one another. As a wife and mother of six children told us: "I am content being wife, mother, grandmother in the traditional ways. I just want to be a contributing part of my family, church, and community in any way I can. My gifts are those of encouragement and deep and lasting faith."

It is not our purpose to criticize those who freely choose and live out the traditional models lovingly and creatively. It is rather to suggest other options and support for couples who wish them, to eliminate the suffering experienced by many women in such traditional roles, and to provide visions of marriage which support the full humanity and contributions to home and world of both wife and husband.

The experience of doing marriage counseling is revealing, where the pains of the old order and the emergence of the new are concerned. In the vast majority of cases, it is the wife who brings the struggle to counseling. Often enough, she comes without her husband, because he is reluctant to admit the need for counseling or to open his life to another person. Sometimes he does come along for the first session, but he is there under protest. This attitude sometimes changes after a few sessions. In a fair number of cases, the couple comes not by the wife's insistence but by a joint decision, as both persons are hurting and do not seem to be able to resolve their difficulties by themselves. What is really rare is for the husband to lead the way in, followed by a reluctant wife, where he more clearly sees the need and takes major responsibility.

It is notable too that when the wife expresses her pain, whether in counseling or in the conversation at home that leads to counseling, the husband is often surprised. He was not aware of any problem. He thinks the marriage is going quite well. He may have noticed that she was a little down lately, but he had not inquired into the reasons or thought much about it. What is often happening here is that the two are moving in quite different spheres, and he is content in his. He cannot understand why she is not content. All he asks of her is to tend the house, take care of the children, and offer him support and affection. It does not occur to him to ask why their ways of life are so different, or how he would like living hers instead of his.

A therapist does not see many cases of a man afflicted with chronic depression. A therapist sees a large number of women who are depressed. Depression is a complex phenomenon with many causes. But the fact that it occurs far more commonly in women than in men should prompt us to reflect on their relative ways of life and their life-prospects. A person who feels trapped in an unsatisfying existence is a prime candidate for depression. This is not to say that a woman cannot be happy in a traditional marriage. Many have been. But it does say that not every woman will be happy in such a marriage, and that it is easy to see why she might not be.

As sociologist Jessie Bernard points out in her book, *The Future of Marriage,* being married has been about twice as advantageous to men as to women.[2] In fact, Bernard speaks of *his* marriage and *her* marriage to indicate how different the experience has been for men and women. The psychological costs of marriage for women have been greater, and the benefits fewer. Wives have made more adjustments and lost more rights. Married women have had worse mental and emotional health as compared not only with married men but with unmarried women.

But traditional marriage arrangements have had negative consequences for men as well as for women. Both women and men are oppressed by assumptions that limit and distort the relational possibilities between them. To succeed in the work world may become an obsession for a husband, and require that he renounce his needs for play and nurturant relationships. He may deny feelings of vulnerability and weakness, to focus on winning in a competitive world. He sometimes takes on the burden of always being the strong one, and ends by asking his wife for nothing but her services. He can lose touch with his emotional life altogether. Yet it is almost always the woman, not the man, who cries out for change in the system. Her losses are much greater.

The recent mass movement of white women into the labor force is one of the factors leading to a questioning of sex roles. In fact, for centuries black women have been dealing creatively with these same concerns: role adaptability, division of household chores, working wives and mothers, and coping with stressful situations.[3]

When Christian women attempt to change roles in an oppressive marriage, they enter into a struggle with many dimensions to it. They have expressed this to us in different ways:

"I grew up being told that the husband was the "Head" and "Authority". He had conjugal rights. My *first* very big step was to speak up and say "No" I won't be used any more. I won't be discounted any more, either in bed or in core decisions in my life. I found that I could make choices and that I had rights. I was fortunate to have a husband who could hear me and also is committed to grow, but it has not been easy."

"I definitely feel a conflict, and as yet I have not resolved it. If I meet my own needs I feel selfish, aggressive, guilty. If I only care for others I feel walked on, taken advantage of, a fool, giving out all the time and not getting anything back. I have a real sense of confusion over where to draw the line between the two."

"I'm a tight-rope walker, trying to balance the needs of my family and the call of my career ministry . . . I just have to accept the struggle. My husband is no Alan Alda. In many ways he is very supportive. The fact that he makes enough money so that I do not need to work has given me tremendous opportunities in education, volunteerism, and, later, career choices. He doesn't, however, like to be inconvenienced in any way . . . meals need to be on time, laundry caught up, house reasonably tidy. It's sometimes hard to know what it is reasonable for me to expect in terms of support since his resistance is so great in some areas. I feel I give him unquestioning support for his career and personal needs while he makes me justify every little meeting or retreat that inconveniences him in any way, for example, in child care."

Sometimes a wife's struggle for liberation comes from a deeper and more desperate place, entrapment in a violent marriage. The sexist organization of society and of marriage is one of the fundamental causes of wife-beating or wife-battering. Conservative estimates indicate that over one million women in the U.S. are victims of such battering. They come from all social strata. As a church we can no longer remain silent in face of such suffering.

Del Martin opens her book, *Battered Wives,* with a letter from a battered wife. The wife writes:

I am in my thirties and so is my husband. I have a high school diploma and am presently attending a local college, trying to obtain the additional education I need. My husband is a college graduate and a professional in his field. We are both attractive and, for the most part, respected and well-liked. We have four children and live in a middle-class home with all the comforts we could possibly want. I have everything, except life without fear. For most of my married life I have been periodically beaten by my husband.

After describing what these beatings are like, she continues:

> Now, the first response to this story, which I myself think of, will be "Why didn't you seek help?" I did. Early in our marriage I went to a clergyman who, after a few visits, told me that my husband meant no real harm, that he was just confused and felt insecure. I was encouraged to be more tolerant and understanding. Most important, I was told to forgive him the beatings just as Christ had forgiven me from the cross. I did that, too.[4]

Her letter goes on to describe fruitless efforts to get help from friends, doctors, and the police.

Marital violence is of course a complex problem, but current research is making clear the relationship between such violence and the subordinate position of women in marriage. The hierarchical nature of the husband/wife relationship, with stereotypical sex roles, is related to such violence in the following ways.

1. The presumption that the husband is the head of the family and the identification of masculinity with aggression lead to the use of violence as an ultimate resource to maintain superior power. Recently in a newspaper account of a wife-battering case in our area, the husband was quoted as saying: "A wife is supposed to know her place and if she doesn't, what else are you going to do?" In such a system male dominance must be maintained at all costs because the person who dominates cannot conceive of any alternative but to be dominated in turn. Violence is used as a means to control another person.

2. The state of powerlessness and dependence in which many women find themselves prevents women from escaping such battering. Many have been taught to accept the authority of their husbands and believe it is right to defer to them. They have been socialized to subordinate roles, to passivity and negative self-images. Many women stay, and do not report domestic violence, because they see no alternative for themselves. Besides their fear of their husband's retaliation, they are held back by the prospect of living the rest of their lives in poverty with their children. They face restricted job opportunities, lower pay for the same job, and doubts about their own abilities.

Clearly this is a problem of major pastoral concern for the church. We must do everything possible to protect women from such violence in the home: provide access to support, advice, and alternate housing; work for better economic opportunities for women and improvements in child care facilities; provide rituals of healing for women who have been battered. But we must also address the root causes of this widespread problem: a delineation of sex role differences which accentuates masculine aggression and feminine passivity, male domination and female subordination. In short, we must repudiate the sexist models of marriage which feed and legitimize wife-battering.

THE EMERGING MODEL OF MUTUALITY IN MARRIAGE: THEORETICAL AND PRACTICAL CONSIDERATIONS

Recognition of the sexist bias in marital relationships and the serious problem of domestic violence has led many couples to search for alternate, more redemptive patterns for marriage. Mutuality is the emerging model. We will speak of mutuality in marriage under three aspects: 1) its general meaning; 2) concrete attempts by couples to work out its implications at various stages of marriage; and 3) the role of scripture passages in supporting or hindering these efforts.

1. Mutuality is foundational to a new vision of marriage. In this model we no longer have two incomplete persons, each presumed to possess only half of the human traits, but two whole persons each of whom has the capacity to develop a wide range of human strengths. Role relationships are based on the actual gifts and inclinations of the two individuals rather than on conventional ideas of what a wife or husband is supposed to be. Mutuality differs from complementarity. It is not just a matter of your strength making up for my weakness, or my gifts compensating for your deficits. Mutuality is a means of empowerment; it fosters the release of new resources in both persons and in the pattern of relating. It creates a situation in which each partner simultaneously *affects* and *is affected by* the other, the goal being a fuller humanity for both. Wife and husband give to and receive from each other in many different ways, beyond the governance of stereotypes.

Mutuality is genuine reciprocity. Without it a couple cannot have real intimacy, for intimacy requires two individuals. Under the hierarchical or complementary model a woman was often taught to believe that the way to happiness was to let her husband's identity determine what hers would be, to build a reflective identity around him. She had very little identity of her own. Under the model of mutuality, intimacy no longer means a woman handing over her life to a man so that the two somehow become one. Instead, wife and husband retain autonomy and self-direction. It is these two full personal identities that are merged in intimacy. Each partner contributes to the other, to the home, and to the public realm.

The shift to mutuality is not easy. As Adrienne Rich has noted: "Truthfulness anywhere means a heightened complexity . . . Women are only beginning to uncover our own truths; many of us would be grateful for some rest in that struggle, would be glad just to lie down with the shards we have painfully unearthed, and be satisfied with those. Often I feel this like an exhaustion in my body . . . the relationships worth having demand that we delve still deeper."[5]

2. Couples are dealing with these challenges in various ways. Taking actual cases, let us examine the impact of change at several stages of the marriage relationship. We will begin at the later end of the marital spectrum, where the impact is often modest. Then we will treat the middle years, where many couples today find themselves in crisis and are feeling both the stress and the satisfaction of major change. Finally we will describe marriages that are just beginning in this new situation.

Memorable was the struggle of a woman in her late fifties for expansion and fulfillment in what up to that time had been a rather traditional marriage. The children, to whom she had devoted herself so completely, were raised and gone, and her husband was nearing retirement. Communication between the two of them had never been too deep, and the woman did not relish the prospect of living out the last twenty or twenty-five years of her life with the deadness she was experiencing. So three years before coming to counseling, with some trepidation, she had taken a full-time job outside the home. She found it a big help. It had strengthened her confidence as well as provided some interesting outside contacts. Now she faced a second major task, talking with her husband about how she experienced their relationship, and trying to get his cooperation in making some changes. With encouragement, she invited her husband to come with her to counseling. Fortunately, he was willing to come, and she began with considerable hesitation to scratch the surface of her discontent. As our sessions went on, she entered more deeply into her desire for more sharing and closeness between them. Her husband was remarkably open to what she was talking about. As they dialogued, it was clear that these two really loved one another, but that both had lived the marriage up to this time our of very traditional scripts. She had asked little or nothing for herself, being content with the role of servant to husband and children. This was no longer going to be enough.

One of the key issues this couple had to face was her fear of his anger. This fear went back to what she had suffered under her father's anger as a little girl. Her husband was actually quite a gentle man, and there had been no incident of severe or destructive anger between them. But her fear of his disapproval had long prevented her from really being herself in the relationship. He, knowing this, was not able to be quite himself either, as he had to try to hold in all irritation or dissatisfaction. This was one of the impediments to their achieving any real intimacy. Once the issues were out in the open, we were able to work on them, and over the next several months this couple made major changes in their way of relating. It turned out that he wanted more honesty and more intimacy just as badly as she did. They said in one session that they wished they had sought counseling thirty years before. That they were able to put their relationship on a more satisfying basis for the final decades of their lives has to be attributed mainly to the wife's courage in facing her discontent and involving her husband in changing a set of assumptions neither of them any longer wanted.

Because our whole society is aging, and most couples now live long beyond the childbearing years, we have greater need than ever to address some of the final consequences of rigid roles: widows who are unable to manage their own lives or who live in poverty; retired men who have had no source of satisfaction or identity other than their work; widowers who do not know how to establish relationships that offer them any emotional satisfaction.

We have said that change at the late end of the marital spectrum is often modest, sometimes nonexistent today. The place where it seems to be hitting hardest is somewhere in the middle years. And there change often comes through crisis and agony. Couples who married under one set of rules find themselves grappling with midlife in a radically different world. The kind of partnership they established may have exacted a high price, so that alternative schemes seem in many ways inviting, but their present pattern is at least familiar and has been manageable. Both partners may feel ambivalence and anxiety about possible changes. The wife may suffer additionally from an accumulation of economic and educational disadvantages which severely limit her options. Then too, her experience of meeting the needs of others may mean that she has not learned to control her own space or time, make her own decisions, or even know how to name her own needs and wishes.

A married woman in her mid-thirties came for counseling. She was depressed and could not understand why. She said she had a good husband, three fine kids, and a beautiful home. Yet she was heavy at heart and down on herself most of the time. It took her a while to be able to say this, but she finally admitted that she did not like being a mother at all. She did not feel good at it, and derived little or no satisfaction from it, though her husband often said she was a very good wife and mother. She did not have many friends, and her activity outside the home was minimal.

In the course of therapy, she went back to school to pursue a graduate degree. She loved it, and felt happier than she had for a long time. She struggled with guilt over the ways her classes and homework took her away from the family. School was expensive too, and she felt bad about spending the money. We began involving her husband in the sessions. He had long been aware of and concerned about her depression, but had not known what to do. Now that she was going to school, he was experiencing other difficulties. He found himself babysitting more in the evenings and on weekends. There was less money available. She often seemed to prefer reading to being with him, and was also beginning to spend time with friends she had made at school. She was no longer available without question to take advantage of his more interesting business trips and go along with him. The children were complaining too.

But he was well aware of another side to the picture. She was happier than she had been in a long time. The time she did spend with him and the children had better quality to it than it had had. She was becoming much more of an intellectual companion to him; in fact, she threatened him at times both with her growing knowledge and the strength of her views. Her finding herself more as a person lifted some of the responsibility he had felt for making her happy. And the children were drawing out the latent father in him. He had less time for TV in the evening, and he even had to come from work at times to drive them somewhere when she could not, but he felt genuinely close to his children for the first time and was proud of his emerging capacities for nurture and play.

Considerable time has elapsed since this couple was in counseling. The wife is finished with school and is working part-time. She enjoys what she is doing, and her depression is gone. She still thinks of herself as an inadequate mother, but it does not bother her so much any more, as motherhood is not her whole life. The couple relationship is strong, stronger than it ever was. Wife and husband have redistributed parenting and household responsibilities more equitably. Their sexual relationship is better. The children have adjusted and are developing nicely. This couple remembers well all the difficulties of their marital revision. But they feel that the risks they took and the deaths they died have definitely brought new life. They also feel more prepared to face whatever challenges future evolution in their marriage may bring.

Couples who are just entering marriage today find themselves in a new cultural situation, where marital roles and general expectations are quite fluid. Most of them realize that they will have to fashion what their own arrangements are going to be. Often vestiges of cultural sexism still cling to both of them, but there is much more awareness and negotiability than there used to be. Two stories illustrate the concerns of this beginning phase of marriage.

A couple in their mid-twenties came for counseling. They had been going together for four years, and had talked many times about getting married. But they were still not married, and wanted help working through why. Exploration revealed that they did indeed love each other a lot, that they already spent a great deal of time together, shared many common interests and values, and were temperamentally quite compatible. It gradually emerged that it was the woman who had the greater reluctance about marrying. The the reasons came clear. She had noticed that her friend was very careful about money, keeping a record of all his expenditures. She had also noted that, in sharp contrast with his financial ledger, his apartment looked like a disaster area. She knew that his career was very important to him, and also that he wanted children. Now she grasped the grounds of her hesitation: She feared getting trapped in a traditional marriage. The scenario which had taken shape in her unconscious was one in which he would pursue his career while she would be at home taking care of the children and picking up after him, and she would have to ask for and account for every penny she spent. Somehow that did not seem very attractive to her. She wanted a career too, she wanted to be financially viable in her own right, and she was not at all sure she wanted children. Once all this was out in the open, the couple began the serious business of negotiation to see whether they could fashion a marriage or not. At this point they left counseling, and we do not know the end of their story. But they are already grappling with the issues which, unaddressed, have brought many other couples to grief down the road.

One such couple were acquaintances of ours who came to their crisis before their first year of marriage was finished. They had moved to Seattle from the midwest on an experimental basis at the husband's suggestion. The wife was very reluctant to leave close friends and family behind, but had agreed on the one year experiment of life in the northwest. As the marriage unfolded, she experienced her husband as making most of the decisions without paying much attention to her input. He liked the northwest (which is indeed wonderful if you don't mind a little rain), whereas she keenly missed friends and family. At ten months, he began speaking of establishing permanent residence. That was when she told him how she had experienced their relationship, and how unhappy she had been. What was unfortunate was that she had waited so long to do that. He got the message, wanted to change, and made some positive moves in that direction. But she was already too far alienated, and filed for divorce.

These two stories, the one of the women who was unwilling

to enter into a sexist marriage, and the other of the woman who quickly made her exit from one, point up one of the principal tasks of marriage preparation today: To support couples in facing the hard questions at the outset. Some of those questions are:

What will the family name be?
Will there be children? If so, how many? When will the couple begin trying to have children?
Who will take care of the children?
How will careers be worked out? Whose career has priority?
Who will be responsible for what household chores?
What is the financial arrangement going to be?
What is the couple's understanding about outside friendships, same sex and other sex?
How will decisions be made when wife and husband find themselves in disagreement?

Planning the marriage rite itself is an important part of getting ready for marriage. Ritual influences us deeply, and wedding ceremonies both reflect and reinforce particular notions of marriage. Many couples are working to make the rite reflect the mutuality they want to have characterize their marriage: eliminating sexist language and sexist scripture texts, removing the word "obey" from the wife's promises, writing vows that reflect the shared roles and reciprocal relationship of their covenant. They are also eliminating a practice which originated in the sexism of the Graeco-Roman culture in which Christianity was born, the giving away of the bride by the father. In ancient times the bride was regarded as the property of her father. In exchange for a price, he turned her over to the groom, who became the new owner. So couples today are with good reason substituting processions in which whole families and sometimes friends are involved, bringing groom and bride to one another.

Efforts to forge more mutually enriching forms of marriage have involved couples at all stages along the marital spectrum in a variety of experiments.

Many women work outside the home because of economic necessity; others, because they want to. They may also want to stay home as much as possible with a baby or small child, not wishing to miss being a part of the child's experiences during those years. Or they may find that the major responsibility for the home is still theirs. This has often led to overload for women: a forty or fifty hour-per-week job plus hours of household responsibilities. Sometimes husband and wife reverse roles to accomplish their goals. Others who reject hierarchy live their equality not by doing all the same tasks but by distributing them according to choice and need, circumstance and personality. One spouse stays home with the baby this year, the other the next year. Or they rotate morning and afternoon shifts of parenthood on the one hand, and shifts on a job on the other hand. Or he works more than full-time on a project while she works part-time and cares for their children until he finishes his task and they reallocate their responsibilities. Give and take. Phasing over the long run of the marital cycle.

Couples attempting this sort of mutuality have learned several things: For it to work, institutions as well as individuals have to change. Employers have to permit job-sharing, part-time work, and leaves. Private and public agencies must provide affordable, accessible child care. Individuals may have to forgo the desire to "do it all," at least doing it all at the same time, and learn to compromise. Mutuality in an intimate relationship requires clarity about one's own wants and, simultaneously, generosity toward the other's wants.

THE INFLUENCE OF SCRIPTURE PASSAGES ON EFFORTS TO ACHIEVE MUTUALITY

In the effort to envision marriage in new ways, certain biblical passages play a key role. They are deeply embedded in social and individual consciousness, and they play a subtle and not so subtle role in how Christian married couples view their relationships. Among these passages, some of the most important are the Genesis creation texts, and the passages in Colossians, Ephesians, the pastoral letters, and 1 Peter which describe the pattern of relationships between husbands and wives. For example, Colossians 3:18 states: "You who are wives, be submissive to your husbands. This is your duty in the Lord." Ephesians 5:21–33 compares the husband-wife relationship to the relationship between Christ and the church. It enjoins mutual love and respect between spouses, but it upholds the dominant/submissive roles of husband and wife. Taken together such texts have been presented as the Christian ideal of marriage and have given religious legitimation to the dominant/subordinate pattern of marital relating. They have been used to argue that the subordinate/submissive roles of husband and wife in marriage are God's law and the "natural" roles of the sexes in marriage.

The good news is that recent work by biblical scholars has given us a new understanding of these passages. The overarching insight in biblical interpretation today is that everything written in Scripture is written in particular social and historical situations. Revelation though it be, the Bible is the work of human hands, and the cultural limitations of its authors, always quite evident, must be distinguished from the divine message. Thus the Bible sees the world as flat. The Bible condones slavery. The Bible is sexist, so sexist that many in the women's movement have simply rejected it as a useful resource.

In contemporary exegesis, the cultural sexism of the Bible is distinguished from the divine message, and this has made a tremendous difference in our overall understanding. In addition, scholars such as Phyllis Trible and Elizabeth Schüssler Fiorenza have closely analyzed some of the particular passages which have lent support to Christian sexism.[6] Some highlights suggest their implications for the theology of marriage.

1. Phyllis Trible's reinterpretation of the second creation account in Genesis as the creation of *humanity* rather than man, of the woman and the man in equality and mutuality, frees this central myth to function in support of a new vision of married relationships—even as a mandate for such relationships. She lays to rest traditional interpretations of the fact that in the story the woman is created after the man and that it is she who first eats the forbidden fruit. She also points out that it is only *after* the fall that the woman's husband rules over her, in other words that this is a sinful situation standing in need of redemption.

2. In dealing with the New Testament, Elizabeth Schüssler Fiorenza establishes the fact that the original vision of Jesus was that of a *discipleship of equals* in which distinctions based on sex, wealth, nationality, or position would be dissolved. This vision is summed up in an early baptismal formula which Paul quotes in Galatians: "There does not exist among you Jew or Greek, slave or freeperson, male or female, for all are one in Christ Jesus

(Gal 3:28)." What happened by the time Colossians, Ephesians, and the pastoral letters were written was that this original vision was sacrificed in the interest of accommodating to the surrounding cultures. The Graeco-Roman as well as the Jewish cultures had stated household rules according to which slaves were subject to their masters, children to their parents, and wives to their husbands. The late New Testament writings simply Christianized this arrangement so as not to rock the social boat too much. But the accommodation is false to the mind of Jesus and even to that of Paul.

The development of our theology of marriage and our work with married couples must now incorporate such fresh interpretations. Recently, for example, while we were preparing to give a workshop to couples on the theology of marriage, we received a letter from the man organizing the workshop asking us to speak to the issue of how he could be a better spiritual director to his wife. When we heard that, we decided to include a session in the workshop on recent interpretation of these late New Testament texts. It was clear, as this couple and others responded to our presentation, that they had been struggling to pattern their relationships on the cultural sexism of these texts.

In several recent weddings we have attended, the couples have used, instead of these passages, sections from the Song of Songs which describe more mutual relating between woman and man or gospel passages which call all Christians to love and forgiveness—simply applying these to married love as a specific form of Christian love.

RECOMMENDATIONS

We have noted both the problems with sexist models of marriage and efforts of married couples to develop models of mutuality. We turn now to our third topic: How can we in the church support the efforts of married couples to relate in more mutual and redemptive ways? We want to conclude with some suggestions for steps the church can take to help heal the sexism in marriage.

1. We need to stop using sexist scripture passages, whether in the marriage ceremony or in work with married couples. We

should, instead, provide biblical study groups to explore recent interpretations of these passages and the socio-historical context in which they functioned. We should also substitute, in our ceremonies and teaching on marriage, texts which call us to new patterns of relationships and mutual love.

2. We should remove sexist elements, such as the giving away of the bride by her father, from the marriage rite, and work to see that the rite's symbolism reflects a mutual convenant between the persons who are marrying.

3. We must end our silence about the problem of marital violence and preach on the evil of violence against women; provide support, shelters, and healing rituals for battered wives; and stop misusing Christian teachings on crucifixion, suffering, and forgiveness in ways which keep battered wives locked into intolerable situations.

4. We need to provide support and pastoral counseling for couples at all stages of marriage to help them become aware of the hidden or overt sexism in their relationships, and enable them to develop skills for mutual relating. Such support and counseling must be based on the conviction that a wife's unhappiness in traditional roles is not her problem to be solved individually, but an opportunity for growth and change in the marital relationship.

5. We must work for equitable legislation, adequate housing policies, and economic opportunities for women, since the lack of these keeps women in subordinate positions in marriage. Reports from the National Commission on Working Women show that women make approximately sixty-two cents for every dollar earned by men; the unemployment rate for minority women is greater than other groups; and the female labor force is clustered in low-paying occupational categories (clerical, sales, service, and factory).

6. We need to develop models of mutuality for exercising authority and power throughout the Christian community. A community of shared gifts rather than a hierarchy of the strong and weak demonstrates and validates alternate approaches to power for married couples. For mutuality to succeed as the new pattern of relationships between wives and husbands, it has to become the pattern of relationships throughout the Christian community.

7. As a Christian community, we ought to explore new ways of raising and answering questions related to role expectations in marriage, for example, how can we care for children in ways that do not require women to forfeit other forms of participation in and contribution to the community, and which enable men to benefit from an equal part in child care? What is the meaning of work done in and for the home and family?

8. We should stop romanticizing and idealizing marriage. Such romanticizing ignores the fact that many women are most at risk in their own homes. We have also found that married couples are not helped by abstract ideals that seem impossible to attain in view of their actual situations; and that women are oppressed by the practice of simultaneously idealizing and undervaluing the roles of wife and mother. Instead we need to develop a theology of marriage which relates Gospel love to the concrete facts of married life as couples know them.

9. We must preach and teach about the evils of sexism. Sexism in marriage is only one manifestation of this larger problem. In all areas of church life we must make clear that the reign of God preached by Jesus is not a reign of men. It is rather a transformed social situation in which all women and men can come to wholeness and selfhood.

10. Finally, if the sexism in marriage is to be healed, there must be an end to the subordinate position of women in the church generally. Marriage mirrors what is happening in the entire community. All that happens in the institutional church affects the relationships of married people. If women are of little account in the church, why should they be of much account anywhere else? One married woman made the point this way: "I am not 'fed' by the church, yet all the while I am expected to do my part and give. My needs are not met in church as a woman, yet I am asked to give all I have to help her grow and others too. Therefore I am in conflict. There is no mutuality." Only as the church becomes a community living out the discipleship of equals, will it be able to credibly enliven and reinforce our efforts as married couples to find new and more loving ways to live out our intimate relationships.

We have tried to do three things in our presentation today: 1) critique sexism in marriage, specifically the models of hierarchy and complementarity; 2) indicate how couples are attempting to develop mutuality in marriage; and 3) suggest ways in which the church can support these efforts.

Many married couples are re-imaging the relationship of marriage, attempting to forge a more Christian and redemptive reality. The prevailing patterns are centuries old and deeply rooted. Changing them is no easy task, yet we see them beginning to change. For us, this is evidence of the reign of God in our midst, a new creation opening up fresh resources of healing and love.

Notes

1. "Hispanic Women: Stress and Mental Health Issues," in *Women Changing Therapy*, ed. Joann Hamerman Robbins and Rachel Josefowitz Siegel. (Harrington Park Press, 1985) 120.
2. Jessie Bernard, *The Future of Marriage* (Yale University Press, 1982) 25ff.
3. See Christine Robinson, "Black Women: A Tradition of Self-Reliant Strength", in *Women Changing Therapy*.
4. Del Martin, *Battered Wives* (Simon and Schuster, 1977) 1–2.
5. *On Lies, Secrets, and Silence: Selected Prose By Adrienne Rich* (W.W. Norton & Co., Inc., 1978).
6. See, for example, Phyllis Trible, *God and the Rhetoric of Sexuality* (Fortress Press, 1978) and Elisabeth Schüssler Fiorenza *In Memory of Her* (Crossroad Publishing Co., 1983).

8

Inculturation, Feminism, and the Dialogue with Rome

Mary Milligan

FIRST OF ALL, I WOULD LIKE TO SAY WHY I HAVE CHOSEN TO address this topic. It was certainly *not* to interest the press, though I do realize that the third element in the triad of the title has great appeal to journalists at the present time. I wanted first of all to speak out of my own experience. It is important for you to have a general idea of what that experience is so that you will understand the limitations and perspective of my remarks and so be able to judge their validity for yourselves. My personal experience for eighteen of the past thirty years has been an international one. Just a year ago I completed a seven-year stay in Rome—my second one. During those seven years, I was challenged frequently to enter into "dialogue with Rome." I bore responsibility within my own congregation for bringing our constitutional process to completion. I was also part of the group of major superiors of women's congregations who spent hours in conversation with John Paul II about religious life. The same group of women religious, along with eight superiors of men's congregations, met regularly with the Congregation for Religious.

My experience has also been one of contact with several continents. That contact has triggered my reflection on inculturation. I have been enriched by witnessing the reality of "church" in various countries—in Mozambique or in Brazil, for example. I felt it might be of some value to share my insights gained from that limited international experience.

The approach I will take is not difficult to guess. In a first part I will look at the challenge of inculturation; a second part will look particularly at the development of feminine religious life in this country. Finally, a third part will try to combine these two aspects to throw light on the very concrete challenge of "dialogue with Rome".

INCULTURATION

Even though the word "inculturation" is fairly new in our theological vocabulary, the reality and challenge of inculturation have been around for a long time. Within a decade after the resurrection, the disciples of Jesus were faced with the demands of proclaiming the word in a culture other than their own. Once faith in Jesus extended beyond the synagogue, the cultural question was posed in a way that would become increasingly complex throughout the centuries.

It is instructive for us to look at the challenge as reflected in our earliest Christian sources. In Chapter fifteen of the Acts of Apostles, the question is vividly posed. The success of the mission among the Gentiles in Antioch raised the fundamental question: How is one to be saved? Though the dilemma is framed in terms of the law and Jewish practices, the heart of the question is "Is it necessary to embrace Judaism to be a Christian?" Among the protagonists at the meeting in Jerusalem, we meet a variety of cultural backgrounds and languages. All had been observers of the Mosaic law when they received the call to follow Jesus in the Way. But the experience of Paul, Barnabas, and other Hellenistic Jewish Christians outside of Jerusalem, their witnessing the power of the risen Jesus among non-Jews gave them a new insight into the nature of the Way they were to follow. Where were the women at the meeting in Jerusalem? Typically they are not mentioned.

It is the Pauline communities which seem to have incarnated the fundamental insight that "in Christ there is neither Jew or Greek, slave nor free, male nor female" (Gal. 3:28). Neither social status, ethnic stock, or sexual identity counted within the Christian community. None of these factors was an obstacle to salvation; none merited salvation. Paul envisaged the Christian community as a "new environment in which one could breathe the air of freedom which was the gift of the Spirit".[1] Within the realm of the Spirit of Jesus, the Christian community, a fundamental equality was to prevail. Just as one did not have to change social or marital status on becoming a Christian (cf. 1 Cor 7), neither did one have to divest oneself of one's cultural background.

Even when the question is solved theoretically, its practice was not easily established. We are told of Peter's ambiguous behavior toward gentile Christians. Certain passages in the letters to Timothy, especially those regarding women, indicate that the primitive vision of an egalitarian community was short-lived.

How to proclaim the risen Jesus in different cultures remained a challenge. According to Acts, Paul's attempt to preach to the Athenians could hardly be termed a huge success. Stoic and epicurian philosophers had little comprehension of his strange message, in spite of efforts to appeal to them through elements of their own culture.

In the quantum leap from the first century to our own day, we will only briefly pose our feet on the stepping stone of the colonial period—the sixteenth through nineteenth centuries. Western culture was, of course, considered (by the West!) to be normative during this period. Christianity had been so clothed in western robes that it had become practically identified with those robes. And so people in newly discovered lands were required to renounce much of their own cultural identity in order to "put on Christ Jesus." Their own non-western cultures were considered to be pagan. We all have seen pictures of missionaries in Mexico, for example, burning whole libraries of Mayan/Incan books on mathematics and the sciences because of their "pagan" (read "non-western") character. Those missionaries who did respect the local culture and who attempted to preach the Gospel through it remain outstanding exceptions to the official practice and policy. One has only to visit the African or South American continent today to find churches which look as if they had been constructed in Spain, Portugal, or Italy and transported as is to the sites where they stand as reminders of both zeal for the

Gospel and cultural domination. One might conjecture to what extent this phenomenon expressed the patriarchal view solidified centuries earlier and anachronistically reinforced to our own day.

It is surely a grace of our times that we are rediscovering the immense cultural values of different groups and are realizing how these values can be a vehicle for those of Jesus. It is just eleven years since the appearance of *Evangelii nuntiandi,* that extraordinary document in which the split between culture and the Gospel is recognized as the drama of our times. According to *Evangelii nuntiandi,*

> For the Church it is a question not only of preaching the gospel in ever-widening geographic areas or to even greater numbers of people, but also of affecting, and as it were upsetting, through the power of the gospel, humankind's criteria of judgment, determining values, points of interest, lines of thought, sources of inspiration and models of life, which are in contrast with the Word of God and the plan of salvation. (#19–20).

Here in the United States, we might think of "inculturation" as applying especially to Africa, Asia, and Latin American, no doubt because the culture of Europe, the basis of our own, is our starting point. And yet, the question of inculturation, of the relationship of the Gospel and culture, must be addressed in all places where the Christian message is proclaimed and lived.

Until very recently, there has been little national attention given to "culture," defined as the values, customs, rituals, art, poetry, and the like which give expression to a people's great spiritual experiences and desires. Unlike many other nations, the United States has no Ministry of Culture, for example. For at least the first hundred and fifty years of our national existence, the myth of the ethnic "melting pot" was the ideal; generations of immigrants strove to leave behind their national heritage and identity—language, customs, social structures—in order to become American. Children were not taught the language of their parents, and so we have first generation Americans of European or Hispanic descent not knowing their parents' native language. That dynamic is changing rapidly, however, as our country finds itself in the midst of a true cultural awakening.

To study the culture of a people, to evangelize the "personal and collective consciences of people" (EN #18) is a mammoth task requiring constant discernment. The values, customs, rituals and other cultural expressions of a people are influenced by climate, geography, topography, and a host of other factors. When we look at our geography here in the North American continent, for example, we recognize that there are, as in most nations, many undefined but quite marked cultural regions. The North is not the South, the East is not the West. Anyone from Los Angeles knows, for example, that that city has more in common with Phoenix, Arizona than it has with San Francisco. A recent book speaks, in fact, of the "nine nations of North America" and situates both Los Angeles and Phoenix in Mexamerica.

One of the essential components in a group's understanding of its identify is a knowledge of its own history. And yet, most American Catholics are ignorant of the unique history and identity of the Catholic Church in America. In an insightful treatment of American Catholicism,[2] John Coleman underlines this uniqueness. "For 175 years, the primary goals of American Catholics were survival and personal and collective achievement . . . Upward mobility and acceptance by American culture constituted core objectives of immigrant Catholics and their leaders . . . " The mid-1960s mark a turning point in American Catholicism. The election of the first Catholic president was the symbol of this turning point, a sort of coming-of-age marked by its own identity crisis. For the American church this turning point coincided historically with the Second Vatican Council. "By the time of the accession of Kennedy (to the American presidency), Catholics had acquired their full share of that upward mobility, status and respectibility they had so long and earnestly pursued". Catholics achieved this status at a time when their own distinctive identity was not clear, thus provoking a crisis in American Catholicism.

Ignorance of our American Catholic history and the geographical diversity of our nation are only two of the factors affecting the culture in which the Gospel is lived and preached in the United States. What challenge is posed to us by the changing ethnic composition of our country? An article of Los Angeles in *Time* magazine last year gave an extraordinarily complex picture of that city, which is mirrored in so many others in our country.

Recognition of the diversity in our church and of our American church helps us to rejoice in our diverse gifts, ministries and ways of acting. We are convinced that this diversity is God-given (cf. 1 Cor 12). But what kind of ongoing discernment is needed in a situation of plurality in order to discover the radical unity of the Gospel which the Spirit creates among disciples of Jesus? As the cultural values of peoples in our own country are recognized as potential vehicles of the Gospel, how will we ensure that the essential unity of the church remains a reality and not merely an empty phrase?

FEMINISM

Several socio-cultural phenomena deeply mark American society today. For our purposes here, I would like to look at only one of these—feminism—as it affects our church and women religious in particular. I speak of women religious for three reasons: 1) they are the group I know best; 2) I was asked to by the planners of this conference; 3) they are an identifiable group whose history is easily documented.

Only future generations will be able to measure fully the depth and extent of the revolution presently in progress in American society. And while the new consciousness of women is by no means limited to the United States, it does seem to have a force here that it does not have elsewhere, with the possible exception of Canada.

In the area of feminism, our continent is forging new frontiers. The effects of our new insights on language and literature alone are extraordinary. New grammatical usages are appearing; libraries and bookstores have whole new categories of books— "women's studies"— which touch theology, sociology, psychology, health, literature, and the like.

And yet our country remains one of inequality between women and men, in the work force, in political life (though the recent primary elections give some hope that change is coming in that area), in health benefits and even, as has recently fascinated the media, at the dry cleaners.

But it is undeniable that a new consciousness has arisen in our country and that consciousness cannot be undone. Not all women perceive the existing inequalities and among those who do, some accept them as inevitable or even as desirable. Others have recognized injustices and, have worked with all their energy to correct them. Within that group there are those who have lost patience and hope in the struggle. What is surely true is that we cannot retrace our steps, we cannot go backwards. The new awareness that exists cannot be undone. If you will excuse the bellicose image, the war has already been won, in my opinion, though there are *many* battles still to be fought.

In a recent dialogue between First-world and Third-world countries, one participant criticized the U.S. and Europe for their failure to situate the feminist issue in the larger context of the struggle for liberation, for self-determination:

> The priorities of the women's movement are different according to the race, class, or nation to which the women belong. For the women of Asia, Africa, and South and Central America their main problems concern the entire social system in which they are involved together with their men. The greater oppression of women in the "Third World" is recognized as related to the ongoing exploitation of the poor countries and races by the rich and powerful nations. These considerations induce the women from the poorer countries to press for a more radical approach to the women's movement. They want women to give priority to overall social transformation within their countries and in international relations.[3]

It would not be difficult to build bridges between feminist theology and other liberation theologies. They have many common traits. Both begin from an experience of oppression and stress praxis as an essential element. Both are based on hermeneutical suspicion. Both revise the Christian tradition from the viewpoint of those who have been rendered invisible—the poor and women. Both proclaim a Jesus who came primarily for those who were marginalized by their society. More attention to these similarities might enable us to build bridges among cultures. It seems to me that what is peculiar to feminism in the United States is the extent to which our entire culture is being penetrated by this reality. Women artists, musicians, and writers, women theologians, scientists, and researchers are finding public expression as never before and thus contributing to a society which one day may truly be able to "ignore gender." Is this phenomenon already an "evangelization" of our culture?

FEMININE RELIGIOUS LIFE IN THE UNITED STATES

Before looking at religious in the United States, let me say that it is important to distinguish in any historical study between masculine and feminine religious life. Throughout the centuries of what we have come to call "apostolic religious life," social factors and ecclesiastical interventions influenced feminine congregations in a way unknown in men's institutes, especially those of priests. These differences have generally been insufficiently recognized, and yet they play an essential part in our understanding of the development of religious life.

Women religious came to our country with the first wave of immigrants from Europe. They played a crucial role within the immigrant church and in the pioneer movement westward. It is especially the second half of the nineteenth century which saw an extraordinary surge in the number of sisters in America. From fewer than 1,400 in 1850, they grew in half a century to almost 40,000. Most of those sisters responded to the needs of their people by providing educational, health, and social services. A decision by the American bishops in 1884 to provide a Catholic school education for every Catholic child determined the choice of many religious institutes to open schools or to staff parochial schools. In the ecclesial context of that period which saw uniformity as a necessary guarantee and expression of unity, religious arriving from Europe brought with them practices born on that Continent. This often meant that "the order of the day in the Mother House" determined the daily schedule of sisters throughout the congregation. European customs, imported, implanted, and cherished by the many dedicated women religious who came to the United States, were at times seen as integral expressions of the essence of religious life. Within the context of a legalistic interpretation of the law which prevailed in the largely Anglo-Saxon Catholic population, many customs were retained in the New World long after they had been discarded in Europe. The lack of cultural adaptation led to deep frustrations in a later age.

An example may help to clarify this point. Within the strong class consciousness of Europe, the distinction, indeed the separation, between choir sisters (those usually involved in schools) and lay sisters (involved primarily in domestic works within the convent) in the same congregation was seen as normal. At its origins this two-tier system was meant to make monastic life accessible even to those unable to read Latin and therefore recite the office; throughout the centuries it also allowed the unmarried daughters of the upper class to live within a monastery much the same kind of life—that is, assisted by domestic servants—they would have led in their own homes. Such a system transplanted on American soil ran counter to the democratic roots of the country. And yet, in some congregations, the system was retained until the second half of the twentieth century. The painful marks of the long retention of the choir/lay division among apostolic religious women are still with us today.

The requirements of cloister are perhaps the most illustrative of how cultural and social roles attributed to women have affected feminine religious institutes. Enclosure was mandated for women religious as early as 1298 (Boniface VIII in *Periculoso*). In 1566, this mandate was reiterated by *Circa pastoralis* which required solemn vows and therefore enclosure of all women in religious communities. Although the apostolic intuition of an Angela Merici or a Mary Ward was contemporary with that of Saint Ignatius, the history of the groups founded by those women indicate that there were strong factors at work in their regard which were not operative in the case of the Society of Jesus. One of those factors was surely the role of women in society—a cultural bias. The idea of women in the streets, outside a convent or a home or a school, was unacceptable. An unaccompanied woman outside such protective institutions was even more unthinkable. It is interesting to notice that the expression "a woman of the street" retains even today a connotation quite different from "the man on the street"! Women were to be protected; their proper domain was inside an institution, generally the home; their realm was the private sphere and not in public.

Any woman wishing to be consecrated to God by public vows of religion had to be cloistered. And yet, as of the sixteenth century, some founders—and I say founders because it was much more difficult for foundresses on their own to do this—some founders devised creative ways of avoiding the restrictions regarding enclosure. In some congregations, the members made promises rather than vows (for example, Soeurs de l'instruction

Charitable du Saint-Enfant Jesus founded by P. Nicholas Barre) or professed one or two vows rather than three. It was only in the early twentieth century (Leo XIII, *Conditae a Christo*) that canonical recognition was given to women religious professing simple vows of poverty, chastity, and obedience and not adopting enclosure. If masculine apostolic religious institutes take the foundation of the Society of Jesus as a watershed, feminine institutes really cannot do the same.

The rules of cloister created great difficulties in our country where distances were great, priests were few, and patrons and dowries rare. And so, the American bishops requested that regulations regarding cloister be modified. In 1864 all American women religious were asked by the Congregation of Bishops and Regulars to take simple vows and adopt a modified enclosure, thus allowing them to respond more adequately to the needs of the church in America.

Service of the people's needs has always marked religious life in the United States. The Catholic Church was a poor church, a minority church. Religious women brought to their service of that church a generous and selfless dedication. The unremunerated or minimally remunerated services of women religious were a major factor in the church's ability to sustain its educational institutions. This dedication was not always accompanied, however, by adequate theological, professional, and even religious formation. Throughout the history of the church, opportunities for the theological education of women have been extremely limited or even non-existent. Recognition of the need for such education led to the foundation of the "Sister Formation Conference" in the 1950's. This event had far-reaching consequences and is, in my opinion, a major factor in the evolution of religious life in the United States. Through the Sister Formation Conference, young religious were assured a solid formation in Scripture, theology and church history, as well as in sociology and psychology. Religious already active were withdrawn temporarily from their various activities in order to study. Summer sessions on university campuses became a normal occupation. Many of those young sisters who were the first-fruits of the Sister Formation movement are leaders in their communities today; others are professional women; others still the mothers of Christian families.

One of the cultural traits of the American people forged by its history is, surely, a spirit of adventure, a willingness to risk in order to discover new frontiers. The pioneer spirit has been evident among both men and women religious in the United States. Their pioneer contribution to the forging of cultural institutions was recognized by Pope John Paul II in his letter of April 3, 1983 to the American Bishops.

> Religious were among your pioneers. They blazed a trail in Catholic education at all levels, helping to create a magnificent educational system from elementary school to university. They brought into being health care facilities remarkable both for their numbers and quality. They made a valuable contribution to the provision of social services. Working towards the establishment of justice, love and peace, they helped to build a social order rooted in the Gospel, striving to bring generation after generation to the maturity of Christ. Their witness to the primacy of Christ's love has been expressed through lives of prayer and dedicated service to others.

When Vatican II called the church to renewal, the response of religious women in the United States was enthusiastic and marked by their characteristic generosity and pioneer spirit. Willing to enter uncharted paths, they often did so spontaneously as a response to the call to renewal. Many congregations were quick to make adaptations. That the first "victims of renewal" were many of the internal practices and rituals which had remained unchanged from their birth in Europe a century previous is not surprising. The more difficult and long-term task of renewal is still underway and continues in the climate of rediscovering the identify of American Catholicism and of a growing feminist awareness.

DIALOGUE WITH ROME

You will surely not be surprised if I confess to you that this third part of my presentation has been rewritten any number of times. At each writing, I was conscious of a good deal of pain within, a pain that comes from recognizing the increasing number of cases where prominent and respected voices in our church are silenced, cases where efforts to respond to pastoral need and to seek to live the Gospel in our American culture seem to be both misunderstood and judged erroneous. The escalation of Vatican interventions this past year is indeed a cause for concern.

It is not my intent here to refer to these recent cases. We are only too aware of them. Rather, I would like to reflect briefly on a few elements which, I believe, underlie the present tension. My purpose is not to be exhaustive but rather to raise areas which need further reflection and then to present some strategies for the future.

The first of the areas I would like to raise is that of unity and its relationship to plurality. Throughout the ages, philosophers and theologians have struggled to understand and express the relationship between the one and the many. Far from being a theoretical question, this one meets us in our concrete everyday life each time we must weigh the common good against the good of an individual. In the face of high tuition costs, parents must decide whether their family can sustain sending a child to the private school of his or her choice. School officials must decide when a student's behavior becomes disruptive of the collective educational climate. Religious leaders must determine when gratuitous service becomes detrimental to the whole body. And in our justice system, Caiphas' opinion that it is better that one person die than that the whole nation perish has been repeated many times over. Gamabel's good advice is much less common. Since Vatican II, our rediscovery of the role of the local church has made us more conscious of the tension between the good of the one and the good of the whole in an ecclesial sense. As the particular identity of local churches is strengthened, how is the unity of the universal church maintained? There is no doubt that many of the recent interventions of the Vatican in the United States church spring from a legitimate concern for doctrinal unity. The tragedy is that they often contribute to division.

One of the greatest challenges on the agenda of the American church in the decade ahead must surely be to find ways of deepening our awareness of belonging to a world community of humankind while growing in our sense of identity as American Catholics. How will we develop our cultural identity as a local church while remaining in communion with all other local churches, including that of Rome?

Another area which needs our ongoing reflection in the decade ahead is the very diverse understandings we have of certain values we hold in common. Yes, a church law does proclaim equality, freedom, and participation of all within the Christian community of the baptized. But how does our cultural experience of those realities affect our understanding of them? What parameters are put on my understanding by the culture in which I live? It is certain that our American understanding of freedom and authority is diverse from that of many other nations. When foreigners come to this country, it is often the exercise of political freedom and freedom of speech which strikes them most strongly. One immigrant from an Eastern European country confessed to me recently that he was shocked by our freedom to criticize our government.

The democratic principles on which our nation is founded proclaim government of, for and by the people themselves. Participation in the selection of our leaders and in the setting of national policy is part of our lives. Until Watergate and the Vietnam war, that participation took for granted the fundamental goodness of our political leaders and their decisions. In war and in peace, God was on our side and the side of our leaders. Finding ourselves inextricably engaged in a "war that nobody wanted," faced with the reality of gross dishonesty within our government, as a nation we had to face the ambiguity of all that is human, authority included. From a naive attitude of unquestioning faith in government leaders, we moved into a stance of responsibility which questioned decisions made by those in authority. Personal responsibility expressed itself in a critical stance as an element of participation.

This same sense of responsibility is reflected in our attitude toward authority within the church. To speak only of religious congregations, we know the change in understanding of congregational leadership in the past twenty years. No longer is blind obedience to superiors seen as a virtue. Rather leaders are seen as exercising a particular service of governing and unifying the group in view of its mission. And during these past twenty years, American religious have been actively involved in chapters of renewal, in writing constitutions, in choosing their leaders and their ministries, in all major decisions touching their life and mission. This participation has not led to a weakened authority but to new ways in exercising it.

The will of women religious to participate extends outside of their community life. They share the growing awareness in American society of global interdependence—of the interdependence of nations, of institutions, of economic and ecological systems. This awareness often leads them to address the causes of injustice as well as its effects, exercising their rights as stockholders, for example, or speaking out against unjust and oppressive policies of civil government. If the participation which so marks our nation and the church on American soil, if our critical and dissenting participation is not seen in its cultural context, it risks being interpreted as disobedience. It could be misread as a lack of respect for authority or as rebelliousness rather than as an expression of a truly adult American church. But unless this way of participating is recognized by our partners in dialogue as a reality and a value, we indeed run the risk of deafness to one another and this brings me to the question of dialogue. I'd like here simply to share with you certain strategies, certain suggestions.

Among the things that struck me when I returned to the United States was how simplistic and one-sided opinions of Rome tend to be. In my first weeks back, some would ask me what "Rome" thought of certain questions, as if knowing that we would know the answer to all uncertainties. Others, when I mentioned that I had spent time in Rome, reacted as if I had uttered a four-letter word—which of course, I had. And the Pope, I perceived, was seen by some as able to do no wrong and by many as able to do no right. We well know from our political scene how difficult if not impossible dialogue becomes when another nation is labeled as the "enemy" as "evil." Our current experiences with Iran, Libya, Russia and elsewhere attest to this. Perhaps my experience in countries where the United States is often regarded as "the enemy" has made me acutely sensitive to this aspect. If we fail to see "Rome" as a collection of human beings like ourselves, both sinful and grace-filled, wanting what is best for God's people but often ignorant or inept and even unique in their ways of proceeding, then dialogue will in fact become impossible. We well know that limited vision, struggle for power, manipulation of people and domination are not limited to one side of the Atlantic.

I have also noticed in this past year that much of what is negative and harsh and little of what is positive gets public attention. Let me give you an example. On January 1 of this year, we celebrated for the nineteenth time the international day of peace. Several months before that celebration each year, a papal message is promulgated. This year's message, "Peace Has No Frontiers", was a particularly powerful and appropriate one, asking that as much attention be given to North-South relationships as is given to East-West. The message calls for increased solidarity and dialogue. A commitment to peace, it states, means "looking at the North-South tensions and replacing them with a new relationship, the social solidarity of all . . . , a social solidarity which faces up honestly to the abyss that exists today but does not acquiesce in any kind of economic determinism."[4] Such a message, in my opinion, is crucial in the United States today and could advance our commitment to both internal and international justice. And yet I found little or nothing about that message in the press; it certainly was not mentioned in any preaching that I heard in the parishes at the beginning of the new year. What I am trying to underline is that unless we do hear another side of the Roman story, we will fall into the trap of identifying Rome as the enemy and so be ourselves responsible for rendering all dialogue impossible.

Another of the tasks before us is to "learn another language," to recognize the way culture affects our understanding of certain words.

Language very much expresses the thought patterns of a people. It arises within a culture and conveys meaning within a culture. The more certain words presuppose the cultural context in which they arise, the more they risk being misunderstood by those in other cultures. Dialogue thus becomes most difficult and charged with tension. A word, for example, like education which in most Latin cultures conveys the whole process of human formation and development is often understood in an Anglo-Saxon context as limited to schools or teaching. International congregations know that it becomes increasingly difficult to use the word "poverty" in a Latin American or African context. I have met young people who struggle for feminist ideals and yet who do not want to be called "feminist." I might add that when the leaders of the International Union of Superiors General met with Pope John Paul II three years ago, it was he who twice said: The church must listen to feminism. How does the content of that word for him relate to its content for us? What are the parameters and presuppositions of our common vocabulary? Only continued efforts to explicitate the content will enable real conversation to continue.

In the specific dialogue which takes place between church representatives in the Vatican and sisters in the United States and on a much more concrete level, we must learn that the direct and forthright American style which we consider "honesty" is often misconstrued in a cultural milieu where diplomacy and diplomatic language are the order of the day. Just as our direct, telegraphic style might shock as Asian or an African, so it is not always helpful in the complex milieu of the Vatican offices.

A crucial task for women in the church is to continue to network with one another. For me, this conference is a great sign of hope in this regard. We do have different opinions, yes! But we must respect one another and refuse to establish deep divisions among us. The feminist has its radical fringes and its committed opponents. Where would we be without those who present certain issues to us starkly, boldly and perhaps excessively? Where would we be without those who received us of certain values we might risk overlooking in the light of the new ones we've discovered. To be divided and separated from one another is truly to be a ploy of the very patriarchal, clerical world vision we want to oppose.

We must likewise continue to network with women in other cultures. Most international religious congregations have a built-in possibility of doing that. Such networking will teach us much about other cultures that allows us to see our own more clearly. In the light of other realities, we see both the strengths and weaknesses and the realitivity of our own. This networking will help us to situate the feminist struggle on our continent in the context of the much broader one for liberation. Both struggles can only benefit from such networking. We know the positive results of networking among leaders of religious congregations. The Leadership Conference of Women Religious deserves much applause for its constitution of such network and the persevering skill with which they continue to dialogue with Vatican offices. That certainly is a sign of hope.

We are at a critical point in our development as a church in the United States. The call to evangelize our culture and to use our culture as a means to evangelize remains strong. The feminist awareness is a growing tone in all of our cultural expressions as a nation. At the very moment when dialogue within the universal church seems to be most crucial in terms of our increasing identity as an American church, it seems also to become most difficult.

To learn again from our earliest Christian sources, it seems we stand very much in the same position as Paul as he also entered into conversation with the church in Rome, a church he knew only indirectly. In the face of the possibility of real and irremediable schism, Paul took a long theological view on history. One gets the impression that he was drawing on his deepest resources as he confronted many of the polarities which characterize our own age as well—freedom and the law; unity and diversity of practice. In writing to the Romans, Paul goes back not to Moses, lest he seem to come down on the side of those urging practice of Mosaic law. His historical arguments rest rather on Abraham, "the ancestor from whom we all descended." And, we add, on Sarah. (4:1)

For any dialogue to work, there must be openness on both sides. We in the United States have the responsibility to do whatever we can to enter into the dialogic process loyally, wisely and with perseverance. But alone we cannot guarantee its success. Only genuine listening and willingness to learn on both sides as well can ensure true dialogue. Will our partners in dialogue be willing to question their presuppositions? To hear women's experience on this continent and elsewhere? Will they allow a deeply rooted clerical culture to be evangelized? I don't know. I do know though that, having waited and worked in patience for a genuine and fruitful dialogue, we like St. Paul, can only hope for what we do not yet see (cf Rom 8:25).

Notes

1. Jerome Murphy-O'Connor, O.P., *1 Corinthians* (Michael Glazier, Inc., 1979) 120.
2. John A. Coleman, *An American Strategic Theology*.
3. John C.B. and Ellen Low Webster, *The Church and Women in the Third World* (Westminister Press, 1985) 11.
4. *Ways of Peace: Papal Messages for the World Days of Peace* (Vatican City, 1986) 239.

9

Self-Determination and Self-Direction in Religious Communities

Sandra Schneiders

EVEN TO RAISE THE ISSUE OF "SELF-DETERMINATION" AMONG WOMEN religious is to announce that it is indeed "the best of times and the worst of times." American women religious are living a tale of two cities. They live with one foot in their American religious communities, where they are committed to developing a life rooted in the Gospel and post-conciliar theology, devoted to justice and attentive to but not enslaved by their own history and experience. They also live with one foot in a Vatican-controlled Roman Catholic Church which is convinced of its right and duty to exercise a virtually absolute control of religious life in its inception, development, and day-to-day unfolding.

In what follows I will first try to set out the scope and underlying theology of Vatican teaching and legislation relevant to the issue of self-determination within religious communities of women. Secondly, I will describe the alternate experience of religious life that is developing among American women religious and indicate its theological and cultural sources. Then I will try to suggest, on the basis of current experience and historical precedent, how this clash of understandings is currently developing. And finally, I will try to image a model of religious life in which adult self-determination might be harmonized with responsible integration into the local and universal church.

PRESENT STATE OF THEOLOGY AND LAW REGARDING RELIGIOUS LIFE

Beginning with chapter six of *Lumen gentium,* the Council's Dogmatic Constitution on the Church, *Perfectae caritatis,* the Decree on Appropriate Renewal of Religious Life,[1] and the implementing documents which followed from 1966 to 1971, the magisterium has developed a body of teaching on religious life that both preserves much of pre-conciliar teaching and claims to be based on current praxis.[2] This teaching has been given legal force in the revised code of canon law[3] which, according to Pope John Paul II, "can be considered the final conciliar document" that "will be for all of you [religious] a valuable aid and a sure guide in concretely stating the means for faithfully and generously living your magnificent vocation in the church."[4] The official teaching of the Council and of subsequent papal and Vatican documents as well as the major provisions of canon law on religious life were summed up in the document "Essential Elements" which appeared in 1983.[5]

Although there are occasional inconsistencies among these documents, this body of teaching and law is quite clear about the expectations of the Vatican regarding the living of the religious life in the church today. Our question concerns the approach to self-determination in this post-conciliar official teaching. Canon 586 maintains that:

> For individual institutes there is acknowledged a rightful autonomy of life, especially of governance, by which they enjoy their own discipline in the Church and have the power to preserve their own patrimony intact . . . [6]

In *Mutuae relationes,* the document on the relationship between bishops and religious orders issued jointly by the Congregation for Bishops and the Congregation for Religious and Secular Institutes (CRSI) in 1978, bishops are reminded that

> Institutes . . . have an internal organization all of their own (cf. CD, 35, 3) which has its proper field of competency and a right of autonomy . . . [7]

Three areas are singled out for the exercise of this autonomy: the determination of the manner of living the evangelical counsels;[8] governance; and internal discipline.[9] However, the interpretation and the restrictions on these areas of autonomy are such as to effectively deny any real autonomy to religious institutes, much less to individual religious. Canon law says that:

> It belongs to the competent authority of the Church to interpret the evangelical counsels, to regulate their practice by laws, to constitute there from stable forms of living by canonical approbation, and, for its part, to the spirit of the founders and wholesome traditions.[10]

It is hard to imagine what autonomy in the interpretation of the vows is left, by this canon, to the institute.

With regard to governance, the law stipulates that

> With due regard for can. 586, [on the autonomy of governance] institutes of pontifical right are immediately and exclusively subject to the power of the Apostolic See in internal governance and discipline.[11]

The same claim is made in *Mutuae relationes* for the bishop in relation to diocesan institutes.[12] In fact, the form and mode of internal government of institutes is determined in detail by canon law, which specifies the establishment and personal authority of superiors at each level of government along with their responsibilities and duties, the functioning of general chapters, and all government matters of consequence.

With regard to discipline, canon 663 spells out in detail the daily observances of religious, down to the recitation of the rosary.[13] "Essential Elements" insists that religious, in order to give public witness, must "willingly accept a pattern of life . . . largely laid down for them" and it is quite clear that that pattern is to be the one specified by central church authority. They are to wear a habit and live in a special residence properly established for them by ecclesiastical authority.[14] They are to have an oratory in their houses in which the blessed sacrament is reserved, participate daily in eucharist, have fixed daily hours of prayer together, have times of monthly and annual retreat fixed for them by authority on local, provincial, and general levels, and so on.[15]

In short, the "legitimate autonomy" recognized for religious institutes in regard to the interpretation of the vows, governance, and discipline is substantially negated by the law. It seems to consist in deciding how, in practice, the institute will carry out the established directives governing even the most minute details of religious life.

Not only is autonomy in the interpretation of the vows, in governance, and in discipline virtually suppressed by current teaching and law, but sweeping claims to control of religious in their life and mission are made, usually in the name of obedience. It is claimed that religious institutes depend "in their origins" on the hierarchy, because each institute "depends for the authentic discernment of its founding charism on the God-given ministry of the hierarchy."[16] Historically, this is not the case. Rather, the hierarchy has often enough been forced to finally accept the discernment of the people of God, which it had resisted, denied, and even tried to suppress. This fact does not seem to offer any challenge to the serene claim to control the origins of the institutes.[17] Furthermore, the church, through the hierarchy, claims the right to accept and approve the constitutions of the institute[18] and reserves to itself the authentic interpretation of them.[19] According to *Lumen gentium,* it is the task of the hierarchy to make laws to regulate the practice of the counsels and to ensure the fidelity of institutes to the spirit of their founders.[20] In "Mutuae Relationes" sweeping powers of control are recognized for the local ordinary.[21] Furthermore, *Perfectae caritatis,* canon law, and "Essential Elements" assert that the apostolate of religious communities is "exercised in the name and by the mandate of the Church".[22] In sum, it is claimed that "[i]nstitutes of consecrated life . . . are subject to the supreme authority of this same Church in a special manner" and the "[i]ndividual members are also bound to obey the Supreme Pontiff as their highest superior by reason of the sacred bond of obedience."[23]

The interpretation in teaching and in law of the notion of the charism of the congregation is particularly restrictive of the self-determination of religious institutes. This theological concept was revalidated by the Council in what seemed at the time to be a healthy remedying of the homogenization of diverse religious families by the code of 1917. Through the joyful recognition of the diversity of gifts represented by religious communities in the church the Council encouraged religious to rejoice in their uniqueness and to offer it to the people of God in service.[24]

However, charism has been gradually equated, in official teaching and legislation, with the specific apostolic work for which the community was founded, for example, teaching or nursing, and interpreted as a principle of double limitation. First, the congregation is not to deviate from or expand beyond the original work.[25] Secondly, no member is to be allowed to exercise a gift, no matter how good or desirable, that is not in accord with this corporate work.[26] Rather than being understood as a gift of evangelical energy empowering the community to discern and respond to the signs of the times, the charism of the institute is defined as a common work, "which the church has recognized as expressing concretely the purpose of the institute. This common and constant apostolate . . . is so closely related to the identity [of the institute]that it cannot be changed . . . "[27] Thus, the charism of the institute, as well as the ministerial involvement of each individual and of the community as a whole, comes under the total control of the hierarchy.

A final, more subtle, but very effective limitation is placed on the self-determination of institutes and individual religious by the reintroduction of a theology of superiority. This elitism has slipped into the teaching about religious life. The basis is actually laid in *Lumen gentium,* where religious are described as "going beyond what is of precept in the matter of perfection."[28] John Paul II has repeatedly emphasized the superiority of religious in comparison with the laity. In his letter to the bishops on the jubilee year he insisted that it has "special value for religious; it affects them in a special way, it makes special demands on their love." Religious have "a special title" to the treasures of grace. In *Redemptionis donum* he devoted an entire section to his understanding of religious life as a "state of perfection," and another to the counsels as a "better" way.[29] "Essential Elements" talks of religious life involving a "closer following of Christ" and religious profession as chosen because of a desire to be "consecrated in a more total way to the service of God."[30] Religious are "predestined" within the people of God so that their legitimate place among the laity is curtailed even while they are denied a place within the hierarchy.

It is somewhat difficult to determine exactly the theological and/or canonical understanding of religious life that emerges from official teaching and law and that functions as justification for the restrictions placed upon the self-determination of religious. There is repeated insistence that religious life is not an intermediate state between clergy and laity but that religious are people called from either state[31] to a life of the evangelical counsels. This state of life, it is asserted, participates in some special way in the sacramental nature of the church, showing forth the mystery of the people of God as transformed in Christ, called to holiness, and participating in His mission to the world.[32]

Because the church legally recognizes this state of life as such, it is *canonical*, and because religious make public profession of the counsels, it is *public*. However, it does not seem to be either of these characteristics that grounds the sweeping claims to immediate, direct, and universal control of religious institutes by the hierarchy. Both are shared with other states in the church which are not so controlled. Thus, it seems that, because religious are understood to constitute a state characterized by *public witness through separation from the world,* the law for them is so much more detailed and restrictive.[33] Separation from the world, expressed in external lifestyle such as some form of cloister in all religious houses[34] and distinguishing garb,[35] is presented as the distinguishing characteristic of religious life in contrast to other canonical (for example, secular institutes) and/or public (for example, matrimony) states. The strange contention of "Essential Elements," that religious witness "is not given" without such practices as wearing a habit and living in a canonically erected house,[36] is perfectly understandable if the distinguishing characteristic of religious life is separation from the world through profession of the vows.

Religious, through their separation from the world, are understood to be attached to, assimilated to, indeed quasi-sacraments of the church in its holiness in a way analogous to the hierarchy's embodiment of the structure of the church as a divinely instituted society. *Mutuae relationes* speaks of the "unquestionable bond of religious life with the life and holiness of the church" as the basis of the bishop's special relationship to religious.[37] "Essential Elements" calls religious life "an outward, social sign of the mystery of God's consecrating action through life."[38] The conclusion drawn from this view of religious life as a kind of sacrament of the church as *mystery* is that religious life must, in its structures, publically reflect the *structure of the institution.* "Essential Elements" says explicitly that the structures of religious institutes "reflect the Christian hierarchy of which the head is Christ himself."[39] Thus, the authority in religious institutes, like the hierarchical authority in the church, "does not derive from the members" and "cannot be shared" because it is conferred on and invested in the person of the superior by the church, within which divine authority is invested in pope and bishops by God.[40]

In short, at the basis of the official understanding of religious life is a christomonistic ecclesiology that legitimates a divine-right monarchy model of the church. We will examine this ecclesiology later in contrast to the pneumatological ecclesiology that grounds the self-understanding of contemporary religious as self-determining agents in the church. A christomonistic view of hierarchy is one in which authority is seen as originating by divine institution in God who communicates it to Christ who, as head of the church, invests it in his vicars, the pope and the episcopal college (and, perhaps, individual bishops and lower clergy, insofar as they participate in the episcopate). Any other exercise of authority in the church, such as that within religious communities, is strictly by delegation. Thus religious are totally subject to the control of a hierarchy that is not only authoritarian in its mode of operation, but totalitarian in its theologically based claims to absolute power in the name of Christ. Any talk of autonomy in such a view is empty rhetoric.

Anyone even vaguely familiar with American women's religious life is aware that the "worst of times" scenario just presented does not describe the self-understanding or practice of American religious today. If the post-conciliar official teaching on religious life does not supply the rationale for the current understanding and if canon law explicitly forbids much of the resulting practice, from where have come the resources for the re-imagination of religious life that has taken place in the last twenty years?

I would like to suggest that there are at least three such sources: 1) the Council's challenge to renewal; 2) an understanding and approach to experimentation very different from the official one;

3) and a pneumatological ecclesiology tentatively suggested in the conciliar documents, which provides an alternative to the christomonistic ecclesiology on which most official teaching on religious life is based.

THE COUNCIL'S CHALLENGE TO RENEWAL

It is important to note that it was the Council as a total phenomenon, with its expansive approach to the world and its enthusiasm for theological renewal and institutional reform, that inspired the renewal of religious life. Although the general treatment of religious renewal in the documents dealing explicitly with religious life was important, the passages that galvanized religious were less those dealing with the particulars of their life than those about the church and the world that were or could be applied to religious life.

In *Perfectae caritatis* the Council gave five principles, which were carefully studied and deeply internalized by religious, and which became their guide to the renewal of religious life.[41] As we look at each of them in the light of subsequent developments, it is easy to see how religious have proceeded to derive from such generally unadventurous documents the radically new forms we are living today.

First, religious were called to recognize that the Gospel itself is the "final norm" and "supreme rule" of religious life. Although no one would have said so explicitly, pre-conciliar religious life was based on the conviction that the constitutions of the institute were the supreme rule. As religious shifted their attention from rules and custom books to the Gospel, they discovered that much in their lives not only did not have its roots in the Gospel but was even contrary to it. Perhaps the most far-reaching of such discoveries was the Gospel call to evangelical equality within the community of Jesus' disciples. The Gospel does not call upon anyone to be superior to or to be separated from others but to love all as Jesus loved us. The rediscovery by religious of their solidarity with brothers and sisters in the church and the world began the movement of the "nun in the world" and signaled, in principle, the end of a life of elitism and privilege. Concretely, this resulted in the surrender of special dress and dwellings, the adaptations of schedules for service rather than for regularity, and the re-examination of institutional commitments and priorities.

Furthermore, there appeared to be nothing evangelical about the plethora of rules governing every detail of daily living and the childish asking of endless permissions by adult women called to mission.[42] The resistance of religious to Vatican insistence on rule-governed existence and the trappings of elite status is not stubborn refusal of Gospel hardship but a deep conviction that such a lifestyle is contrary to the Gospel call to equality and freedom for mission.

The second principle for renewal was the recognition of the Spirit-inspired diversity of religious congregations. This affirmation of the role of the charism of the founder in the resulting life and mission of the institute grounded a new sense of autonomy and responsibility of members for their communities. It no longer appeared appropriate to ask Rome who women religious were or should be, much less to accept a self-definition imposed unilaterally by those who did not share the life of women religious. Religious began to consult their history and to trust their lived experience as a guide to their particular present and corporate future. They claimed the right to interpret the vows they had professed and the rules they had written according to the traditions of their own congregations. Although revised constitutions were to be submitted to the Vatican for approval,[43] *Ecclesiae sanctae,* which supplied the norms for the implementing of *Perfectae caritatis,* recognized that "it is the institutes themselves which have the main responsibility for renewal and adaptation."[44] This document, which was without doubt the most open and adventurous of all in encouraging experimentation and legitimizing new ventures in religious renewal, was taken very seriously by most congregations. Charism was recognized by religious, not as a principle of limitation, but as a gift of the creative Spirit through the congregation to the church. Like the talents in the Gospel, it was not to be wrapped in the napkin of tradition and buried in the ground for safety; it had been born of the risks taken by our founders and was to be invested today with creative ingenuity in hopes of a new harvest in an unknown future.

The third principle of renewal was that religious were to make the church's initiatives in the areas of biblical, liturgical, pastoral, ecumenical, missionary, and social renewal their own. In other words, religious were to become women of the church, fully engaged in the glorious task of opening ecclesial windows onto the twentieth century world. No group in the church plunged into this adventure with more zeal than women religious. They read, studied, attended summer schools of theology, experimented liturgically, took part in ecumenical projects, and ventured into the ghettos and onto the picket lines. By an energetic praxis they internalized the Council documents and soon followed the trajectories initiated in those documents beyond what even the Council had envisioned. Small wonder that when CRSI, in "Essential Elements," serenely declared that the period of experimentation was now over and that religious were to put on their habits and repair to their convents, there to take up again a Tridentine lifestyle of cloister and institutional apostolates largely laid down for them by ecclesiastical authority,[45] the declaration was met with astonished disbelief and generally ignored.

The fourth principle of renewal was that religious were to have a proper understanding of humanity and the modern world so that they could participate in the church's mission to the world. Perhaps more than any other, this invitation led women religious beyond the confines of cloister and traditional institutional works. They interpreted this principle in the light of *Gaudium et spes,* the Dogmatic Constitution on the Church in the Modern World, which declared that

> The joy and hope, the grief and anguish of the people of our time, especially of those who are poor or afflicted in any way, are the joy and hope, the grief and anguish of the followers of Christ as well. Nothing that is genuinely human fails to find an echo in their hearts.[46]

This ringing proclamation of solidarity with the world confirmed the rejection of "separation from the world" as an acceptable or appropriate stance for the modern religious. Even contemplative religious began to question the purpose of a rigid material understanding of cloister that prevented education about and solidarity with the suffering of our world.

No doubt it was the new and positive approach to the world which first exposed many women religious to a new cultural movement that would change their lives: feminism. Religious began to analyze the patriarchal structures of the church and to repudiate male domination of their own life and that of others. The more totalitarian the claims of the Vatican males to control of women's lives, the clearer the feminist agenda became. Religious women began to realize that their claim to full adult personhood in the church, including the recognized right to self-determination and access to all ministries in the church, was fundamental to their agenda. When Theresa Kane, RSM, announced this conviction to Pope John Paul II on national television,[47] she spoke as president of the Leadership Conference of Women Religious, which had begun to function as an effective source and resource for the agenda of women religious in this country. When the first draft of the new code of canon law appeared, the LCWR, at the invitation of the Canon Law Society of America, formulated a powerful response in which it predicted the non-acceptance of almost every provision of the present law that has, in fact, been ignored or refused by women religious.[48] The struggle between an increasingly feminist religious life in the United States and a resolutely patriarchal Vatican is only beginning. It cannot be called off by a unilateral order to retreat from the world into which the conciliar documents plunged us or to abandon a claim to adult status to which evangelical feminism calls us.

The fifth principle for renewal, although seemingly the most traditional and innocuous, has been perhaps the most radically transforming: spiritual renewal. Again, women religious gave themselves to such renewal with zeal. They replaced routine retreats preached exclusively by male clerics with transformative, directed, individual, and group retreats often enough directed by women religious. They surrendered routine community prayers that fulfilled obligations but had little effect on life and accepted instead the challenge to discover personal and communal forms of prayer that would make them new persons for a new world. And as they struggled with the failures and the renewal involved they grew up in the Spirit. From the years of renewal emerged a spiritually mature group of women whose struggles for justice in the church and world were solidly rooted in a deep union with Christ. The courage to stand resolutely, whether against grape-growers and weapon builders, or against Vatican hierarchs demanding the expulsion of their sisters, has been born of long hours of struggle in prayer and deep decisions about what counts in a life of consecration.

The Council has contributed to the rethinking of religious life. First, in recognizing the universality of the call to holiness and the lay status of non-ordained religious, the Council gave religious women a way of understanding themselves that called for a new humanity and a new solidarity. They could no longer define themselves as those "called to perfection" in some exclusive way nor understand themselves as a separate caste, "a little less than the clergy but crowned with glory and honor." Deprived of the ascribed status that went with strange clothes and stranger practices, women religious had to earn, by deeds, the respect and love of fellow Christians. And in that earning, they have experienced a new solidarity with the rest of the laity, a solidarity in commitment to the transformation of the world and a solidarity in oppression with the church. But with this equality and solidarity has come new freedom. Religious are not quasi-clerics, agents of the institution whose duty is to impart and enforce the "party line." Their first duty is prophetic witness to the Gospel involving both denunciation of injustice and the energizing of new hope.[49] This realization has involved religious individuals and congregations in serious struggles with institutional authority, particularly over political involvement of religious and over theological dissent. The struggles are not over, but the theological foundation of the position of religious life is quite clear.

A final conciliar contribution is the recognition that ministry, in the life of apostolic congregations, is not a secondary end, an "overflow" or a "by product" of the seeking for perfection. Rather, "the apostolate constitutes an essential element" of these institutions.[50] While the document, "Essential Elements," attempts to circumscribe that apostolate by limiting it to tasks carried on with members of one's own community in traditional works and to root it in religious obedience rather than in baptism,[51] *Mutuae relationes* calls for "a certain apostolic diligence . . . in order to devise new, ingenious, and courageous ecclesial experiments under the inspiration of the Holy Spirit" and declares that a "responsiveness rich in creative initiative . . . is eminently compatible with the charismatic nature of the religious life."[52] Paul VI, in *Evangelii nuntiandi,* takes a similarly positive approach to the "originality" and "genius" of religious' ministerial involvement.[53] There is no doubt which position motivates American women religious. The tensions created by the full integration of ministry into the self-understanding and praxis of religious are enormous, but the resulting life is far more meaningful than the dichotomized existence of pre-conciliar days.

EXPERIMENTATION AMONG WOMEN RELIGIOUS

Following the adventurous prescriptions of *Ecclesiae sanctae,* Paul VI's 1966 norms for implementing *Perfectae caritatis,* women religious began an extensive program of so-called "experimentation." Actually, the term "experiment" is misleading, for those experiences that were beyond and even contrary to established understandings of religious life were not laboratory procedures which could be simply abandoned at some later point. Even those which yielded negative results permanently changed their participants. Religious *lived* a different experience of their vocation and they "could never go home again." Among the deliberately undertaken experiences of the immediate post-conciliar period were a variety of living arrangements such as small-group, intercommunity, and solitary forms; an expansion of ministries beyond the collective and institutional which involved religious primarily in work with adults outside their own communities; the personalizing of spirituality; and new forms of government which were participative rather than hierarchical, involving adult to adult rather than child to adult relationships between community members and their leaders.

Although Pope Paul seemed to think that the "period of experimentation" would end with the writing of new constitutions based on the learnings produced,[54] such a classicist view of history is incompatible with modern historical consciousness. Not only can religious not return to pre-conciliar self-understanding and lifestyle; they can no longer espouse the ideal of a permanently valid and henceforth unchanging rule of life that lays down detailed and uniform prescriptions for all members of the institute. What Bernard Lonergan has called "historical-mindedness" is the result of the period of experimentation. Change is not a path to some future state of stability. The stable state is change. While this terrifies Vatican officials, it energizes the religious who have taken responsibility for determining their own forms of life.

CONFLICTING ECCLESIOLOGIES

The leaders of women's religious life in this country have come to explicit awareness that the underlying conflict between Vatican officialdom in its attempt to dictate the parameters and control the practice of religious life, on the one hand, and women religious in their claim to self-determination and adult responsibility, on the other, is not only a clash between medieval patriarchs and modern democrats but, more deeply, a clash between two incompatible ecclesiologies. We can be grateful to Edward Kilmartin for his incisive explanation of this subject.[55]

As Kilmartin explains, the documents of Vatican II, especially *Lumen gentium,* do not provide us with a single vision of the church. There are at least three discernible, and not entirely compatible, ecclesiologies woven throughout the documents. First is the major pre-conciliar juridical ecclesiology within which the power of jurisdiction comes not from orders but from juridical constitution, through election, appointment, or delegation. The Council is concerned with correcting the inadequacy of this model that uproots church order from its sacramental base.

Secondly, there is the major ecclesiology of the Council itself, a christomonistic communitarian model that grounds all ministry in the church in sacraments—baptism for the laity and orders for the ordained—with the two being distinct not just in degree but in kind.[56] In this understanding of church, the power of jurisdiction comes directly from the sacrament of orders and cannot be bestowed on an unordained person, even by the pope. Because the church's hierarchical structure reveals its inner mystery, the headship of Christ over his body, the church, the sacramental basis of authority, is subverted if authority is not unipersonal, personally possessed, and reserved to the ordained.

The power of jurisdiction is ontologically grounded in ordination. This understanding of the church is operative in the Vatican treatment of religious life. Religious are thought to be bound to the church as a sacramental embodiment of her mystery. Because there can be no separation, much less contradiction, between the church's inner mystery and her outer structure,[57] the structure of religious life must depend upon and mirror that of the church if it is to reveal her mystery. Thus, just as Christ is personally and solely the head of His body, so his vicar, the pope, is such among the bishops, as is the bishop among the priests and the priest among the faithful. But there this ontologically-based structure of headship ends. The head of the religious institute (and heads of its subdivisions), who must be singular and personally possessed of delegated authority, is the representative among the religious of the authority of the hierarchy. Consequently, there can be no real sharing of authority in the community, anymore than the laity can actually participate in the power of jurisdiction of the ordained.

However, because the authority of the religious superior is delegated, it remains always and totally dependent upon the real authority that grounds it, namely, that of the hierarchy. Even conferences of major superiors can exist only as "approved by the Holy See, by which alone they can be erected . . . and under whose supreme governance they remain."[58] Here we see the ontological basis of the constant reiteration of the claim of immediate, direct, and absolute control of religious life by the hierarchy. This is not simply a "power grab" on the part of the ordained, but a necessary deduction from the christomonistic understanding of the nature of the church as the Body of Christ. Furthermore, those who espouse this ecclesiology are convinced that it is divinely instituted and therefore irreformable and unchallengeable.

The third ecclesiology in the Council documents Kilmartin calls a "trinitarian/pneumatological" model. This model, based upon such passages as 1 Corinthians 12:4–13 and Ephesians 4:5, is present but not strong in the documents. We find it operative in *Lumen gentium* 8 and 48 and in *Unitatis redintegratio* 2.[59] In a pneumatological ecclesiology, the supreme model and principle of the mystery of the church is the trinity of equality of Persons in God. The Holy Spirit, poured out on all the baptized, stands between Christ the head and the his body, the church (including ordained as well as lay), uniting the church to Christ and bestowing gifts upon all. Thus, the ordained are not ontologically distinguished from the laity by the personal possession of "holy power" which they can only delegate to others, but the ministries of all the baptized derive equally from the gifts bestowed on them by the Spirit, which are ordered to one another for the building up of the body. This ecclesiology can ground the qualitatively equal responsibility of all the baptized, who all have spiritual authority and who all represent Christ and the church before the world, for the mission of the church.

Obviously, the claim of religious to self-determination with regard to their life and mission is operating out of this third ecclesiology. They do not see religious life as existing solely by permission of and in dependence upon the hierarchy, or themselves as exercising their ministry by delegation. They do not claim absolute independence from the hierarchy, but act rather from a conviction of mutual interdependence based on equality and mutuality. This conviction of mutuality stands in sharp contrast with the notion of dependence based on the essential inequality insisted on by Pius X in *Vehementer nos* and *Pascendi*, which is an inescapable conclusion of a christomonistic understanding of church and ministry.

The interaction among these three factors, namely, the conciliar call to renewal, the experience of religious during the period between the council and the present, and the gradual espousal of a pneumatological ecclesiology, has led to a self-understanding and praxis among religious which is in definite conflict with official teaching about religious life and church law regulating it.

Women religious today see themselves as a voluntary association of free and equal adults who have embraced the life of consecrated celibacy in community. They see religious life as a particular way of living their baptismal identity and mission, but not as a superior way. They reserve to themselves, in interdependence with the rest of the church and its leaders, the interpretation of the vows they make, the inner governance and discipline of their communities, and the choice of their ministries to which they are called by baptism, community charism, personal gifts, and the needs of the church. In other words, religious claim adult status, equality, interdependent autonomy and self-determination in a church whose pastors are, in general, a long ways from sharing this view.

THE INTERSECTION BETWEEN OFFICIAL POSITION ON RELIGIOUS LIFE AND SELF-UNDERSTANDING AND PRACTICE OF RELIGIOUS LIFE

We have passed the point, historically, at which the contradiction between official teaching on religious life and the practice of that life by religious can be overlooked or disguised. That point was the promulgation of the revised code of canon law in 1983. A power struggle has begun between religious congregations committed to self-determination and the Vatican attempting to reassert its control over religious life. The promulgation of "Essential Elements" accompanied by a letter of the pope not to religious but to bishops (as is appropriate within a christomonistic ecclesiology) was an effort to settle, in favor of the hierarchy, the issue of who is in charge of religious life. Needless to say, the widespread rejection of the document by religious is eloquent testimony to the failure of that attempt.

The ensuing papally mandated "study" of American religious life did not achieve the purpose most suspected it had, namely, to bring American women religious into line with official legislation. The intelligence and pastoral sensitivity of Archbishop Quinn and his commission, who turned an investigation into a very fruitful dialogue between religious and local ordinaries, succeeded in educating the latter on the experience, hopes, and intentions of religious and, in many cases, convincing the bishops that the religious in their dioceses were the last people who needed official repression. What it did not do was intimidate religious into submission to Vatican claims of control.

The struggle is also being waged over the issue of approbation for revised constitutions. As the documents formulated by chapters of renewal are being sent to Rome for approval, both the "hot" issues and the inconsistencies of the process are coming to light. Some congregations have been ordered and/or forced to include in their documents provisions for habit, convent dwelling, or daily practices which they do not now observe and do not intend to implement. Others have been forced to include a recognition that the pope is to be obeyed in virtue of the vow of obedience. Still others have had their current forms of government rejected or unilaterally modified to reflect the monarchical assumptions of the Vatican. On the other hand, some constitutions have been approved without amendment even when they lacked the very provisions demanded for others. Finally, some congregations are engaged in what will surely be lengthy negotiations as they refuse to betray the consensus building processes which have produced their constitutions or to give up on the possibility of gaining approbation.

Surely the most desperate form of the struggle has centered on individual religious who, with the knowledge and/or consent of their congregational leadership, have acted outside or against current law for religious. In the case of Sister Agnes Mary Mansour, RSM, the Vatican sent a personal representative, Bishop Bevilaqua, to force her from her congregation over the defense of her legitimate superiors by presenting her with an impossible ultimatum.[60] This caused the LCWR to organize to prevent future use of the surprise factor to attain repressive ends before adequate preparation could be made. The now infamous case of the "24 signers" of the *New York Times* advertisment on dissent in the church ended differently with a costly but a real victory for the major superiors, who refused to threaten or to expel their members upon command, and who eventually negotiated a satisfactory settlement in almost every case, something that would be difficult to imagine if the LCWR had not been organized for such an event. This success is particularly significant, for in negotiating the settlements, neither the community leaders nor the sisters involved accepted the application of canon 696 by the Vatican, which would have involved accepting the interpretation of the signers' action as "pertinacious disobedience to . . . superiors," namely, the Vatican.

The escalation of efforts to force religious to accept the conception of religious life contained in the new code testifies to the seriousness of the issue. The Vatican is attempting to prevent two real possibilities from becoming fact. The first is widespread non-reception of the law by women religious. If religious congregations never put into effect the newly promulgated law in their constitutions and practice, it will eventually die as effectively "law" for them. It will be, in effect, "non-received." Those congregations which are refusing to put into their particular law what they honestly cannot accept and do not intend to live are participating in this rendering null of unacceptable legislation. Those congregations which are allowing their members to act outside of and/or contrary to the law, while remaining in good standing, not by way of exception or dispensation but as expressive of community consensus (for example, those engaged in political ministries), are similarly participating in this process.

Secondly, many congregations are developing practices, especially in regard to government and the "missioning" of their members, which are contrary to the law. If such "customs" remain in effect for thirty years or more they become "customs contrary to law" which themselves have the force of law.

While both these strategies, non-reception of official law, and the development of customs contrary to law, seem strange and even dangerous to American religious raised in the post-Tridentine period, it is important to remember that at each of the five major turning points in the history of religious life the newly emerging form was regarded as not genuine religious life because it departed from the then effective official understanding of what constituted that life. In their turn the Benedictine monastics, the mobile mendicants, the non-monastic clerics regular, the non-cloistered congregations of simple vows, and the "worldly" secular institutes have been denied official status. With the inclusion of secular institutes in canon law under Institutes of Consecrated Life we see happening in their case what happened in each of the foregoing. Gradually, the new form, which is religious life in the theological sense of the term, is assimilated to the canonical understanding of that life.

It may be that the so-called "non-clerical communities" are the emerging form of our day. These groups, whose members make vows of celibacy, poverty, and obedience and live a particular form of community life, are a non-canonical but quite public and corporate form of the life of the evangelical counsels. What makes them non-canonical is their insistence on self-determination vis-a-vis official church authority. There is already some talk among currently canonical groups that surrendering canonical status may be the price they will have to pay to maintain the form of religious life to which they feel called. This would not be a desirable development; but canonical status is not to be clung to at the price of loss of corporate integrity. If our nineteenth century founders had valued canonical status above the following of Christ according to their charisms, religious today would all be cloistered and the church in this country would no doubt still be in the ghetto.

IMAGINING AN ALTERNATIVE MODEL OF RELIGIOUS LIFE

But what about a "best of times" scenario? What might religious life look like if both the legitimate demand of religious for self-determination and the needs of the church for order and ministerial coordination were to be taken seriously.

First, the theological basis of such a form of religious life would have to be an ecclesiology grounded in the assumption that all adult members of Christ are full and equal participants in the church, however different their roles and responsibilities may be.[61] The equal status of the baptized is the only viable ground for the mutuality that religious see as the only acceptable type of relationship with Church leaders. The sacralized patriarchy in which only ordained males are considered adults and the rest of the church, especially women, must relate as dependent children to father-figures is both theologically and humanly offensive. However long it takes, this form of ecclesial organization must be consigned to the museum of history.

Secondly, it would seem useful to emphasize and develop the implications of the lay status of women religious. At the present time religious exist in a no-person's land. *Lumen gentium*,[62] while on the one hand denying that religious inhabit a "middle way between the clerical and lay conditions", on the other hand defines laity to mean "all the faithful except those in Holy Orders and those who belong to a religious state approved by the Church."[63] Thus, religious have neither the rights and privileges of the clergy nor the freedom and autonomy of the laity. But they have the obligations and restrictions of both. Religious, as lay persons, should enjoy the same freedom as the rest of the laity to participate actively in the affairs of the world for the sake of its transformation in Christ. Only the definition of religious commitment in terms of separation from the world, a definition which modern religious do not accept, or a definition of religious as clergy who officially represent the institution, would necessitate the removal of religious life from the public sphere. Religious themselves, in their increasingly active involvement in justice issues, are claiming their historical prophetic role in human society and it would seem that, as lay persons consecrated by vows of poverty, celibacy and obedience, they are uniquely qualified for precisely that role.

Thirdly, religious consecration needs to be understood in analogy with the public consecration of matrimony rather than by analogy with ordination.

While ordination is something done to a person by the church in order to assimilate that person to the church's hierarchical structure, religious consecration is effected, like marriage, by the free response of the individual to a personal vocation, in this case, to live consecrated celibacy as the determining characteristic of his or her life. In regard to both matrimony and religious profession the church gives the state of life legal sanction, thus making it a canonical state, and sets it forth liturgically as a state of consecration to God.[64] In both cases the persons involved make themselves socially accountable for the fulfillment of the evangelical obligations they assume, thus constituting themselves in a public state in the Church. It seems reasonable then to inquire why, if the sacramentally married who are in a public, canonical state of consecrated life by profession of marriage vows retain their full lay status with all its attendant responsibility in and for the world and all its freedom of exercise in the fulfilling of those responsibilities, religious must necessarily be considered shorn of that status by religious profession. This situation seems to be the result of historical confusion between the clerical and religious vocations. It could be argued that the basis of the confusion is the imposition of mandatory celibacy on the clergy, thus assimilating them to religious life, which in turn is clericalized. In any case, it would seem, theologically speaking, that religious are lay people and their right to act accordingly should be recognized. This would involve, automatically, the recognition of a certain autonomy, self-determination, and self-direction as fully appropriate for lay religious.

The problem which the recognition of the right of religious to autonomy and self-determination raises is that of the appropriate validation of religious congregations and their practice and the orderly integration of religious, as communities and as individuals, into the life and mission of the local church. There have been enough cases of unbalanced individuals claiming to be religious and even gathering together disciples into unhealthy lifestyles to make it clear that religious institutes should be validated in some publicly accountable way if they are to present themselves as Roman Catholic religious. At the present time the Vatican claims the sole right to recognize pontifical institutes and assigns the same right to local ordinaries in regard to diocesan groups. It would seem that the time has come to recognize that this function properly belongs to the leadership groups of religious themselves, that is, to national and international bodies constituted of and by religious. Such groups exist. In the case of women, the International Union of Superiors General and the Leadership Conference of Women Religious are eminently qualified to exercise this responsibility. The pastors of the universal and local church ought certainly to be consulted, and to exercise a "negative check" regarding the Christian character and evangelical practice of the proposed institutes. But an appropriate decentralization of authority, along with the exercise of subsidiarity and good sense, would seem to suggest that hierarchical validation is no longer necessary or appropriate in the case of institutes of women religious.

Finally, religious, like other laity, are increasingly involved in the ministerial life of the local church, and as such must be integrated into the pastoral plan of the diocese in an orderly way. As *Mutuae relationes* points out, pastors, laity, and religious (note the threefold distinction repudiated above), share a true equality[65] which is the basis of their cooperation in the ministry. But, the ministerial activity of all must be coordinated, a function which belongs in the first place to the bishop, not because he is ontologically superior to the others but because of his role as leader.[66] *Mutuae relationes* goes a long way toward suggesting how this pastoral leadership of the bishop can be coordinated with the appropriate internal leadership and charism of the religious institute so that religious can function appropriately in the ministry of the diocese. The only basis acceptable to religious for the working out of appropriate ground rules for the actual functioning of this cooperation is mutuality based on equality. Neither the total dependence of children or slaves nor the total independence of free agents "doing their own thing," but the mature interdependence of autonomous and self-determining adults is the appropriate form of relationship among the baptized.

CONCLUSION

In summary, religious women are claiming an autonomy and self-determination befitting baptized adults within the community. This claim is compatible with both good theology and good order. However, it seems that there will be a long struggle and perhaps much suffering before an entrenched and theologically argued monarchical ecclesiology gives way to full participation and mutuality. In the meantime, conviction and experience must be buttressed with collective strategy if religious are not to surrender their personhood once again to the demands of a patriarchal system which is destructive of both oppressors and oppressed. Perhaps one of the great services religious women will render to the post-conciliar ecclesial community is their contribution to the realization of a church in which there are no longer slaves and masters, male rulers and female dependents, but free and equal co-disciples sharing community in the Spirit. The path to justice and freedom is long and so we must heed the word of God to the prophet Habakkuk:

> Write the vision down, make it plain upon the tablets . . . For still the vision awaits its time . . . If it seems slow, wait for it; it will surely come and will not delay. Behold, the one whose soul is not upright will fail, but the righteous shall live by their faith (Hb 2:2–4).

Notes

1. *Lumen gentium* VI, 402–407; *Perfectae caritatis* 611–123. All references to conciliar and post-conciliar documents are to the English translations in *Documents of Vatican II,* ed. A.P. Flanner (Grand Rapids: William B. Eerdmans,

1984) unless otherwise noted. Documents are refered to by title, section number(s) where appropriate, and page number(s).

2. "Essential Elements in Church Teaching on Religious Life," *Origins* 13 (July 7, 1983) 133–142; see III, p. 140; Conclusion, p. 142.

3. All references to canon law are to the English translation in *Code of Canon Law: Latin-English Edition,* tr. under auspices of the Canon Law Society of America (Washington, D.C.: Canon Law Society of America, 1983). Canons are refered to by number and page.

4. John Paul II, *Redemptionis donum, Origins* 13 (April 12, 1984) 2, p. 723.

5. "Essential Elements," 2, p. 134.

6. *Canon Law* 586, p. 223.

7. *Mutuae relationes, Origins* 8 (August 31, 1978) 161, 163–175, III, p. 167.

8. Cf. *Canon Law* 598, #1; "Essential Elements" III, I, 7, p. 141.

9. Cf. *Canon Law* 586, p. 223.

10. *Canon Law* 576, p. 221, emphasis added.

11. *Canon Law* 593, p. 225.

12. Cf. *Mutuae relationes,* II, p. 165.

13. Cf. *Canon Law* 663, ##1–5, p. 251.

14. Cf. "Essential Elements," 41, p. 138.

15. Cf. *Canon Law* 663, 664, 665, 666, 667, 669, pp. 251, 253, 255.

16. "Essential Elements," 41, p. 139.

17. Peter Fitzpatrick, CFX, gives a number of examples of this in a private paper entitled "The Pope's Letter to the U.S. Bishops and the SCRSI Document." For example, he mentions that at the First Provincial Council of Baltimore in 1829 the hierarchy could not determine whether the Black Oblate Sisters of Providence were persons or things—a singular lack of discernment! The hierarchy's repressive treatment of Mary Ward, foundress of the Presentation Sisters (IBVMs) is a legend among religious.

18. Cf. "Essential Elements," 10–11, p. 134.

19. Cf. *Canon Law* 576 and 587, #2, p. 221; "Essential Elements," III, III, 16, p. 141.

20. Cf. *Lumen gentium* VI, p. 405.

21. Cf. "Mutuae Relationes," II, p. 165.

22. Cf. *Perfectae caritatis* 8, p. 615; *Canon Law* 675, #3, p. 257; "Essential Elements," II, VIII, 32, p. 142.

23. *Canon Law* 590, ##1 and 2 respectively, p. 225. Emphasis added. See also "Essential Elements," 16, p. 135.

24. Cf. *Perfectae caritatis* 1.

25. Cf. "Essential Elements," II, 3, 24, p. 136.

26. Cf. "Essential Elements," II, 2, 22, p. 136.

27. "Essential Elements," II, 3, 25, p. 136.

28. *Lumen gentium* V, p. 402.

29. *Redemptionis donum* 4, p. 724, and 9, p. 727 respectively.

30. "Essential Elements," I, 7, p. 134 and II, 1, 14, p. 135 respectively. Reference is to *Lumen gentium* VI, 43, 44, pp. 403–405.

31. See, e.g., *Canon Law* 207, ##1 and 2, pp. 69, 71; 588, #1, p. 223; *Lumen*

gentium VI, 43, 44, pp. 403, 405; *Renovationis causam*, Introd., p. 634; "Essential Elements," II, 6, 38, p. 138

32. Cf. "Essential Elements," II, 6, 38, p. 138; *Mutuae relationes*, III, p. 166.

33. It suffices to compare the 102 canons on religious life with the 20 on Secular Institutes and the 15 on Societies of Apostolic Life to establish this difference.

34. Cf. *Canon Law* 669, #1, p. 255; "Essential Elements," III, IX, 37, p. 142.

35. Cf. *Canon Law* 669, #1, p. 255; "Essential Elements," III, IX, 37, p. 142.

36. Cf. "Essential Elements," II, 6, 34, p. 138.

37. *Mutuae relationes*, 2, p. 165.

38. "Essential Elements," II, 7, 38, p. 138.

39. "Essential Elements," II, 9, 49, p. 140.

40. Cf. "Essential Elements," II, 9, 49, p. 140.

41. *Perfectae caritatis* 2, pp. 612–613.

42. For an excellent personal description of this conversation process see J.D. Chittister, "No Time for Tying Cats," *Midwives of the Future: American Sisters Tell Their Story*, ed. A.P. Ware (Kansas City: Leaven, 1985) 4–21.

43. Cf. *Ecclesiae sanctae II*, II, I, 8, p. 626.

44. *Ecclesiae sanctae II*, I, 1, p. 624.

45. Cf. "Essential Elements," III, introd., p. 140.

46. *Gaudium et spes* 1, p. 903.

47. For text of Theresa Kane's remarks, see *Origins* 9 (October 18, 1979) pp. 284–285 (margins).

48. *LCWR Recommendations: Schema of Canons on Religious Life* (Washington, D.C.: Leadership Conference of Women Religious, 1977).

49. See W. Brueggemann, *The Prophetic Imagination* (Philadelphia: Fortress, 1978) for an excellent biblical treatment of the vocation of the prophet.

50. *Mutuae relationes*, II, 5, p. 170 and its references.

51. Cf. "Essential Elements," II, 3, 26, p. 137.

52. *Mutuae relationes*, I, 4, p. 168.

53. Pope Paul VI *Evangelii nuntiandi*, available in translation as *On Evangelization in the Modern World* [Apostolic Exhortation—Dec. 8, 1975] (Washington, D.C.: United States Catholic Conference, 1976).

54. *Ecclesiae sanctae II*, I, 6, p. 625.

55. E. Kilmartin, "Lay Participation in the Apostolate of the Hierarchy," *Official Ministry in a New Age*, ed. J.N. Provost [Permanent Seminar Studies 5] (Washington, D.C.: Canon Law Society of America, 1981) 80–116.

56. *Lumen gentium* I, 10, p. 361.

57. Cf. *Lumen gentium* I, 8, pp. 357–358; also see *Mutuae relationes*, II, 5, p. 171.

58. *Canon Law* 709, p. 271.

59. *Lumen gentium* I, 8, p. 357; VII, 48, pp 407–409; *Unitatis redintegratio* I, 2, pp. 453–455.

60. For the official documentation on the case see *Origins* 13 (May 26, 1983) 33, 35–36; 13 (September 1, 1983) 197, 199–206.

61. This equality is explicitly recognized in *Canon Law* 208, p. 71: "In virtue

of their rebirth in Christ there exists among all the Christian faithful a true equality with regard to dignity and the activity whereby all cooperate in the building up of the Body of Christ in accord with each one's own condition and function."

62. *Lumen gentium* VI, 44, p. 403.
63. *Lumen gentium* IV, 31, p. 388.
64. Cf. *Lumen gentium* VI, 45, p. 406.
65. *Mutuae relationes,* I, 1, p. 163.
66. Cf. *Evangelii nuntiandi* 69, p. 50.

10

Breaking the Grand Silence: A Diocesan Process

Rita J. Burns

IT IS VERY MUCH AN ACCIDENT THAT I AM HERE TODAY TO ADDRESS this session of Time Consultants' Conference on Women in the Church. The conveners of the conference had hoped to have a bishop use this time to address the topic of writing a diocesan pastoral letter on women. When repeated attempts to arrange such a session were unsuccessful, conference planners gave up and chose instead to explore other possibilities regarding diocesan level statements on women in the church. They selected a process which occurred a few years ago in the archdiocese of Milwaukee in which a task force on the role of women conducted listening sessions among women of the archdiocese and subsequently published a report on these sessions in the diocesan newspaper, the *Catholic Herald*.

I take this opportunity to express my gratitude that all of those bishops who were invited to speak were unable to be here today, for whatever reasons.

I am grateful because of my conviction about the value of processes like the Milwaukee one. While I believe that bishops' pastoral letters on women are significant, different values are at stake in the process I will describe and it is my opinion that, at this point in our history, it is of crucial importance that at least some of the voices that speak about women in the church be those of women themselves.

I will describe various components of the process which took place in the Milwaukee archdiocese and reflect on the values which were at stake in it.

DESCRIPTION OF THE PROCESS

The process which took place in Milwaukee preceded the hearings which have occurred during the past year or so in conjunction with the U.S. bishops' decision to issue a statement on women. If you are familiar with the U.S. bishops' hearings, you will recognize some similarities and some differences between them and the Milwaukee listening process.

In March of 1981 Rembert Weakland appointed nine persons, myself included, to a task force on the role of women. The archbishop gave us a two-fold assignment: 1) analyze the present role of women in the archdiocese and 2) make recommendations where adequate representation of women was not present or where women were not assuming functions that were open and available to them. The archbishop's letter of appointment reminded us of the limitations that are present in church law and that there was nothing that could be done about them at the diocesan level.

The task force met and pondered our options regarding how to proceed. Very early on it was clear that, by ourselves, the nine of us were in no position to do what we had been asked to do. Analysis of the roles of women required raw data which we simply didn't have. So, we designed what we called a listening process. Over the course of eight months (October 1981 through June 1982) we met with seventeen different groups in various geographical parts of the archdiocese. We contacted parish council presidents and pastors and asked that they use every means available to invite participation in these listening sessions. In addition, invitations were sent to church women's organizations and announcements of the sessions were made by the local media.

Participants. Our invitation was accepted by nearly five hundred women (and a few men) who ranged in age from early twenties to mid-eighties. They were black, white, Oriental, Hispanic, Native American, single, married, divorced, widowed, canonical religious, mothers, grandmothers, homemakers, and women who work outside the home. The majority were what we all recognize as the backbone of church activity, that is, those who hold things together at the grassroots level of church: parish council members, Girl Scout leaders, directors of religious education, Catholic school principals and teachers, youth ministers, liturgy committee members, Renew leaders, eucharistic ministers, lectors, and so forth. In addition to these highly-involved women, there were some who care very deeply about the church but whose experience had alienated them so that they no longer participate in church gatherings or activities.

Sessions. The design of each of the listening sessions was very simple. After all present introduced themselves, someone from the task force spoke very briefly about why we were there. To focus the session, we presented a short slide presentation about the roles of women in early Christianity and in today's church. The slide presentation ended with a question: where is God calling us now? Participants were then invited to share with us two things: 1) their experiences as women in the church and 2) their hopes for the future. As participants in the listening session spoke, members of the task force recorded notes about what was being said and, after everyone present had had an opportunity to speak, we concluded the session with a prayerful reflection on Luke's account of Jesus and the bent-over woman.

In general, the listening sessions were characterized by a spirit of honest, open communication. The experiences women described were typically very personal, and often, very painful ones. In almost all instances, participants listened to one another with careful attention and respect. It was clear that participants regarded the task force as a legitimate "ear" of Archbishop Weakland and many expressed gratitude to him and to us for inviting them to speak. They said that nothing like that had ever happened before.

Before I report what the women said during these sessions, let me note parenthetically two things about what we did. First, in asking women to speak about their experiences and hopes, the task force took a step beyond the archbishop's original assignment, which was to analyze the *roles* of women and to report where adequate representation of women didn't exist or where women were not exercising roles which were open to them. In other words, the archbishop asked us to address the *roles* of women and instead we asked women about their experiences and hopes in general. I don't recall now whether we were conscious at the time that we were going beyond what the archbishop had told us to do. Neither am I certain that in asking the broader questions we were acting contrary to the archbishop's intent. Whatever the case, our decision to ask about experiences and hopes turned out to be significant insofar as women spoke about much more than just roles. Secondly, let me note that once we decided to ask open-ended questions about experiences and hopes, we thought it inappropriate to pass on to participants in the listening process the archbishop's reminder about the limitations which church law prescribes. We didn't feel we could ask about experiences and hopes and then say, "But you can't talk about X experiences or X hopes."

What the Women Said. You must be asking, "What did they say?" I am about to address that question but as I do, please be aware that I am condensing at least thirty-four hours of women's speech into just a couple of minutes. I encourage you to read the full report where what the women said is recorded in detail. The broad generalizations I am about to make in no way do justice to the concrete experiences which are described in the report.

If anything surprised me about what we heard from the women in the Milwaukee archdiocese, it was the remarkable similarities in the experiences of very diverse groups of people. As I see it, the most prominent similarities were women's experiences of feeling demeaned, invisible, and powerless within the church.

Feeling Demeaned. Some women who came to the listening sessions were those who serve their communities in traditional ways. Generally, these are nurturing or domestic roles—making coffee, preparing and serving church dinners, contributing to church bazaars, and the like. They don't aspire to different roles. However, they know themselves to be responsible adults and they ask not to be taken for granted and not to have their contributions minimized in relation to other forms of service. They don't seek the proverbial pedestal, just respect and courtesy.

More voices shared the self-perception of the first group but they want to serve in non-traditional roles. They ask not to be accused of ego-tripping and being power-hungry. They ask not to be trivialized by jokes or teasing remarks. They ask that others not assume they're incompetent until they prove themselves. They ask not to have to ask permission so often. They ask to be treated as adults. Women who already are pastoral ministers ask for support instead of resistance and to be recognized as legitimate ministers alongside the clergy. Women who aspire to the permanent diaconate ask that the church acknowledge its neglect of their gifts and training.

A third group of women asks very little. These are the women who no longer participate in church gatherings. They explained their decisions as stemming from experiences of having been demeaned within the church. For example, women associated with shelters for victims of domestic violence were well represented at the listening sessions. They told of having sought help from parish personnel or church agencies and being made to feel that they were to blame for the troubled or violent situations in which they found themselves.

Although the women I've described (those in traditional roles, those who aspire to non-traditional roles, and those who no longer look to the church for a role) are very diverse, they share the experience of being demeaned.

Invisibility. The experience of invisibility is, of course, most profound among those women who would like to be part of the church but have been pushed to the point of total alienation. We heard, however, that invisibility is also experienced within the church itself. Whenever the liturgy was mentioned at a listening session, the problems of non-inclusive language were raised. When words like "he," "brothers," "sons," "men" are used in the liturgy, women feel like they're not present. Women likewise feel invisible when it comes to the preaching of God's word in the liturgical assembly. When women are never present at the altar, some women must remind themselves that the mediator between God and the world is humanity in general and not man.

Women ask that the visibility of women be recognized by the church's effort to preach and teach about Jesus and women, women in Christian tradition, and women's spirituality. They ask to see women counselors and spiritual directors. They asked to see their daughters serve at the altar alongside their sons. Women who feel called to priestly ministry ask that the church stop talking about its vocation shortage.

Powerlessness. Finally, the experience of powerlessness is shared by diverse groups of women within the church. Hispanic women know their people and, because of this familiarity, are ready to preach, lead prayer, and make decisions but they are powerless to assume these roles. A few other women who spoke are troubled about the direction of the post-conciliar church and are prepared to do what they can to restore the clarity and stability of preconciliar days but they feel powerless to do so. Still others are happy to serve on parish councils and committees but feel powerless in the face of their peers' "Father knows best" attitude or, worse yet, in the face of the pastor's right to do as he wishes, regardless of the council or committee. Women feel powerless when their priests are unprepared to preach with depth, to interact with adults, or to understand family problems, divorce, single parenting, rape, widowhood or the mutuality of roles in marital relationships. They feel powerless when there are no clearly established procedures of accountability for their priests. Those who are employed within the church feel powerless when it comes to wages, benefits, job security, and financial assistance for ongoing ministerial education. All seemed to feel powerless in the realization that ultimately the place of women in a parish or diocese depends on the views of the particular priest or bishop who is assigned to them.

Women who wish to return to the pre-Vatican II era hope to have some say about seminary training, as do women who are impatient with what they see as the church's slow pace in renewal. The bottom line in all of this is that women in Milwaukee want to be there when decisions are made in their church.

VALUES AT STAKE IN THE LISTENING PROCESS

In a very abbreviated way, I have addressed the first topic given to me by the conveners of this conference: what we did in the Milwaukee archdiocesan listening process. I turn now to the second task, that of addressing the values that are at stake in processes like the one in Milwaukee. I will focus on the listening process itself and I do so with the conviction that it is significant in ways that pastoral letters about women cannot be. To be sure, I do not wish to discount the value of official church statements about women. But, it is my opinion that to bypass processes like the one I've described is akin to not planting our mustard seeds. Before explaining why I say this, let me return briefly to what happened in Milwaukee.

In several ways I think our task force anticipated the value of the process itself when we designed the listening sessions. First, we didn't presume to speak for and about the women of the archdiocese until we had heard them speak. Second, although we invited and received written responses from women, we thought it important that we actually hear and see women and that women actually hear and see one another. Third, we did not go out to meet women in the diocese with an already-established agenda. That is, we did not ask questions about specific topics. The areas of concern which appear in our report came from the women who spoke, not from the archbishop and not from the task force. Fourth, our goal in each of the listening sessions was that all of those present have an opportunity to have their voices heard. We made it clear that there was no need to reach consensus in any of the groups.

If the task force anticipated the importance of the process itself, what we had not anticipated was that the listening process would change us and our direction. Before the listening process actually got underway, we thought of ourselves very much as the *archbishop's* task force. We understood ourselves to be the "ears" of the official leader of the archdiocese. But, as we listened to more and more women, something happened that altered this perception of our role. With all due respect to the archbishop, our loyalties changed. We were compelled by what we were hearing to become the voices of the women we heard. We became the *women's* task force. Thus, our goal in preparing the document we submitted at the end of the process was to report faithfully just what the women had said. We did not intend that our report serve as background material out of which the archbishop would issue a statement about women. We intended simply to bring the voices we had heard into a wider arena so that many more might hear.

This decision did not come easily. I recall vividly the task force's first meeting after all the listening sessions had taken place. It was time to decide what to do about a report. The group's cynics were ready to abandon the whole project, saying that nothing would come of it anyway. Those with more pleasant personalities were ready to report what the women had said but they suggested that we couldn't really say it like it was said to us. They thought we needed to tone it down a bit; the disillusionment and alienation and anger were just too raw. After all, church-related documents are almost always happy talk—ideals, hopes, promises. The die-hards among us (those I would call the "pure in heart") won out. The task force agreed to say what was said in all its rawness.

When we composed the report we consciously set out to write for publication. Fortunately, Archbishop Weakland responded well. He saw to it that our report was published in its entirety and exactly as it was handed over to him. The only change was that the archbishop prefaced the published document with a letter to the church of Milwaukee. In it he wrote:

> I beg all of you to read carefully and weigh all they have written. At times it may be painful, at times it may make you angry, at times it may make you defensive. (But) I have no doubt that the members (of the task force) heard what they write, and we must join in their process of listening if we are to be Church.

In fact, once the report was published, the listening went on. There were many gatherings throughout the archdiocese in which our report served as a springboard for discussions in which others brought their experiences of church to expression. As the speaking and the listening continued, people contacted one or another of us to say, "Oh, yes." There was a compelling truth in what those women had said and there was something freeing in finally having it spoken.

Now let us explore at a theoretical level why that process is so important. Why is it important for women to speak their experiences and what is the significance of issuing the statements of women instead of a church statement about women? My reflections on these questions come from three directions: When a woman speaks her experience, what is at stake for her? What is at stake for other women who hear? And, what is at stake for the institutional church?

First, when a woman speaks, what is at stake for her? In an essay entitled "Women's Stories, Women's Quest," Carol Christ suggests that, without speech, the stuff of life is just that, "stuff"—a sort of formless mass of data.[1] Human speech takes that raw data (which we call life experience) and puts it "out there." Only when it's "out there" (named) can it be analyzed, understood, and judged. In a very real way, we say and then we see.

To be human is to speak and to be authentically human is to speak our own words and not those of someone else. Speech is a means whereby one becomes a self. We become who we are through speech. Without it, we don't really know ourselves and a potential self just shrivels up and gets lost in the formless mass of data. In other words, to abandon speech is to abandon ourselves. We give the only thing we've got over to others who then will shape it (and us) according to their particular frameworks. Others will tell us what our experience is and what it means.

It is of critical import, then, that a woman *come to terms with* her experience in a very literal way. At the most fundamental level, what is at stake is herself.

Speaking one's experience is especially important when the experience is one of suffering. To avoid "coming to terms with" pain is not to acknowledge it, to repress it. As Dorothee Solle has pointed out, this fosters hopeless and apathetic behavior wherein a person lets herself be controlled by her situation.[2] Ultimately, Solle says, unspoken unacknowledged suffering engenders neuroses which are expressed in numb brooding or sudden explosions.

To bring suffering to speech, on the other hand, is to take the first and necessary step toward changing the pain-producing situation. One gets it "out there" where it can be understood and dealt with. Again, we say and then we see. Bringing pain to speech is the necessary link which transforms inward-directed suffering to outward-directed movement, personal isolation to solidarity with others, being dominated by one's situation to shaping one's situation.

I recall one of the listening sessions wherein a woman described being treated in a particularly insulting way by the pastor of her parish. When she finished, another woman in the group blurted out: "Well why do you let him treat you that way?" I have to believe that it was not business as usual when the first woman returned to her parish!

The point is that when a woman speaks her experience, she is coming to terms with herself and when she is able to speak pain, she has come to a point of being able to do something about it. But, you say, there's so much in the church situation that women are powerless to change. This leads me to another observation about suffering speech and the listening process.

Walter Brueggemann has written about suffering speech in the Bible. In an article published in 1974, Brueggemann points out that the lament psalms typically feature a description of the person's distress.[3] In the psalms this is usually sickness, loneliness, danger, shame or humiliation. The psalmist then petitions God to intervene and the psalm ends on a note of confidence or thanksgiving. The rhetoric of the Bible's suffering speech thus moves from hurt to joy. The description of the situation of suffering is the first step in this transformation.

The lament pattern extends beyond the psalter. Only after Israel groaned under its bondage did the exodus begin. Only after the wilderness community named its hunger and thirst was it satisfied. Only after the blind men called to Jesus were they able to see. Only when Peter screamed was he rescued from his bold experiment of walking on water.

But, do real parallels exist between the Milwaukee listening process and the biblical pattern of lament? I think so, although one must proceed carefully. Biblical figures directed their suffering speech to God, thus placing their hurt in the lands of some One they believed was in a position to effect change. Women who participated in the listening process described pain-filled experiences to the task force. However, they regarded us as the archbishop's personal envoys, sent to search them out with the express purpose of listening for him. I don't think it would have been the same had we been a self-appointed group. When they spoke to us, most women really envisioned that they were placing their suffering in the hands of someone whose position made change possible, namely the archbishop. While one must be cautious about drawing direct parallels between God and members of the hierarchy, what I want to point out is that the potential for change is a necessary prerequisite for bringing suffering to speech. If the woman herself is in a position to shape her situation differently, speech is the key that makes that possible. If she is unable to shape the situation, she must have a forum for speaking her pain to someone who is in a position to effect change.

When a woman speaks her experience, what is at stake for other women? Frequently in the Milwaukee process, when one woman gave her formless experience shape by bringing it to speech, it happened that other women said, "Oh, yes." The "oh, yes" phenomenon indicates that what one person says rings true to, authentically brings to expression, the experience of others. I am not referring to putting words on other people's lips or ideas into other people's heads, which is what one of my former professors said happens when men permit their wives to go to those "women's things." Rather, I'm talking about one person describing her experience, putting it "out there" and having another person see her own experience, perhaps for the first time. We say and then someone else sees. It's not capitulating to someone else. It's finding oneself through the words of another. We do this whenever we read a great book or hear a great speech. It's discovering ourselves in the intrinsic truth that someone else places before us.

Carol Christ writes:

> When one woman puts her experiences into words, another woman who has kept silent, afraid of what others would think, can find validation. And when the second woman says aloud, "Yes, that was my experience too", the first woman loses some of her fear.[4]

Christ suggests that when one woman speaks and what she says rings true to the experience of others, the women not only find themselves, they also find one another. The environment is ripe for authentic Christian community to come to birth.

If this is true of speech in general, it is especially true when the speech is about suffering. I can testify from having been present at the listening sessions in Milwaukee that one simply does not go away from spoken pain unmoved and unchanged. I'm confident that you recognize the truth in this if you have ever had someone in pain speak to you about that pain. The movement that occurs in the hearer is a movement toward the speaker who suffers. If the hearer has even an ounce of empathy, the hearer actually feels the pain with the speaker. A bonding occurs and where it does, authentic Christian community is born at an even deeper level.

When women expressed pain during the Milwaukee listening sessions, other women were being issued an invitation to respond to the person in need—to be with her and find ways to change the situation. It was a direct invitation to be church. It was a challenge to those others who listened or who read the report to be the people of God we say we are.

In his book, *The Emergent Church,* Johann Metz articulates a probing question in this regard:

> Have we not interiorized the paternalistic church to such an extent that we think everything connected with church renewal ultimately depends on one thing: on change happening to those who take care of us, which means above all the pope and the bishops?[5]

The fact is, Metz continues, "a dependent people has to transform itself, and not just behave like a people being taken care of."[6]

If members of the church want an alternative to a hierarchical church, it seems that, by definition, the hierarchy cannot create that alternative. We can. Speaking with one another and really listening is a first step in realizing that alternative. I can't say whether or not this challenge has actually been taken up by those who heard the women in the listening process. The task force report includes recommendations about how people can help one another as well as how official church structures can make changes that would benefit women.

Having explored the importance of women's speech for those who speak and for other women who hear, let us proceed to a third and final question: *when women bring their experience to speech, what is at stake for the institutional church?*

When women speak about their experiences with church institutions or structures, the institution has the opportunity to see itself through the eyes of its otherwise silent majority. We say and then they see. Precisely because we are in the margins women have the potential for a different perspective. And, when women say that there's something amiss and in need of change in the institution, the institution is invited to examine itself and take steps to become more authentically what it is meant to be. In other words, women are in a position to exercise prophetic ministry with regard to the institutional church.

In saying this, I am using the understanding of prophetic

ministry which is proposed in Walter Brueggemann's work, *The Prophetic Imagination.*[7] Brueggemann suggests that the ministry of prophets is a two-fold ministry of speech: they criticize and they energize through speech. Prophetic criticism, he says, has its beginnings in grief. At some point we realize that "things are not as they should be, not as they were promised, and not as they must be and will be."[8] The criticizing word of the prophet, according to Brueggemann, "is not carping and denouncing. It is asserting that false claims to authority and power cannot keep their promises."[9] Saying this out loud in some way pronounces that a world has come to an end. And, it is this dismantling, Brueggemann says, that allows a new world to emerge.

Energizing speech, which must always be held together with criticism, brings another world within the range of vision. It promises "another time and situation toward which the community of faith may move"[10] and awakens "fervent anticipation of the newness that God has promised and will surely give."[11] Brueggemann continues: energizing speech creates "the sense of new realities that can be trusted and relied upon just when the old realities had left us hopeless."[12]

Certainly when women in Milwaukee said, "I dream of a church of sisters and brothers," or "I hope for leaders who are servants," or "I envision that my daughters will have the same opportunities as my sons"—women were weaving new possibilities with their words.

Any church that is rooted in the biblical tradition cannot but consider itself rich indeed if it has prophets. It may feel uncomfortable, but if it is honest at all, the church must consider it a grace when prophets are in its midst. I would contend that what is at stake for the institutional church in processes like the one in Milwaukee is the prophetic dimension of a believing community. Those prophets bring to public expression our tired, worn out realities and, in the process, evoke new possibilities.

It reminds me of the fairy tale in which the dishonest weavers knew, the old prime minister knew, and the ruler himself knew the truth about the emperor's new clothes. But no one would tell. Hans Christian Andersen tells it:

> There marched the Emperor in the procession under the beautiful canopy, and everybody in the streets and at the windows said, "Goodness! The Emperor's new clothes are the finest he has ever

> had. What a wonder train! What a perfect fit." No one would let it be thought that he couldn't see anything, because that would have meant he wasn't fit for his job, or that he was very stupid. Never had the Emperor's clothes been such a success.
>
> "But he hasn't got anything on!" said a little child. "Goodness gracious, do you hear what the little innocent says?" cried the father, and the child's remark was whispered from one to the other.
>
> "He hasn't got anything on!" the people all shouted at last.[13]

We say and then we see.

In conclusion, I have suggested that processes in which women speak their experiences and their hopes with regard to the church are full of possibilities. I believe that my conviction about this was shared by the Milwaukee task force when it designed the process and by the archbishop when he invited the entire church of Milwaukee to read the report and thereby enter into the listening process.

The values that are at stake in this process are these: 1) women come to terms with their experiences and thereby take a deeper step into their reality as authentic human selves; 2) women discover bonds among them which effectively serve as an invitation to be authentic Christian community; 3) the institutional church has the opportunity to see itself in a new way and likewise be called to greater authenticity. In a word, what is at stake for everybody is authenticity, conversion, liberation. And, is not this what it is all about? The apostle Paul said it this way:

> . . . we know that up to the present time all of creation groans with pain, like the pain of childbirth. But it is not just creation alone which groans; we who have the Spirit . . . also groan within ourselves as we wait for God to make us (God's) children and set our whole being free.[14]

Notes

1. See Carol P. Christ, *Diving Deep and Surfacing* (Boston: Beacon Press, 1980) 1–12.
2. Dorothee Sölle, *Suffering* (Philadelphia: Fortress Press, 1975).

3. Walter Brueggemann, "From Hurt to Joy, From Death to Life," *Interpretation* 28 (1974) 3–19.
4. Christ, *Diving Deep* 23.
5. Johann Baptist Metz, *The Emergent Church*, trans., Peter Mann (New York: Crossroad, 1981) 82.
6. Ibid.
7. Walter Brueggemann, *The Prophetic Imagination* (Philadelphia: Fortress Press, 1978).
8. Ibid. 21.
9. Ibid. 20.
10. Ibid. 13.
11. Ibid.
12. Ibid. 23.
13. Hans Christian Andersen, "The Emperor's New Clothes," *Eighty Fairy Tales*, trans., R.P. Keiwin (New York: Pantheon Books, 1976) 67–68.
14. Romans 8:22–23.

THE VISION

11

Spirituality: Finding Our True Home

Madonna Kolbenschlag

TODAY WE KNOW THAT SPIRITUALITY, ESPECIALLY AMONG WOMEN, IS one of the most subversive influences in our time. Spirituality has been the foundation and the shaping ethos of our civilization—and today, it is being challenged by a new spirituality, one that people are living and not talking about very much because we don't have a language for all of it yet. People are also being persecuted for it and are dying for it.

In our concern today with issues of peace and justice, and poverty and tyranny, we can sometimes forget that reality is fundamentally spiritual rather than material, and that consciousness pervades and shapes the world that we live in. Nothing changes unless that changes.

And today women are probably the most important catalysts in the change that is taking place, because they have discovered the Great Lie about the spirituality that has shaped our world. They are in the process of revealing an authentic, life-giving spirituality brought forth from their own experience. We are creating a new wisdom literature.

In the past the spirituality that we have been given—and many of you are old enough to remember it, and it's still being given—in many ways was a caricature and a distortion, a kind of disembodied spiritualism or asceticism. It was a spirituality of repression and messianic righteousness. Today we are awakening to a spirituality of passion and a mission of solidarity.

Why are women crucial to this transformation? To understand this I do want to discuss the origins and the beginnings of the spirituality that has shaped us.

Some see the whole question of spirituality as a sort of contest between Father-God of the tradition and the Mother-God of women's liberation. And there are those who say that spirituality has very little to do with either of the images of God and more to do with our own self-image and with the liberation of human beings from oppression. Both of these perspectives represent half of the reality.

Anyone who has spent time with small children has observed their instinct for domination and control. Kids compete with each for the attention of adults; they grab each other's toys and they push each other out of the sandbox. But behaviors like these are usually discouraged by adults, and by parents and older siblings. These experiences are not allowed to become models for behavior—they are de-legitimated.

But when we become adults, our behavior is legitimated or de-legitimated by the prevailing, dominant myths of our culture. (Reagan and Rambo are, in their own way, legitimating myths.) The most powerful, comprehensive, and energizing engine of legitimation and de-legitimation in most cultures is the myth of God.

The myth of God that prevails in our culture is a projection of a privileged, dominant caste. It is the ultimate legitimating metaphor and model for our social and political structures, for our language and for the dynamics of our interpersonal relations. The myth of the Father-God is not only a theological concept, it is an anthropological reality of our culture. In its contemporary form, it is largely a product of the Judaeo-Christian tradition. Now, we could argue, in theological terms, whether this myth of God in the cultural sense is really a caricature of the Holy One who is Truth beyond all images, and perhaps even a caricature of the God who delivered his people in the Old Testament and brought us into the New. The point is, the myth is still the God of our culture. And the God-construct comes to resemble our social values and arrangements and it becomes a gatekeeper for selecting myths which legitimate and reinforce distorted social arrangements. The myth of our God is as much a reflection of our world as those sculptures that you see in Mexico of the Aztec Jaguar God, with its gaping receptacles for human hearts ripped out of their living human sacrifices. The values and the power structure of the society make the God-myth necessary.

The paradigmatic myth of God in western civilization is found for us in the creation story of Genesis. And I'm sure you've heard many times what is depicted there; a world created in one momentary flash of divine power as a finished product; at least that's the implication. Monotheism is very emphatic. The Creator is an anthropomorphic patriarch. The patriarch sets up the hierarchy of life systems. The implication is that each one will "rule over" the next one down in the ladder of life. And so God is at the top, man is next, then women and child, then animals, earth.

The God of western civilization is transcendent, remote, judgmental, omnipotent, omniscient, and by implication, white, male, and celibate. A "good old boy"—associating intimately with only two other divine males—a workaholic who has been busy replicating himself in patriarchal structures of dominance everywhere. Thus, a metaphor and a myth that has been used to legitimate religious bigotry, racism, classism, imperialism, clericalism, and all the other "isms" that you can think of. The myth of our God has reinforced a world of dominance and dependency, divided us between "control" and the fear of chaos, between a world of "haves" and "have-nots."

Now, the Genesis creation myth also presents us with a paradigm in which humanity is disobedient. And we know Genesis was written by several authors, but the myth that has become most influential in our civilization and in shaping it, is not the myth that says that He created them male and female in the image of God (Genesis 1); it's the one that comes in the third chapter in the passage about the fall that has become so overwhelmingly influential in our civilization. Eve is portrayed as the occasion of the human fall from grace—a curse as the foundation of human society and source of death and pain. Authority is vested in the male. Man is required to rule over woman, and subdue the earth.

It's amazing, working here in Washington, to hear how often public officials—especially those of a certain biblical persuasion—defend their policies by saying that we been commissioned "to rule and subdue the earth."

There are two things happening to this myth of God today. Both are essentially spiritual phenomena—expressions of spirituality—that are destined to have far-reaching effects on human events and global politics.

One, and I'm sure you are very aware of this, is the hardening of this dominant myth of God into a rigid, fascistic and narrow-minded fundamentalism—whether that is expressed in the Islamic extremism of the Iranian mullahs, or in the creationism and moral puritanism of the neo-Right in the United States, which at this very moment is being debated in the courtrooms of our land.

The other is the dissolving of that myth and image, the recreation of the myth of God through the process of alienation from the old myth, and the reconstruction of a God myth through the lens of another experience of humanness. This phenomenon was captured so wonderfully by Alice Walker in her novel *The Color Purple* when her character, Celie, rejects the image of God in that wonderful conversation about him being imaged as white, male, bearded, uncaring and distant, and Shug says to Celie in that conversation, "You can't see anything at all until you get man off your eyeball." Patriarchy, embedded in the creation myth of Genesis is the universal religion, and the spiritual journey of women today in exodus from that caricature of the divine is the most profound sign of our times—and the most threatening. It explains the vehemence, the viciousness, and the relentlessness of the backlash. It also explains why the transformation of women's spirituality so visibly images the journey of the oppressed people of the world from dependency and subservience to freedom, to self-determination, and ultimately to interdependence.

Some will say, "Well, Genesis, the creation story—that's all prologue and past, we live in the spirituality of the New Testament." Is it? Go back to the New Testament that records the early church experience and you will find in a chapter in Timothy:

> A woman must learn in silence to be completely submissive. I do not permit a woman to act as teacher or in any way to have au-

> thority over man. She must be quiet. For Adam was created first, Eve afterward. Moreover, it was not Adam who was deceived but the woman. It was she who was led astray and fell into sin and she will be saved by childbearing, providing she continues in faith and love and holiness, her chastity being taken for granted.

That is the dominant myth that has come to shape our world and certainly our church. What explains the persistence of the myth? What explains its selection? There were other myths available at the time. For example, the Sumerian myth in which a male was the source of the fall and the curse upon humankind. In fact, there were many myths in which men who aspired to divine knowledge were blamed for bringing evil into the world. The means by which humans acquired divine knowledge was always portrayed in these myths as being acquired through eating, drinking certain substances, and through sexual experience. Typically, we find all of these elements in these early parallel myths: the tree of knowledge, the forbidden fruit, the snake. But the Genesis story inverts many of the tropes of earlier myths. Why?

The creation myth of Genesis marked the establishment of monotheism and the legitimation of patriarchy as a way of nature, as "God's will." Social historians and cultural anthropologists, building on the work of biblical scholars, have in recent years offered some new insights on the myth. Gerder Lerner in her study *The Creation of Patriarchy* points out the significance of the prohibition not to eat of the tree of knowledge of good and evil. She said it resulted in a double transgression.

First, a sexual transgression. "They knew they were naked." In the ancient world, images of the snake were always associated with the goddess of fertility, the goddess of life. Thus, the snake is the symbol of preeminent female power, also of the threat of chaos—female power out of control. The banishing of the snake is the banishing of the goddess and symbolically Eve's free and autonomous expression of her sexuality. From henceforth its only expression would be through motherhood and pain and sorrow.

The second transgression: "You shall be as gods." It is a transgression of power. Because of her autonomous act, her curiosity, and her "aggressive" desire to know, she is to be punished by being excluded from knowledge and experience that is power. Eve is cursed, punished by being subordinated to her husband—"he shall rule over thee." Eve will have the power to reproduce, in the physical sense, but no creative power, in the social sense.

And so the curse of Genesis—visited most visibly and one-sidedly on woman—is the split in civilization between procreation and creativity. We are the inheritors of the world that Genesis legitimated. When we ask, who creates life? Who speaks to God? Who rules over and names creation? Who creates culture? The answer is *man*. And when we ask, who bears children, and gives her body and cares for them, and who brought sin and death into the world?—the answer is *woman*.

There is no way to put a gloss on Genesis that makes it seem any better for women. It's not just the triumph of the one true God over the fertility goddesses and the cults. It is a clear condemnation by Yahweh of female sexuality exercised freely and autonomously. It is, above all, a condemnation and prohibition of the exercise of female power and authority.

So now we see what a seamless web this is: the Vatican preoccupation with contraception, abortion, female altar servers, ordination, nuns' habits and constitutions. This is all of a piece. It's not about the "mind of Christ." And the abortion controversy is not only about life, it's also about control over women's sexuality and power.

Let's look at some further implications of myth. The social historians also tell us that the development of monotheism was an evolutionary leap that advanced human beings in the direction of abstract thought and toward the definition of universally valid symbols. And so the birth of the process of symbol-making—the fundamental process that shaped our society—occurred under circumstances which marginalized women. Monotheistic patriarchy advanced human capacity, but institutionalized the exclusion of women from the creation of symbol systems. From this comes a philosophy of history, the split between the mind and body, and between spirituality and sensuality. Class society begins with the dominance of men over women in the creation of culture, and develops into the dominance of some men over other men and all women. Thus gender dominance and preference underlies all forms of invalidation: class, race, and caste.

And we see the effect on women over the centuries. We have been excluded from the primary symbol-making, legitimating castes of our civilization. Excluded from *politics* in the beginning by not even being granted citizenship; excluded from full participation in *religious traditions,* the split in ministry exactly mirrors the split between the procreative functions and the creative functions. Those who create and name—theology and sacraments—are divided as a separate caste from those who are supporters and care-givers. Women were also separated from the *arts* and *sciences* by being restricted from training in analytical and abstract thinking for so many centuries.

To make matters worse, Aristotle used the structure of the patriarchal household as a model for the government of the body politic. I suspect if we look carefully at canon law, we would find the same model at work. Thus women, according to the cultural myth, have been limited to pro-creating the material substance of creation, and caring for it—but excluded from the creation of symbol-systems that name, that validate, define, and judge. We have been faithful daughters in that patriarchal household.

The God-myth has not only given us a spirituality and a psychology, it has legitimated and reinforced structures that are founded on this myth and perpetuated them. It has given us not only moral codes but public policies and socio-economic structures that govern our lives today.

The separation of procreative caring activity from the creation of civilization has given us a spirituality that separates the personal from the political, and the private from the public. The closer we look, the deeper we go, we see to what extent what culture has done with gender is at the root of this. It really means that we are not divided between East and West or North and South, or black and white, or even between the haves and the have-nots in this planet, so much as between the *valued* and the *not-valued,* the ones who count and the ones who are disposable. And the model is still functioning in the pair-bond between man and woman.

This is a spirituality. It has created the world we live in. Spirituality of a different kind will create the world we want to live in. I see spirituality as a kind of hologram of consciousness in which a person is in touch with all dimensions of reality and struggles toward a synchrony between those dimensions. It demands that we be in touch with, in truth with, our own inner world, the outer world of phenomena and relationship, and the world beyond the senses, through the world of symbols. For most women today, cognitive dissonance, alienation—or its alternative, illusion—distorts this hologram of authentic spirituality. The myth of God, the myth of the creation story as the parent-paradigm of our civilization has distorted our own self-image, alienated us from valuing our own experience, and excluded us from the power to shape our society and civilization, and tyrannized us with the mask of a false God.

That's why women are the key to the transformation of the culture, not only because they are the chief supporters and clients of patriarchy, but because women are clearly the catalysts for the formation of the new spirituality. It is women, above all, who are in the process of reversing Genesis, of turning the myth on its head by validating and feeing their sexuality, by theologizing out of their own experience, by taking responsibility for symbol-making in the public sectors.

For people who are alienated and in exodus—on the way to something else—the notion of God degenerates, becomes tentative. It has to be recreated on the personal experience of the journey. This new logos, this new myth then begets a new social architecture. Luther's concept of the "mask of God" has some relevance here. He wasn't very kind to women but he had a few good ideas. Luther proposed that God as the ultimate Holy One, as the Absolute Other, can only be known by finite creatures through what God is not, through the opposite sign of God. So that only through some kind of "antithesis" can God's total otherness somehow be revealed.

So why should we be surprised that the Holy One is breaking through the consciousness of humanity as a Goddess or as an uppity Woman? When we ask ourselves, where is God's face, where is God's otherness today, we will find it in what society has devalued.

Surely this is the meaning of so much of the New Testament and so many of Jesus' authentic parables, so many of his encounters with women. God is the Unexpected One, the Surprise. And so the notion of God as Woman, and almost anything as Woman, comes as a shock and a surprise.

Someone once asked me, what can we salvage from the traditional God-myth that is not destructive? I don't think that salvaging is any concern of ours. Faith is the process of continually replacing our metaphors for God. If we do not, we get backlash and fanatical fundamentalism. I've often wondered if this isn't the explanation for that mysterious and profound saying of Meister Eckhart: "I pray to God to free me of God for God's sake."

A symbolic system is in the process of redemption. It is a reflection, a sign of a world turning upside down and inside out. "You have put down the mighty from their thrones and have exalted the lowly."

What will it require of us? What will the new spirituality look like?

First of all, it is a spirituality of *passion*. In the ancient times the Church Fathers, as well as the secular philosophers, were convinced that women were morally and spiritually weak. And so they encouraged them in the practice of andreia, or "manliness," as a way of mortifying their carnal passions and overcoming the handicap of being a woman. Then in the nineteenth century, the pendulum of popular belief swung the other way and held that women were instinctively more moral and spiritual than men, and the bourgeois woman had to conform to the idealization of the Eternal Feminine, the pedestal myth.

Women today must reclaim their reality from these fantasies, especially through the power of a holistic sexuality and the right to a free and personally responsible expression of it. We cannot accept numbness and sterility in the name of the Gospel. We cannot internalize a masculinized spirituality, based on the false asceticism of power and toughness, of control and dominance, that has left so many men desiccated, their feelings neutralized, and their drive for power overfed. Women have always experienced the interconnection of sexuality, affectivity, religious zeal, and the creative impulse. And so we have to ignore the Great Lie that denies this. Women have to pour out their passion on creation, even as the woman in the Gospel poured the precious ointment over the feet of a loved One.

This spirituality then is ultimately a passion for life, and it reaches beyond the mere expression of self to the survival of the human society and the regeneration of social structures. There is another side to passion that complements holistic love for creation, and that is rage and anger. We have to be capable of outrage for the sake of the reign of God. There is a wonderful Greek word that recurs in very interesting places in the New Testament that combines the meaning of boldness with passion—I believe the word is *parrhesia*. When that word appears in Scripture, its moral context is always one of conflict. It's a word you find in Luke and John and Acts, especially. It is a gift of the Spirit. It is a gift of audacity that overcomes fear, shyness, weakness and above all, self-doubt. It is precisely this *parrhesia* that patriarchy has repressed in women and that must erupt today—a sense of outrage against injustice, of boldness in confronting the abuse of power, of passionate witness in the face of all forms of violence.

There are many things that should evoke our outrage. Working with human rights cases evoked a great deal in me and helped to change me. There was once a picture that I saw that I felt summed up what should evoke our outrage in terms of our situation as women, and should evoke the outrage of men as well. I was preparing material for a Congressional hearing on international development, and I ran across a picture of a young, very attractive Indian women, clad in a sari, sitting for a portrait with her three children. The background suggested a very urban setting, and she looked as if she were by no means destitute. In the photo her nine year old son was holding one of her other children, a baby, on his lap. And that baby looked robust and alert and very squirmy—as a child of that age might. And she held another baby in her lap. But this infant looked emaciated, hollow-eyed, and listless—very much like those pictures we've seen of the starving Ethiopian children. And the caption under the picture said this:

> The emaciated baby girl on the left and the sturdier baby boy on the right are twins. The difference in their condition is entirely due to the boy being nursed first, his sister getting what was left over. The healthier boy cries for attention and gets it, and the glazed little girl no longer even tries.

I don't think I have ever seen a more graphic picture of the situation of women throughout our civilization, and it should evoke our outrage. The deprivation of everything, from basic nurturance, to access to training and skills and education, to economic and political power, to respect in the public dialogue, to confidence and self-worth, and so on. What keeps this system in place? The picture tells us what perpetuates the myth: the universal phenomenon of *son preference;* the universal phenomenon of *male privilege* and *entitlement* to *power* the universal phenomenon of what I have called *androlatry,* the worship of what is male-identified, whether that's work or writing or professions or the color of a person's skin or whatever—all of this is connected with what male experience has set up as the preferred norm.

And, of course, the flip side of that false consciousness, the devaluation, diminishment and abuse of whatever is female-identified. Indeed, as every culture reveals, whatever society wants to debase or invalidate, it will feminize. All languages have epithets as evidence of this. We even have social research that reveals that we learn patterns of relating to minority groups and outsiders by "practicing on women." We should never become numb to this—we should feel and reflect outrage.

I suppose it would be evident by now that another aspect of the spirituality we need in the contemporary situation is *resistance.* And this will demand of some, martyrdom. Nobody should go looking for it, nobody will go looking for it but it may come to some, and has, judging the growing lists of martyrs in recent months and years. So others will retire to the catacombs, or take to the hills as guerrillas; and to begin to think like a guerrilla is a good idea in these times, to build the consciousness and alternatives for the new society without losing your leverage on affecting the system. That's one way of looking at it. While the old forms harden and fossilize with an implacable rigidity, we can be about shaping something for the future. And others will spend their time simply rescuing the wounded and the victims. Everyone can have a role to play, but no one will be allowed the luxury of release from the struggle, because this is our time in history and our moment of truth.

We will have to be a people who believe in the possibility of change. This requires that another characteristic of our spirituality be *imagination.* I think probably of the many things that I've learned from my years of working in government, the most discouraging has been the failure of the imagination which seems to doom our system to go on repeating the past, going in circles, repeating the old agendas, replicating the old logic—whether it's legislation or foreign policy—we keep coming up with non-solutions. Certainly my work with human rights abuses taught me something about the lack of imagination, the mindlessness and the compulsiveness that is responsible for so much terror. It really did change my notion of evil.

I used to think that all evil was the result of intentional acts, willed by bad people, or at least morally defective people. And I don't believe that anymore. Evil so often is our failure to face up to the painful process of change.

There's a logic that is built into systems that persists long after the system's capacity to fulfill its purpose has degenerated. One theologian has said, "What is evil in our time? What is the demonic? It is that which imprisons us in the past by its investment in its own self-perpetuation."

To believe in the possibility of change demands imagination. It is to believe in surprising systems by introducing creative, imaginative, unexpected responses to the same old problems.

Some years ago three Stanford psychiatrists proposed a theory of behavioral change that suggested a new approach to problem solving. They made a distinction between first-order change and second-order change.

First-order change, they suggested is the way we usually approach problems. When confronted with an obstacle—a situation that requires change—we generally resort to emphasizing its opposite, opposing force with force. We assume that when something is bad, its opposite has to be good. When resolution is not immediately forthcoming, our response is usually to double the intensity of our effort. The opposite so easily becomes more of the same.

Genuine change most often occurs through a *second-order response,* one which rethinks the solution previously tried and suggests something altogether unexpected. This imaginative thinking is at the heart of a Jewish proverb that came out of the Polish concentration camps: "Faced with two alternatives, always choose the third."

The quality of paradox and surprise is at the heart of second-order change. It requires a radical breaking out of the framework, in the conceptual blocks that limit our imagination. That is why second-order change occurs so often in what Belden Lane and others have called "impasse situations." In a genuine impasse, every normal way of action is brought to a standstill. The left side of the brain, with its usual application of conventional thinking, grinds to a halt. The impasse drives us back to contemplation, forces the right brain into gear, seeking intuitive, unconventional answers to the situation. It's very close to revelation.

And certainly what we've seen in our nation's capital, in our national policy, and certainly in many revolutions and reform movements, have been attempts at first-order change. Our entire political system in the United States, our judicial system, our competitive market, our pluralistic, free information society—everything is geared to first-order change; everything stands in some kind of adversarial relation to something else.

At this very moment we are seeing being played out on the world scene two contrasting dramas: one is a study in classic first-order change, and the other is a very fragile experiment in second-order change. In South Africa first-order change is escalating. On the other hand, what is happening in the Philippines is the direct result of an effort to explore alternatives to violent revolution, and this effort began in the early 1970s.

Enough Filipinos dared to imagine a third way and prepare for it. President Corazon Aquino, herself, is symbolic of the unexpected alternative. She is also symbolic of why women are destined to be a crucial factor in fundamental social change. Women who are conscious of their disempowerment, and women who are not co-opted by the privileges of their class are not invested in the survival of the old order. And they have of necessity learned how to make change in other ways than through sheer strength, or force of arms or power. Women understand, and for centuries have understood, something about how to create change when one is not standing in a position of dominance. The world has need of this reality.

There are many women less privileged than Corazon Aquino, who could change the repetitive, patriarchal cycles that we go through, that go on begetting violence and sterility and human deprivation. They need to find their voice, to realize their strength and to gain practice.

And I'm thinking when I say that of something that I discovered when I was in Peru—having the wonderful opportunity of meeting hundreds of women over the period of a month, poor women, some privileged women, women in between, urban women, Andean women, women from the pueblos and the barrios. I spoke with some women who work in teams, helping to empower other women.

And I heard this story from one of them about their work in the barrio. They said one of the worst things about the condition of women in the world is their isolation from each other. They could be living two inches from a woman in another shack but be totally isolated from sharing her spirit with her. So the first thing they do is go into the barrio and bring the women together to share in a way that they have never shared before—their inner feelings, their life, their story. And then after a while, the women get the hang of this and then they begin, as women will do, to talk about their problems. One woman told me in this one barrio they discovered that most had a similar problem in common—wife beating. And so you see how they move very naturally into a little social analysis. The next stage was questioning: was there anything they could do about it? Many of the men would get drunk on the weekends and come home and beat them up. Someone proposed an idea: they scraped together enough money to buy whistles for everyone. And they made a pact, a pledge together that when the man of the house came home and began his beating, either the woman or her oldest child would run out into the street, blow the whistle and everyone else would come out with their pots and pans and set up a din such as never been heard in that barrio. Well, they did it; they shamed the wife-beaters, and they created change.

Can you imagine the sense of empowerment that those women experienced for the first time in their lives? For the first time they experienced having a little bit of control over what happens in their world, which is a very small world. They experienced the spirituality that makes change possible—the sense of their own self-worth, the passionate determination and the imaginative solution to create change, and certainly a sense of shared fate and solidarity.

This kind of *solidarity* is perhaps the most obvious characteristic of the new spirituality, and the one that is the most difficult to achieve. If the women's movement in North America has failed in any way, it is certainly in this area. And it is the greatest challenge that the women and men leaving this conference will face. In spite of the plurality of our society, the inclusiveness of the Gospel message, we have not yet learned to transcend socio-economic barriers, to bond across class, across culture, across religious, and even canonical divisions, across so many social and political boundaries. Until we do, these barriers are holding us back from action for the future.

I know that I have emphasized the virtues that are the "hanging on" and the "hanging-in-there" virtues in describing the new spirituality: *passion, resistance, imagination,* and *solidarity.* I have emphasized these because they are in short supply. But there are other virtues, too: the "letting-go" virtues. And for each of us, it is a matter of finding the rhythm between them. The letting-go virtues are important at crucial times.

- Giving up the need to be right. As Marie McIntyre says in her book, "Being right does necessarily have anything to do with the truth."
- Giving up our frustrated urgency for change *now.* None of the guerrillas in the hills of Central America believe that change is going to come in their generation, but they work as if it were. Redeeming our relationship to time.
- Renouncing our desperate need to control; reclaiming our sense of grace, our sense of creation as play.
- Being grateful for adversity, for our times, or our own ambivalent situations.
- Knowing that the end of anxiety is awe, the goal of politics is life, and the function of theology is to protect, cherish the Mystery.

Women are learning this spirituality through an often painful process of trial and error, and they have already come a long way on the journey. Today, I want to say particularly to men that we are in a new moment now that requires something more of them, and it is to them that I address the most challenging message that I have today. You have stood back on the sidelines, waiting and hoping that the change will come in the conventional masculine way, through an executive order from the CEO, whether that's in Rome or in Washington, or wherever. Some of you have been supportive of our cause, some of you have laid theoretical groundwork to support change, you have encouraged small innovations along the way. But your belief in the future of women and its importance for the survival of our planet hasn't cost you anything yet; no relinquishment of power, no rejection slips, no blood. Now there are some obvious exceptions, and we know who they are. In a patriarchal system of power, change is not going to come from the top down. Women are not going to be integrated; they are going to remain "outsiders." My brothers, it is time for you to join your sisters as "outsiders." It's time for you to resign your membership in the male club and join us in the back of the bus!

Let me tell you just a brief incident that describes what I mean. There was an ecumenical group made up of Roman Catholics, including some priests and one bishop, and their colleagues, men and women who were of a Protestant denomination. They scheduled one of their meetings at a Catholic monastery. On the day of the service, the time for the liturgy came and the abbot approached the group and said he was very sorry but only the men, according to tradition, would be allowed down to the nave of the chapel where the altar was. The women would have to remain in the balcony. Some of these women were ordained ministers in their faith. The ecumenical group, of course, by this time had become friends; they had been meeting for many years, and so they sat together and discerned their way to a decision. They decided unanimously that the men would not join the monks in the nave of the church but would join the women in the balcony. Needless to say that did lead to some subsequent change in the monastery.

This is the kind of solidarity that is required of us, and especially of those who are privileged. It will demand much of men, a relinquishment of power. If Christ were walking the earth today, do you think he would expect it to happen any other way? What an incredible notion it is for the patriarchs of the world—whether it is in the Vatican or the Ayatollahs of the world, or the tele-evangelists—what an incredible idea it is for them to keep using the argument that it is "the mind of Christ" that only men be ordained to ministry in the church, that only men be "heads of families," that men be always first and preferred. And it's still being said.

The drama we see being played out in our own house today on the West Coast reveals the two Gorgons that most threaten patriarchal peace of mind. Whatever Archbishop Hunthausen's intentions, he has, in the eyes of Rome, failed the patriarchal litmus test in two areas in particular: he has shown tolerance and flexibility in matters affecting sexuality and women; and he has apparently indulged in participatory and democratic structures of consultation. Both of these attitudes undermine "control," and so they are heresy.

Allen Boesak of South Africa has observed very knowingly: "The question of orthodoxy is always raised when we cannot face the problems that overwhelm us."

But it doesn't matter. The exodus has begun. The age of the patriarchs is over. They will be left behind in Egypt. And so, to believe in Exodus is to hope, it is to believe that the God of history is the God of Surprise, and is leading us somewhere. It is to understand also that the way to the promised land and to the new covenant is through the wilderness. That's why we need *passion, resistance, relinquishment, imagination,* and *solidarity*. Only those gifts and deep prayer will sustain us on the journey. It is to believe that if some women are disobeying the Pharoah's commands, we should take note; it may be divine grace breaking through our defenses.

Perhaps if we squint a little at Genesis we will see the subtext emerging, visible only in the light of the end time. Eve, reaching for the tree of life, for the fruit of knowledge and power, full of desire for Godlikeness—Eve is the ancestor of those disobedient women who began our redemption, the midwives and the holy women who first resisted Pharaoh.

True daughters and sons of Eve will, in increasing numbers, reach for the tree of life and the fruits of knowledge and power, seeking Godlikeness. The question is how long will other men and women go on reaching for the fruits of patriarchy?

Resistance and relinquishment will be a scandal to patriarchy. But our elder brother, Jesus, was a scandal to patriarchy. Women and all who would be sisters and brothers of Jesus will be a scandal.

I believe that is our true home, now. That is the wilderness in which we find ourselves.

12

Sexism in the Church: Agenda for the Next Decade

Joan Chittister

THERE ARE TWO STORIES, PERHAPS, WHICH INDICATE WITH GREATEST precision the purpose and the power of this conference, which is neither club nor parochial convention but the coming together from everywhere and from nowhere in particular of each of us and all of us, one at a time, and together, to talk about the unfulfilled promise of the creation of women that daily, daily, nags for resolution.

The first story is from the life of Margaret Mead. They asked the great anthropologist, "Doctor Mead, what are the most important periods of human development in all of history?" And, it is said, Margaret Mead responded without hesitation: "There are four periods in human history, she explained, "after which nothing was ever again the same—and those times are the period of evolution; the period of the ice age; the age of industrialization; and the period of the woman's movement."

The other story is much older—and much more demanding. Among the religious literature of the ancient East comes this other insight. A woman whose whole struggle in life had been the unrealized search for full human development, complained to the holy one that, despite herself, destiny made the personal fulfillment for which she sought so sincerely unachievable. And the holy one said, "But that is impossible. It is you who make your destiny." But the woman protested, "Surely you are not saying, holy one, that I am responsible for being born a woman?" And the holy one answered: "You don't understand: Being born a woman is not destiny. Being born a woman is fate. Destiny," the seer said, "is how you accept that womanhood and destiny is what you make of it."

The messages and meanings are clear: In the first place, the woman's movement is a growing, swelling, ongoing, cultural current of social change. And secondly, it is all up to us. The prophetic power of transformation of the face of the church, no, of the world, is in this auditorium today. And, God knows, the world is in need of transformation. Things simply must not go on as they have been and still are now for women:—unwhole, unhealthy, unrepentant, and unfulfilled—but the real problem is that whether things go on for women in the future as they have in the past depends on what you and I do with things as they are.

What, indeed, must be our own agenda for the 1990s? And, most of all, where do we get it? And how shall we recognize it when we see it? And how shall we distinguish between the false gods and the true in a movement called alternately both good and evil? How shall we know that we are being good church as well as good feminists?

Science and the Oppression of Women

There are signs in the culture, of course: the oppression of women has finally run out of scientific steam. What was once scientifically posited simply cannot be scientifically proven. There is no scientific proof whatsoever to the old philosophical truism that women—as a class—are inferior to men as a class. It's just not true, the research confirms, that women are less intelligent, or less emotionally stable, or less physically capable, or less biologically complete, or less socially equipped, or less spiritually insightful than men. The Maccoby studies confirm the fact that women are just as bright—or brighter—than male students, all the way to college. Then, the Horner research shows us, young women begin to fear that being too bright will bring them social disapproval, will make them less marriageable, and so, then young women deliberately begin to limit their academic performance—or, at least, to do the fellow's homework.

What was once explained, in other words, as a spurt of development for men is really a curb on development by women. More, according to NASA, space travel research indicates that pound for pound, inch for inch, muscle for muscle, women show more physical endurance than men. Biological analyses reveal that the aging process—the human deterioration problem—is a function of the male hormone, not the female hormone.

The Smith-Rosenberg studies in their critique of the Freudian hysteria data uncovered the fact that the one emotional factor common to each of Freud's women patients was not their envy of men. It was their rage at having been dismissed themselves as ineffective because they were women.

The Broverman work in mental health research, contends that the most mentally healthy people are androgenous people—people who have fully developed both the masculine and the feminine sides of their personalities and that the neurotics of our time are the macho males and the female females, the Rambos and the Twiggies of society, which is exactly what our culture has been intent on producing.

Hospital statistics show us that prior to the women's movement 8 percent of the men and 20 percent of the women receiving psychiatric help were hospitalized for depression. But the statistics also show that following the women's movement—after women began to see opportunity and affirmation and recognition in life, just as men always have—that then, after women's liberation became a possibility, still 9 percent of all the men but only 8 percent of all the women receiving psychiatric help were hospitalized for depression.

No, science will not confirm a basis for the oppression of women. And society is certainly no sign of the inferiority of women either. Women have run governments, and discovered comets, and guided major exploratory expeditions, and counseled popes, and developed businesses, and led not-violent movements and created alternative communities in the church—even despite the church—and, by now, have worked in every major arena in society, at least with obvious competence if never with equity, and, at the same time, did it all alone, and with no help from anyone.

No, society, like science, is no testimony in favor of the inherent inequality of women. And surely the best doctrines of the church are not. We do baptize women, after all, and we insist on shriving and absolving them, and we marry them in the same full sacramental recognition that their husbands get, and we bless their bodies and reconcile their souls, and we communicate them, and we confirm them,—just like the males with them—in their obligation to spread the faith as well as to keep the faith.

We say always—at least right up until where it counts—that God made women in God's own image, and that God talked to them just as God talked to men and that God trusted them with free will just as much as God trusted men. And we say that in the incarnation Jesus redeemed women, too, and will raise them from the dead, just as well as men, and that in their lives God gives them grace, too, though sadly it is also said that women may not be carriers of grace, or dispense it, or preach it or use it in the church in any official way. God's grace, it seems, goes sour when it gets to women.

But, nevertheless, the good news is that science and society and theology all say that women are grand, equal, human beings, and some women have been able to prove that so. But the bad news is that so few women have been given the chance. So what is there left for us to do about it that will not, of course, blight the plan of God for us? Perhaps the only way to be sure that what we do in the future as women and for women will not corrupt the design of the eternal for us is to look at the women whom Yahweh God raised up as models, and look at the women whom Christ affirmed and ask: first, what was the agenda of these women? And, second, has that agenda been satisfied? And, finally, if not, then what, in the name of creation, must we do about that if we are to be true both to the Gospel and to *Pacem in terris* in which John XXIII says clearly: "Those who discover that they have rights have the responsibility to claim them."

Ruth and Naomi

Let us look, for instance, at the agendas of the widows Ruth and Naomi. Naomi was a widowed old woman, and Ruth was a younger one in a society that had no room for widows. Only Ruth, the younger woman, was still sexually attractive and sexually acceptable and so she did the only thing a woman could do to take care of the people she loved more than her very own life: Ruth gave herself to a man, not for his love, not for his holy companionship, but for his money and for his security.

But our society has no room either for single women or for widows. Our young women—most of them—work in the lowest of low class jobs for the lowest of low wages, without future and without just recompense. The Bureau of Labor Statistics tell us that 80 percent of employed women are segregated in twenty of the 420 job categories in the United States and that there is "women's work" even in the "non-sex-stratified" areas: in sales, for example, 83 percent of those who sell apparel are women who earn an average of $171 a week. But car and boat sales*men*—and 92 percent of them are—earn an average of $400 a week. The bureau tells us, too, that even professional women earn only 71 percent of the wages earned by professional men in the same profession.

Three-fourths of our old women, the U.N. Decade of Woman shows, live below the poverty line. In fact, two-thirds of the elderly women of the U.S.—the richest and supposedly the most feminist nations on earth—live on a fraction of their husband's Social Security checks. If she dies first, of course, he will continue to receive the entire Social Security check, despite the fact that she's no longer his dependent. But if he dies first, before the age of their retirement this society, if it gives her anything at all, for years will withhold from that woman whole portions of what should have been that check—despite inflation, despite need, despite the fact that rent and light and heat and food cost old women exactly what they cost old men. As a result, retired men in this country receive an average of $5500 a year, but retired old women are living on an average of only $3300 a year.

Take that information into the pulpit on Mother's Day and see if you can convince women how much church and state really value their work in the home. Oh, yes, the message about whose money their money really is, is very clear. And no, Ruth and Naomi's agenda has not been satisfied. The feminization of poverty is still with us still and getting worse by the day.

Moses' Mother and Pharaoh's Daughter

Let us look, then at the agenda of Moses' mother and Pharoah's daughter. Moses' mother and Pharoah's daughter lived in a society where "men were men," and differences were solved by destruction and might made right and the innocent were sacrificed for the sake of the powerful. Moses' mother and Pharoah's daughter wanted no part of the domination and destruction that characterize the male power paradigm. Moses' mother and Pharoah's daughter believed in compassion instead of conflict, and collaboration instead of coercion, and cooperation rather than competition. And together, secretly, those two women—one inside the destructive system and one outside the destructive system—reached across the boundaries of their lives to subvert it by refusing to be enemies, by saving the child and therefore saving the race.

Well, our society doesn't want the woman's viewpoint in conflict resolution and important social arenas, either. Women aren't tough enough, they fear, to push the nuclear button—in some circles apparently a skill to be envied. Our society, in fact, works hard to glorify the masculine ideal, and institutionalize male modes of response and denigrate feminine values and smile-down feminine strategies and dismiss feminine social models. Our society works hard, as a result, to take the "woman" out of the recruit, to make a boy a man, and to make the man a killer. Our society plans, in fact, to eliminate 100 percent of the women and children of the world in the nuclear wars men have designed to "protect" them. And no one is even asking those women if that is all right!

There is no doubt about it, the agenda of Moses' mother and Pharoah's daughter has definitely not been satisfied. The theology of domination and the machomania it breeds is with us still and threatens now not simply a people but an entire globe.

Esther

But let us look, then, at the agenda of Esther, the woman who is expected to be an ornament in the court of the king. They call her "queen" but only in things that do not matter to an autocratic and hierarchial world. "No one can go to the king," she reports to the people who look to her for help, "unless the king calls them. And I have not been called to the palace of the king for over thirty days." And then risks her life to do what must be done.

In our society, too, women may give advice—when and if

they're ever asked—but women are seldom official advisors except in token ways and women are almost never decision makers. Only 10 percent of the government positions in this country are held by women; and only 5 percent of the corporate executive positions are held by women; and no percentage at all of the decision-making positions of the church are held by women.

Like Esther, what women finally do for right and truth they do at their own peril. They can lose their homes, and their jobs and their reputations and their faith for it because no one is really obliged to listen. They can wear their bodies and their hearts and their souls completely out trying to be heard but no one, absolutely no one, is obliged either to hear or to respond.

By all means be clear about this: Whatever now the number of token women in the boardrooms and the chanceries of the world, Esther's agenda of influence and presence and participation in the charism of power has definitely not been satisfied. It is the males of the system who shape, control, administer, and own it. Sometimes beneficiently, true, but always totally and finally.

Judith

But let us look, then, at the agenda of Judith. Judith wanted the harassment to stop once and for all. Judith wanted free of male intimidation and male bondage, and male abuse and male threat. And in desperation, and with deep faith, she finally confronts it.

But in this country yet, according to Geller, Steinmetz and Brown in *Behind Closed Doors* two million women are beaten yearly, because men "take dominion" over women's bodies and men have forever encouraged men to do so in booty, in brothels and in economic bondage.

In two-thirds of all marriages women are beaten at least once; one-fourth of the women of this country are beaten weekly; 20 percent of all the emergency medical services given to women follow a beating; 25 percent of all the female suicide attempts are a result of repeated domestic beatings. 25 percent of all female murder victims are murdered either by their husbands or their boyfriends. A woman in this country is beaten every eighteen seconds and raped every three minutes. Pornographers make four billion dollars every single year on the abuse of women. Violence toward women in this country and in every country is not sometimes. Violence against women is always.

No, indeed, Judith's agenda of freedom and personal security has definitely not been satisfied for women.

Mary of Bethany, the Samaritan Woman, Mary Magdalen, the Women at the Tomb

So let us look then at the agendas of Mary of Bethany and the Samaritan woman and Mary Magdalen and the women at the tomb. The Samaritan woman simply didn't fit any of their social standards. Mary of Bethany simply didn't accept any of their role definitions. Mary Magdalen was indeed a bold and brazen woman. And they made no bones—any of them—about their commitment to Jesus. No bones at all about either his call or their intention—in fact, their compulsion—to carry on his will and his wonderful presence in their lives.

The Samaritan woman faced them head on. Mary of Bethany persisted in her vocation. The women of Jerusalem went on ministering to him while all the others hid. Mary Magdalen, remember, went right into their midst—it was a forty hours gathering, or perhaps a synod, I think—to minister to him and to proclaim his resurrection.

"What is that woman doing in here," the men said. "Send her away." And they went to the tomb to see for themselves, "because they did not believe her," the Scripture reads. "We have no more need of you," the men of Samaria said. "Our place is in the kitchen," Martha, the well-conditioned woman said.

But Jesus said back to all of them: "She is doing what you are not doing; she's preparing me for my burial." And Jesus said, "But she has chosen the better part, and it shall not be denied her."

And Jesus said to the woman, and to the woman only, "I am the Messiah." And Jesus said, "Mary, don't stay here. You go and tell Peter and the others . . ."

Well, we live in a society where women are still not allowed into the Holy of Holies. We live in a society where they turn women away from their empty seminaries in droves, while in a sacramental church people lack the sacraments.

We live in a society where a girl-child, ironically, may not even officially carry a cruet to the altar, because the church that teaches "the gates of hell shall not prevail against it" can, apparently, be brought to its knees by a little eleven-year old girl.

We live in a society where women are no longer allowed to preach the Gospel, or minister the sacraments to the dying, or teach Scripture to the ordinandi. And if and when they do, they do not believe her. Oh, yes, the message is very clear and it is still the same: There is nothing that a man of the church can learn about God and faith and Gospel from a woman of the church. Never forget, full inclusion in ministry was the agenda of Mary Magdalen and Mary of Bethany and the Samaritan woman and the women at the tomb, and that agenda is not yet, two thousand years later, despite the words of Jesus, satisfied.

Eve

Let us look too at the agenda of Eve, the mother of the human race. Eve was created, like Adam, directly by God. Eve was given paradise, like Adam, and on a par with him. And Adam, like Eve, heard the serpent. And Adam, like Eve, sinned anyway. And Eve, like Adam, was gloriously redeemed.

But when history tells the story of Eve, there is little recognition that the sin was, after all, only half hers. Neither Adam nor Eve, after all, kept the commandment of God—they both heard the temptation together and neither one of them refused—nor did he even question, the big rational hunk: ("Now, Honey, you know how emotional you get about these things; let's talk about it tonight after supper . . .") Even, surely, the Office for the Doctrine of the Faith is willing to admit that they found two sets of teeth marks on the apple.

Indeed, the result of that joint sin was the rupture of relationships between human beings and God, and between the human beings themselves. But if that is so, then redemption depends on our transcending and repairing the ruptures, not on our institutionalizing them. But we still live in a world where the official texts of the church say only that women, as a result of the sin, are devoted to less noble ends than men. And on the basis of that reasoning women are still being denied education, and autonomy, and economic independence, and full human adulthood this whole world over.

And no one has officially declared those texts wrong.

You bet the agenda of Eve—the recognition of women's real moral equality—is long unfinished.

Mary the Mother of God

Finally, let us look, as well, at the agenda of Mary the Mother of God: Mary, the unmarried mother; Mary, the political refugee; Mary, the homeless one; Mary, the disciple and prophet; Mary, the Third World woman; Mary, the one full of grace.

Mary simply took things into her own hands. The standards of the society and the norms of the synagogue meant absolutely nothing to her next to the deep, clear, commanding call of God in her life. Mary knew that what the law demanded she could not do, because what God asked she must do under any circumstances. Mary knew that the gift given to her by God had to be brought to fruit no matter who thought otherwise.

Mary's agenda was fullness of personhood. Mary was the liberated and the liberator. Mary changed God into the body and blood of Christ; she called for miracles and got them; she made the *Magnificat* the national anthem of women everywhere.

And yet, still, this very day, women are being married for dowry and sold for bride price and denied an inheritance and deprived of money, and work and land and housing and food-stamps and child care services and health and welfare benefits. And they are sacrificed daily in one way and another for the political, military, economic, and theological sins of men. And what are we doing about it?

The 1990s

Oh, indeed, the agenda of the 1990s is far too clear because it is far too long in being satisfied. The women raised up before us by God: Ruth and Naomi, and Moses' mother and Pharoah's daughter and Esther and the Samaritan woman and Mary of Bethany and Mary Magdalen and Eve, the mother of the human race, and Mary, the Mother of God, have spoken to every century about the needs and rights and burdens of being woman. Over and over they call to us about the feminization of poverty, the destructiveness of the theology of domination, the destructive lack of participation in the power that rules them; the need for affirmation of the feminine; full inclusion in ministry; the recognition of basic moral equality and fullness of female personhood. And what the church teaches and models about women's nature, place, and role gives credibility or contradiction to these realities.

But in this generation, too, though we may have awareness, we definitely do not have equality. In their lives is still our life. As long as we live, they live. With a Gospel call.

The question of the 90s is creation. The agenda for the 90s is to claim it fully. Everywhere.

But to do that as church we must have a new theology of family and a new kind of Cana conferences where the concepts of mutuality and parenting bring truth to old, unfit, one-sided notions of obedience and mothering. We must write and research and question and question the limited states of women's lives until the questions are heard and the answers make both good sense and good church.

We must give the lie to the lies. We must press for a resolution of the tension between the definition of church and the practice of clericalism. We must be about the retelling of Scripture in ways that give light to the dignity and the dreams and the gifts of women there and everywhere. We must link and bond together to affirm and promote the hopes and the needs and the rights of women who, regardless of how comfortable you and I may see our own individual lives, are as a class still degraded, rejected, ignored, used, exploited, deluded, homeless, and poor.

Most of all, we must not let ourselves be divided from one another in our struggle for women everywhere. We must, if no one else will, hear the voices of women that sound different than our own and care about hurts unlike our own until all women's concerns are seen as human concerns.

We must reassess the meaning of the incarnation and its implications for ministry. We must as church bring ourselves to choose between sacraments and maleness. We must see the links between militarization and the domination and deprivation of women and their children around the entire globe. We must realize that women of color are doubly burdened and do everything possible to end our own national policies of economic deprivation and social irresponsibility which contribute to that.

And, finally, we must, if we cannot change them, change ourselves, which is to say that we must, after all this time, wait no longer: to refuse abuse, and refuse victimization, and refuse trivialization, and refuse the invisibility that invades every institution in society, even the language of the church. And we must find non-violent ways to do so.

We must begin to target our donations for women's projects; we must make public our discontent and disapproval of the absence of women from important state and church affairs; we must swamp the chanceries and congresses and corporations of the world with petitions for change.

And finally in the face of opposition we must not give up. We must develop the virtue of tenacity. We must develop strong organizations of women. We must support the ones that already exist, weary after years of effort in our behalf. We must educate the next generation to understand why what is, is. And we must take as our lifelong truth: "If not for us, then because of us." We must question and claim and care enough to go on when going on seems fruitless. And most of all, we must not be silent. We must speak up and speak to and speak on until sexism is seen for the sin it is and repented.

That is the agenda for them as church and for us as church, all together and alone.

It is not that much has not already been said on women. It is simply that it is not possible to have a conscience and say nothing. When Jesus was crucified, many "followed at a distance," Scripture records, but they are not the ones we remember, nor are they the ones we emulate, nor are they the ones who stand for the best in the church. It was two women and one non-violent male who went all the way to the foot of the cross professing truth publicly.

Well, once again, we need women of courage and men of conscience to bring the tenor of truth to a time when turning back is impossible and turning to is unclear.

And is there any hope at all? Well, only this perhaps, but good enough for me: Remember, on the hard days, that when the church of Jerusalem debated the legitimacy of accepting gentiles into Jewish Christianity, the struggle was bitter. Jesus had never done it, they argued. Judaism was for the Jews, they argued. But Peter proclaimed then: "If God was giving them the same gift we were given, who was I to interfere?" And Gamaliel argued when the Jews resisted new revelation: "Let these people alone. If their purpose or activity is human in its origins, it will destroy itself. If, on the other hand, it comes from God, you will not be able to destroy them without fighting God." (Acts, 5:38) In both instances, the men of the church were converted from smothering the Spirit of God. My hope is that the men of the church can be converted again.

But most of all my hope lies in the sign of a woman whose life was also finally unbent.

The Scripture reads: "On a Sabbath Day Jesus was teaching in one of the synagogues. There was a woman there who for eighteen years had been possessed by a spirit which drained her strength. She was badly stooped, quite incapable of standing erect. And when Jesus saw her, he called her to him and said, 'Woman, you are free of your infirmity.' And he laid his hand upon her and immediately she stood up straight and began thanking God." (Jn 13:10)

Indeed there is great hope. All we need in this next decade are the prophetic insights of Peter and Gamaliel, the faith of the afflicted woman, the memory of Jesus and the courage of the powerless who went protesting publicly to the foot of the cross.

"To be born a woman," the holy one said, "is not destiny. To be born a woman is fate. Destiny is what you make of it."

"There is no cure," the Africans say, "that does not cost." The cure the church needs now may well cost many of us, but that will be little enough price to pay for a goal so great, the church—full, equal, and undivided.

This time it is you whom the next generation will thank or not for both the conscience and the courage it will take to unbend their stooped lives.

13

Challenge for the Future

Remi J. De Roo

IT IS GOOD TO BE HERE. I BELIEVE THAT WHEN SO MANY FAITHFUL members of the church gather in love, despite the difficulties, the pain, the temptations to discouragement, Jesus keeps his promise to be in our midst. With you, I trust in the power of Christ's Spirit who always sustains our hope.

You are to be commended for the particular service to the church that you render here. Your lucidity and courage illustrate your dedication to the realm of God. The church is alive and growing, and the gifts which you bring to that dynamic process are reasons for hope and celebration.

In preparation for this event, I worked on a pile of notes. I ended up with a written text, which I've given to the media. It is really far too long, so I am not going to read it to you. Rather, I will just relate to some key thoughts, ideas that run through my mind as I live this experience. And I do it by trying to cover five points.

First of all, some elements drawn from experience; then some initial questions that arise out of this experience; some observations about social analysis; a review of some of the shifting paradigms in understanding what is happening both in church and in society. Finally, I will address myself to the challenges and possibilities for the future.

A SURVEY OF EXPERIENCE

Personal Experience

Going back to my youth, I remember how I experienced, like other people, the paradigms, models, metaphors, images of symbols, if you will, the various cultural artifacts through which we perceive reality. They condition very much our perception of what is happening, even our self-understanding. In my youth, most Catholics, who tended to look inwards, perceived the church as an unconquerable fortress, defying the forces of evil; or as Peter's barque, weathering the stormy sea, a haven of refuge; as the perfect society, calling for obedience and submission. Many of us felt like members of the chosen flock, as sheep guided by an omniscient shepherd who provided directions to heaven in black and white.

For those who looked outwards, at the world, church and society were generally perceived as being opposed to each other. It was a virtue to avoid "contact" with the world. Meanwhile, the world was moving. Society as a whole had come to accept unlimited scientific progress as unquestioned dogma. There was no problem we couldn't solve. Predictions which we see today were based on limited and reductionist historical pre-determinism, were in those days anticipated as a fact. Whatever was predicted, would happen. We fought wars to "end all wars." We trusted that democracy would solve all economic and political ills, (and we expected women to know where they belonged).

I know that is too brief a review, too simplistic, but it reminds me how conditioned I was by these paradigms or symbols. My point is that our historical conditioning in those days remained unquestioned. It was only gradually that it dawned on us that this situation had to change.

I remember my own awakening to the exciting early days of Catholic Action when I was out of the blue appointed a Diocesan Director and asked to work with people who knew a lot more about Catholic Action than I did. I heard the repeated calls for recognition of lay responsibility. I thrilled to the first stirrings of liturgical reform; to the efforts of lay leaders to reconcile their full temporal engagement in the world with fidelity to Catholic doctrine and practice, efforts which were often instinctively questioned.

To me Vatican II was the major turning point, not only for this century, but for my own life. I bless God who called me to serve as a bishop during that first Council session. It gave me an unusual opportunity to see life in a whole new dimension. Overnight, wave after wave of new perceptions swept over us as we argued and debated in the Vatican Council chamber at St. Peter's.

The fortress church on the mountain assumed the shape of a pilgrim people struggling in the valley. Other Christian churches were recognized as communities of salvation, (believe it or not!). They were even allowed the status of "sister churches." The ecumenical movement shifted from official rejection to pontifical promotion, through the recognition that indeed there was a hierarchy of truths. The Council encouraged everyone to make distinctions between essential doctrine and less central teachings.

Collegiality was an idea barely known on the eve of Vatican II. I remember Father Congar telling us it had first been used in an exclusive circle by a theologian in 1937. Almost immediately it became a word on everybody's lips, a central theme in theology. It was one of those experiences where I could say I visibly lived the movement of the Spirit.

A hierarchology, which is what we really had in those days, centered on church structures and canon law, gave way to a renewed ecclesiology based on baptism, a universal call to holiness and ministry, and that profoundly dynamic notion of the church immersed in the stuff of history as sacrament to the world.

The Council recognized the competency of the laity and invited them to speak up. I believe it was Joan Chittister who reminded us that Pope John XXIII in his encyclical, *Pacem in terris,* said that those who have rights have the corresponding responsibility to claim them.

A new definition of marriage as community of life and love, beyond the previous formal contract, enhanced the partnership of women in the family. However, there were weaknesses too. The Council, of necessity (coming so late after so much movement), had its ambivalence and its compromises.

In retrospect, I think it is only fair to say that little progress was achieved in the treatment of women as persons. The sparse references to women in Vatican Council texts reflect an attitude that still considers the male gender as normative.

Vatican Council determined to be and defined itself as resolutely pastoral. That doesn't mean it wasn't doctrinal, but I learned that maybe the pastoral dimension is the most effective doctrine. I experienced more deeply there how doctrine means more than intellectual knowledge. Jesus taught with his entire person. His actions preceded his words and often didn't need any words. His death and his resurrection were his ultimate redeeming gestures initiating the visible reign of God.

It was thus that I came to realize more fully what had always been accepted in theory and pastoral practice, namely, that the first mission of a pastoral leader in the church is to model the example of Jesus. Christ was a person for others, one who came to serve by revealing to people their inalienable dignity and capacity to love.

Parallel to Vatican II we had the social phenomenon of the "angry 60s": civil protests making headlines; university students demonstrating; growing anxiety about the atom bomb; an awakening to the implications of the many social diseases resulting from our ambition to manipulate nature, to dominate, and to destroy.

Where we once hailed the modern revolution and progress born of the Renaissance, the Enlightenment, and the industrial era, we are increasingly conscious how conditioned our western world has been by the ideologies that underlie the utopia of endless progress through science.

There are two groups of people who helped me to see how our attitudes must change dramatically if our fragile planet is to survive. They were the futurists and the feminists scholars. The feminists particularly awakened me to my personal need to develop those qualities which would balance the left brain as we call it, the characteristics commonly associated with male attitudes. That experience began in my own diocese, on the Pacific west coast, a diocese long blessed with the ministries of gifted women. They have greatly enriched the life of our local diocesan church.

Diocesan Experience

Thanks to the Council the contribution of women to the life of the Church on Vancouver Island increased substantially. By 1967 we formed a diocesan Pastoral Council where women carry equal responsibilities with men. Shortly after, a Bishop's Council or diocesan governing body, which meets regularly, with equal representation of women. Parish Councils became commonplace, frequently and very effectively chaired by women. The principle, at least, of equal participation by women in all non-ordained ministries was promulgated, readily accepted by most parishes, even if not always fully applied.

With the collaboration of women from many parishes, a survey was conducted on Vancouver Island, in 1975. It led to the formation of a permanent Women's Committee, which became more formalized as a diocesan Women's Commission in 1984.

While much remains to be done, I consider myself privileged to have been able, in this manner, to work closely with an outstanding group of women in many areas. These contacts have helped me immeasurably in developing a sensitivity towards women's issues that I would never have known otherwise. And while I realize that I will continue to need assistance, I am very grateful for the experience I have had already.

The Canadian Scene

Let me shift now to the broader scene across Canada. Our central office in Ottawa published a calendar detailing the events and the initiatives at the national level undertaken over the past years, with respect to the role of women in society and in the church. I will not burden you with the forty items spanning fifteen years, but just mention a few highlights from those years that begin in 1971.

We have a national Catholic Women's League in Canada. Women from the Edmonton (Alberta) Archdiocese had sent a brief to Ottawa questioning the Canadian bishops. There ensued a colloquium as we call it, a dialogue, at our April plenary assembly. From this resulted a series of recommendations which cover a range of ideas, as follows: equal rights for women; removal of discriminatory barriers from canon law or custom; women to participate in church bodies dealing with matter of common concern; women to be ordained; clergy to be taught to respect the inherent dignity of women; clinics to counsel women on responsible family planning; solidarity with women working outside the home; and special attention to working women suffering injustice through economic pressures.

As a result, the plenary assembly, the following September

accepted a proposal to ask the pope for a mixed commission to study the question of ministries for women in the church. Cardinal George Flahiff intervened at the October, 1971 Bishops' Synod, outlining the proposal and urging that women share responsibility and participate more fully in the community of society and of the church. A movement had started in Canada, and it has not ceased to grow.

In March of 1972, the Administrative Board, now known as the Permanent Council of the CCCB, established a committee to prepare a working document for studies at the diocesan and regional levels and to propose follow up plans for the 1971 Synod on justice. And these reports came back in both languages, English and French (since we always work bilingually) in May of 1974.

Then from Canada a request was sent to Rome in 1975 to extend non-ordained ministries to women. In February 1976, Bishop Emmett Carter, now Cardinal Archbishop of Toronto, in the name of the Administrative Board, requested that the Vatican initiate a theological examination of the question of women's ordination. I am very proud that Canada took the leadership in that regard.

But I can't give you all the details . . . just to say that in 1978, we had a major pastoral project in promoting study on women in society and church ministry. In 1980 Bishop Robert Lebel spoke again at the Synod, calling for a positive recognition of the modern feminist movement, out of fidelity to the word of God.

In 1982 an ad hoc committee on women in the church was set up. It contacted thousands of women across the country. Archbishop, now Cardinal, Albert Vachon of Quebec attended the 1983 Synod. He spoke about male and female reconciliation in the church. He called for "recognition of the ravages of sexism and of male appropriation of church institutions."

It was in October of 1984 that the ad hoc committee reported to a plenary assembly of Canada's bishops. Twelve recommendations were advanced and discussed. They covered a whole range of issues: application of the principles of social justice to women involved in the church or suffering injustice in society; inclusive language; official pastoral mandates for women; revision of educational materials to promote equal partnership;

scholarships for lay women in training; adequate representation on committees; women sharing in the formation of priests; a study of the ministries of women; better representation on the National Pastoral Team; regular local gatherings to promote dialogue, with theological and pastoral reflection; a schedule for an on-going review, with full participation by women in the process itself.

Recommendation #9 as we now refer to it, achieved a certain notoriety. It proposed for circulation a kit of discussion starters and background materials. Its purpose was to promote understanding of the situation of women in the church and society with a view to appropriate remedial action.

All these recommendations were accepted by the Plenary Assembly with only minor modifications, most of them proposed by the women themselves in discussion. The kit was later published and all the materials were set to the CCCB commissions, to all dioceses and relevant Catholic organizations across the country.

Increasing exchanges between women and bishops in the diocesan, regional and national spheres had prepared the Catholic population for the recommendations. They were generally well received and acted upon. Widespread use has been made of the kit, published in an attractive green folder, which earned it the name of "The Green Kit". (It sold over fifteen thousand copies which in Canada is considered quite a success.)

The Kit invited people to dialogue about the life experiences of women in twelve sessions covering specific themes. The titles reveal the main thrust of these themes: signs of the times; the place of women in the church; their image; the church and sexuality; liturgical language; co-responsibility; equality; speaking out in the church; ministries; leadership; the question of identity (who am I? who are we?) and so on. (The Kit is available from the national office, 90 Parent Ave., Ottawa, K1N 7B1).

As a result, a national network is gradually developing. Over half the dioceses already have contact; persons. Discussion is widespread, and the general reaction has been overwhelmingly positive.

However, opposition to these initiatives had developed in some areas. A group of women alarmed by the new trends, especially the Green Kit, are promoting what they call a "statement of affirmation" and a counterkit which we now call the "Blue Kit".

Through all this we recognize the pain of many responsible women, of leaders of various spheres, caught between the clashes of these different visions of women's place in church and society.

It shows once again the problems encountered by people with varying perceptions of reality, different paradigms, different models of the church. Real tensions exist, not only with vertical authority structures, but also between men and women with conflicting visions.

This experience of dialogue in 1984 was re-lived again with a broader lay representation, men and women and clergy, at our October Plenary Assembly in Ottawa. All those who participated were free to name their experience, in small discussion groups and then in general reporting sessions. And this process is being repeatedly validated at the national as well as the local spheres.

I would be naive, however, not to see that serious discrepancies still exist in Canada between published statements and the reality most women experience. I know many women in my own diocese are still waiting for effective proof of co-equal participation. But I do want to celebrate the progress already achieved, while humbly admitting the need for on-going conversion.

INITIAL QUESTIONS

By reading feminist literature and sharing in these experiences, I come to ask myself a number of questions. For instance, how decisive were the attitudes of Jesus towards women in shaping the evolving ministry of the early church? Why the apparent reversal of these attitudes through the centuries? Did Vatican II really facilitate the promotion of women, or did it set us back? Will feminist theology and activism succeed in their goals? Is feminism in other words doomed to die? Must we ask that Gamalielian question that Joan Chittister, I believe, referred to: "is it of God?" Will feminist ideas be co-opted by increasingly sophisticated patterns of male dominance? And finally, can we achieve mutually in ministry without dividing the church? Certainly, serious issues that we have to face. And in doing so, I want to stress once again the importance of what you have already heard spoken about: social analysis.

THE ROLE OF SOCIAL ANALYSIS

To me, social analysis is central. Because, conditioned as I am by my own environment, I know how difficult it is for me to be critical of my own experience, of my own culture. So I need a different perspective, a critical set of criteria with which to assess the strengths and weaknesses of the environment, the forces that shaped my own identity. Looking critically at my own identity can be threatening. And that is why I have learned to value social analysis in its multiple forms, as it becomes increasingly sophisticated. It helps me to situate my faith in a realistic context. It deepens my understanding of what the incarnation means in the here and now. Unless my gaze of faith penetrates deeply into the substance on which rests my hope, today's enthusiasm can easily give way to disillusionment tomorrow.

I recognize that you are already doing a lot of social analysis. I just want to stress the importance of continuing to deepen this probing into the heart of the issues, the causes, not just the consequences or circumstances, because the signs of the times can be manipulated by other than the forces of good. So asking the right questions is crucial. We have to discern realistically what are the forces at work, the relationships, the orientations they impose almost unconsciously on our society. What relationships of power are interacting here? Are they inspired by Gospel values. Do they scheme to ultimately solidify existing structures, by co-opting our efforts? And how can we effectively apply the "preferential option for the cause of the poor" that we so readily talk about. How can we facilitate the gestation of necessary grassroot networks, through the long process of birthing and growing; how develop strategies for effective structural transformation?

But I mustn't go on. I want to speak briefly of the influence of women scholars in my life. Earlier I referred to them, but I want to recognize not only the writers, but other disciplines as well: art, poetry, dance. These also call people to liberate their effective and creative potential. And church leaders could benefit immensely from more trusting familiarity with these creative endeavors.

Let me mention some, even briefly: Elizabeth Schüssler Fiorenza, with her feminist theological reconstruction of Christian origins; her challenges to the value-laden assumptions of our contemporary scientific paradigms; her hermeneutics of suspicion; her call for a feminist re-appropriate of the power of naming; her outlining of the parameters for a meta-critique; her proposals for a transformation of a patriarchal church into a discipleship community of equals.

All such endeavours represent for me a highpoint in contemporary thought. I could say the same about others like Rosemary Radford Reuther, Joan Chittister, Monica Hellwig, (eventually recognized as president of CTSA); and the many other talented people, Mary Collins, Rita Burns, Lucy Vasquez who thrilled us last night. What a wealth of talent! But I mustn't burden this talk with multiple quotations, I just want to recognize my indebtedness to all these feminists who have helped me to search beyond the Enlightenment and the Renaissance, to find the contemporary problems and discover their roots in the development of the cultural mind-sets, the socio-economic relationships of primitive patriarchal patterns and dualistic paradigms. The dehumanization caused by misguided technology, the dichotomy between public and private ethics, can in some part be traced back to earlier dualistic or reductionist concepts of reality and of the image of God. And I understand better now, thanks to them, how the conditions brought about by post-industrial trends have awakened oppressed womanhood to basic problems. For women now perceive their enduring cultural and political marginalization as having been further aggravated by our greater economic marginalization.

SHIFTING PARADIGMS

I know this is all familiar to you. So let me just refer briefly to some of the shifting paradigms that give us a renewed vision, both of the world externally as a delicately balanced, interdependent system, and the church internally, where the members are achieving a renewed and growing sense of human dignity and responsibility, and claiming their personhood based on the sacrament of baptism and confirmation.

Many lay people have taken to heart the call to spiritual adulthood and the inward search for the experience of God's Spirit. Thus I come with them to appreciate better the meaning of the incarnation and the reflect on the profound interplay of relationships between faith and culture. I have noted how Pope John Paul II keeps reminding us (it runs like a theme through many of his speeches, it animated his talks in Canada) telling us that while culture is not the norm of faith, faith must become culture, if it is to be properly grasped, clearly proclaimed and effectively lived.

A Trinitarian Paradigm

Here are some of these new paradigms that I feel have special significance today. First and foremost, a renewed Trinitarian paradigm, because our first image, our first example or model, concerns our idea of God. How do we image this mystery, which is so profound, which influences how we perceive reality? And that's where the Trinitarian paradigm is to me absolutely foundational to a renewed church. Our Catholic tradition reveals to us, at least in theory, a Trinitarian model of total equality and unlimited mutuality. God is one, and at the same time, trinitarian, in the sense of relational, reaching out to us in Christ, and simultaneously drawing us into communion and unity in the Spirit of love.

Pneumatology: Role of the Holy Spirit

My second paradigm is pneumatology, the role of the Holy Spirit, slowly rediscovered at Vatican II, thanks to the assistance of our brothers bishops from the Eastern Churches. This renewed pneumatology has already enriched our ecclesiology and our models of church. It has completely transformed our liturgy (consider the new prefaces). We appreciate better the creative role of the Holy Spirit who, constantly causes new ministries to emerge from the fountain of Divine Life.

Male Images

The other paradigm concerns male images. We need to reflect further on the problem that arises when God is imaged primarily or even exclusively as a male. This is familiar to you. (I have to move on because my watch keeps speeding up as I talk!) Let us remind ourselves of the series of feminine images that we find in Scripture: The Spirit brooding, hovering over creation; motherhood; the divine energies of "sophia"—wisdom and love; spiritual life imaged as an intimacy between two lovers; the term *perichoresis*, meaning to dance around another, though not uniquely feminine, an image which has been used to describe the inner trinitarian relationships in God, the two natures in Christ, grace, the reception of the eucharist.

Rosemary Radford Reuther speaks of the primordial power of the mother symbol as the ground of being. All of this could help to redress the balance which is now weighed down on the side of patriarchy.

The Model of Jesus Paradigm

We would have to speak of the model of Jesus as another very important paradigm. Time does not allow us to go into detail. But you know full well how Jesus showed a total balance, in his recognition of the equality of women and men. And these Gospel attitudes of Jesus in some ways could be applied as the ultimate paradigm. Why was this paradigm shift that Jesus so obviously wanted, not fully realized? Could it be that the cultural limitations of his disciples inhibited their capacity to transmit these attitudes integrally to the early Christian community? Could it be that their audiences were not prepared to receive or to understand them, given their formation? The explosive power of the Good News that Jesus brought to oppressed women transcended all cultural categories. Was the cultural myopia of male church leaders one reason why the anti-feminist attitudes of pagan society succeeded in modifying this thrust towards total equality and mutuality? Difficult questions! But we must consider them, not evade them.

A Paradigm Shift in Tradition: Feminine Models

We could go on to the feminine models. Here is another paradigm shift in position which I rejoice in: all the models the

Christian Scriptures give us. I am sure you read about them. Briefly, let me recall Elizabeth, inspired to recognize the divine motherhood of her cousin: Mary, shown pondering in her heart; blessed in her physical motherhood, Mary is declared by Jesus even more blessed in her faith.

At Bethany, Martha and Mary, examples of equality and discipleship, both specially loved by Jesus, learning that contemplative listening is essential; Mary Magdalene, called by name into discipleship; the bent woman of Luke, telling us all that we need to stand erect before God as redeemed people, touched by the healing power of Jesus; Mary of Magdala, and the other women, who were the initial "apostles to the apostles," in those early hours after the resurrection. And who but the women stayed faithful to Jesus all the way to Calvary? I could go on, through Matthew and John, the woman from Samaria, challenging Jesus in discussion at the well, receiving from him the revelation of the waters of life, becoming an effective apostle to her own people. I could recall St. Paul, but time does not allow more than a passing mention: Pheobe, Priscilla, Junia, the other female leaders in the front ranks, presidents of the numerous house churches. Sad indeed that so many feminine models have been lost in history, obscured, distorted, even used negatively! I recognize those scholars who enrich our tradition by bringing back this rich dimension of our history.

Societal Influences

There are many influences in society that give us problems. Maybe one of the most profound, (I referred to it earlier,) I would call reductionism. It is a peculiarly western trait—the tendency to see things as "either/or" instead of accepting "both/and," recognizing that frequently what appears to be contradictory can simply be different dimensions of mystery. Reductionism has played havoc in the field of doctrine, emphasizing secondary teachings while ignoring the deeper and richer doctrines of the church. It has devasted our understanding of the human person, and of gender relationships. It has led to gender being considered as constitutive of the person, and all the resulting deviations that have occurred in relations between male and female can serve as examples. But I should move on, as time is passing. I do want to commend on how I see the future. What are the challenges we face?

FUTURE CHALLENGES

First, let's begin by effectively recognizing the gains that have been made. From my limited experience, in the last twenty years, more has been achieved than in any number of centuries—maybe way back to the fourth century. I am convinced that we have reached a turning point in history. As was said yesterday, things will never be the same again. Traditional church teaching reminds us that the permanent value of revealed doctrine or discipline is ascertained through its universal reception by the total body of the church. And Vatican II (you may recall) raised this issue of reception (we could call it the Cardinal Newman issue) to the fore of our preoccupations. We've only begun to cope with that issue. What happens when a substantial body of the church says: "We no longer perceive certain things as taken for granted"?

Women in Ministry

Unless we are prepared to dismiss out of hand the imposing body of evidence concerning the cultural conditioning of early church ministry and its developing forms, do we not have a reason for a reconsideration of our traditions with respect to women in ministry? If the apparent reversal of the attitudes of Jesus can be shown to have resulted from anti-feminist societal pressures, then the question follows: could not the current tradition of exclusion eventually prove not to be unchangeable?

The Galatians 3:28 issue also has to be faced. What some call a baptismal creed of total equality between women and men, as well as Paul's readiness to confront Peter when he perceived Christ's central teaching and his supreme command of love as being transgressed, must give all of us pause for reflection.

And another question arises: Is the church called today to greater fidelity as it seeks to fulfill its mission as representative of liberated humanity?

The Question of Ordination

And so we reach the question of ordination. With respect to orders, are the charisms of women who claim that their attraction to ordination is a call of the Spirit, not worthy of testing by the entire believing church? The issue of women's ordination, as I see it, has become a symbol. It is perceived by many as a symbol of the willingness or the refusal of the church to come to grips with the challenges presented by contemporary society. It also has serious implications for continuing ecumenical dialogue. An Episcopalian bishop (in Canada we call them Anglican), John Baycroft, spoke to the CCCB Assembly in Ottawa. He is on the ARCIC II (Anglican Roman Catholic International Commission) which has to pursue the unresolved issues of ministry. He spoke to the Canadian Bishops about "the other side of the ecumenical coin." It is this: ARCIC II will have at its center the question of a possible unity of mission between Christian churches expressing a diversity of ministry. And now, the question arises from the Anglican side. Will such diversity allow the sharing of koinonia, of communion, among churches who interpret the mind of Christ differently with respect to the ordination of women? Evading that ecumenical problem would cause irreparable harm to the credibility of the Catholic Church. There may be no meaningful solution within the present clerical framework of ministry, but the effort to resolve these issues must be made. More is involved than just the matter of a desire for orders expressed by individual women. At stake here is a re-examination of our anthropology (are there two ways to be human?); of how we continue to effectively image God; how we understand our membership in the Body of Christ; how we define our ecclesiology; how we envisage church mission and ministry. This inescapable agenda will require earnest prayer, for discernment and for the courage to act. The courage to act, this is the ultimate question!

Now, although the issue of ordination looms high on the present horizon, there is a deeper issue and a broader question at stake, as I see it. Because our entire understanding of ecclesiology (how we identify ourselves as church) rests on, and should be permeated by, a thorough-going pneumatology (doctrine of the Spirit that I referred to earlier) (we are indebted to the Eastern Churches for its recovery). If the gifts bring to visibility the Holy Spirit and its operation in the church as well as in the community (the presence of the Spirit), then we have to ask ourselves the question: Who is the real minister in every one of the churches' ministries? Perhaps St. Augustine points the way when he deals with the ministry of the ordained priest as one of "instrumental causality": in other words, the one who unites matter and form (brings them together and allows the power of the Spirit to act). It is both a humbling and kenotic experience to admit that we, no matter what our ministry, are only instruments of the Spirit. So it is the Spirit who operates through all of us, no matter what ministry we perform.

Ministry to the World

I want to go on, to broaden once again our horizons, to get us out of this "reductionistic cage" that we put ourselves into, in the western world and in the church. Another broad question is the whole issue of the lay apostolate, of lay activity. Ministry is too frequently equated with internal church structures, with institutions controlled in some way by church authorities. We must keep reminding ourselves that the church is servant to the realm of God. The Church is not an end in itself.

As a Council Father with twenty-four years of experience as a bishop, I see that many insights of Vatican II are in real danger of being lost. We could have a new clericalization of the laity (through primarily internal ministry), and forget what we are here for in the first place: "Go, proclaim the Good News to all the world," to the entire cosmos.

Ecclesiology Renewed

And so we return to the question of ecclesiology. It lies at the heart of everything we do here. We are led to the deeper issue of the re-appropriation by all the baptized, (and this is so important I have to repeat it) the re-appropriation by all the baptized, of their responsibility for the proclamation of God's word, for sacramental celebration, for global, cosmic ministry and ultimately for political activity as well.

I remember intervening at the Vatican Council, at the request of the renowned Dominican scholar, Father Chenu, to stress once again that the creative and redemptive purpose of God are one. God did not create the world and then later recognize a mistake to be corrected by the redemption. There is one loving purpose of creation and redemption, and the mission of all the faithful as baptized and confirmed participants in Christ's global eucharist is one.

Time does not allow me to touch on liberation theology. I am sure you've heard a lot about it. I just want to say we have much to learn from liberation theology, properly understood and applied to North America in the sense that we don't have to import outside models to recognize that the Holy Spirit is also at work liberating North America.

Building Bridges

What remains to be done? In a certain way we can say that the movement has only begun. And so I invite you, as you have done here, to continue reaching out to people, men and women alike. Put your best loving energies into awakening those who are unaware of the cultural and social conditioning which inhibits their growth to fuller humanity. Continue to form popular groups, to develop networks with other grassroots initiatives, to promote creative dialogue, communion, with the goal of ecclesial and societal wholeness. And of necessity we should come to consider issues of social justice which we cannot detail here. But I think I've given you the underlying approach. Your common concern will inevitably impel you to involvement in the major social issues of today, and political action for their resolution: the rampant pauperization of women; our reductionistic, limited approach to the idea of work (it has to be redefined); our inadequate labour system, of which women are the first victims (primary producers and victims of our food systems); the inappropriate answers given to issues of social welfare. We can no longer hesitate in identifying these basic structural distortions of our society as a condition of social sin. This will not happen without dialogue with the clergy. Parish priests' attitudes can have a decisive impact on women, at times of crises or in the face of serious options. I know this is one of the most painful things I experience as a bishop. Priests, like many other men, are threatened by feminism, particularly in the realm of ministry as it relates to their identity, their authority, and their perceived roles.

Full equality in the church will not be achieved without enduring the mystery of the cross. The kenosis required will test our compassion, our ability to maintain Christian love in the midst of suffering.

CONCLUSION

And I conclude. We are pilgrims on a historic mission, the end of which is not yet in sight. But in many ways, my experience has been that the journey itself is already its own reward, as is my presence here with you. I feel I have grown immensely through the challenge you offered me to present this closing talk.

The ultimate challenge is to actualize anew the Gospel of Jesus Christ in a post-industrial society, where one of the surprises of the Holy Spirit may well be to present us with a culture, a soil secretly thirsting for transcendence. Society may prove to be open in new ways to inspiration, by the example of how Jesus himself related to women. And then we might see once again demonstrated the enduring value of the Gospel beyond all cultural mutations. We must never forget the resurrection was the bursting forth of hope out of powerlessness. As we labor to bring forth an agenda for mutuality in the new millennium the Risen Christ will manifest himself to us once again as he appeared to the women disciples: "Do not fear, it is I."

The experience of presenting this talk brings to my mind T.S. Eliot's *Four Quartets*. You will remember where in "Little Gidding" he muses: "To make an end, is to make a beginning. The end is where we start." And further on, "We shall not cease from exploration. And the end of all our exploring will be to arrive where we started and know the place for the first time."

My heart tells me that in reviewing these issues affecting women in the church today and in the future, I too have experienced familiar terrain for the first time. Thank you for accompanying me as I explored the hope-filled reality of our mutual interdependence. Scripture reminds us that the tensions and struggles, the pain and travail announce the birthing of the Reign of God. They are as nothing compared to the resurrection which will crown our fidelity and our hope.

Contributors

Donald Senior, C.P., is Professor of New Testament at Catholic Theological Union in Chicago. He holds a doctoral degree in New Testament Studies from the University of Louvain and has published numerous books and articles on biblical topics.

Richard P. McBrien, priest of the Archdiocese of Hartford, Connecticut, is Professor of Theology and Chairman of the Department of Theology at the University of Notre Dame. He is the author of fourteen books, including *Catholicism, Caesar's Coin: Religion and Politics in America,* and *Ministry: A Theological-Pastoral Handbook.*

James Provost is the Executive Coordinator of the Canon Law Society of America, managing editor of *The Jurist,* and Associate Professor of Canon Law at The Catholic University of America. In the work, *The Code of Canon Law: A Text and Commentary,* he wrote the section on rights and obligations of all the Christian faithful.

Mary Collins, O.S.B., Associate Professor at The Catholic University of America and formerly president of the North American Academy of Liturgy, is co-director of *Concilium's* Advisory Committee on Feminist Theology. Her book *Worship: Renewal to Practice* was recently published by The Pastoral Press.

Mary Catherine Hilkert, O.P., is Assistant Professor of Systematic Theology at the Aquinas Institute of Theology in St. Louis and has been a visiting professor at both The Catholic University of America and Notre Dame University. She preaches regularly in Catholic and ecumenical circles. Her articles have appeared in *Spirituality Today, Worship, Thomist,* and *Theology Digest.*

Fran Ferder, F.S.P.A., currently co-directs a ministerial counseling and consultation service for the Archdiocese of Seattle. She has a Ph.D. in clinical psychology and a doctorate in ministry. Her most recent book is entitled *Words Made Flesh: A Biblical-Psychological Reflection on Human Communication.*

Kathleen Fischer and Thomas Hart are a married couple from Seattle. Kathleen has an M.S.W. with a specialty in aging; Tom has an M.S. in marriage and family therapy. Both have doctorates in theology. They have written several books, primarily related to marriage, their latest being *Christian Foundations: Faith in Our Time.*

Mary Milliagan, R.S.H.M., currently serves as Provost of Loyola Marymount University in Los Angeles. She holds a doctorate in theology from the Gregorian University in Rome. As superior general of her congregation from 1980 to 1985, she travelled extensively and was a member on the Executive Committee of the International Union of Superiors General.

Sandra M. Schneiders, I.H.M., is Associate Professor of New Testament Studies and Christian Spirituality at the Jesuit School of Theology and Graduate Theological Union in Berkeley, California. Dr. Schneider's most recent publications include *New Wineskins: Reimagining Religious Life Today* and *Women and the Word: The Gender of God in the New Testament and the Spirituality of Women.*

Rita Burns is Assistant Professor in the Department of Religious Studies at St. Mary's College in Notre Dame, Indiana. She holds a master's degree in Hebrew and Semitic Studies and a doctorate in Religious Studies with a specialization in Scripture. The paper contained in this volume rose out of her work with the Task Force on the Role of Women in the Archdiocese of Milwaukee during 1981 and 1982.

Madonna Kolbenschlag, H.M., formerly a senior fellow at the Woodstock Theological Center at Georgetown, is presently a visiting ecumenical fellow at the National Cathedral, Washington, D.C. She holds a doctorate in the Philosophy of Literature from the University of Notre Dame. Her best known book is *Kiss Sleeping Beauty Good-Bye*. She has written two more books which consider political issues and the Catholic Church: *Between God and Caesar* and *Authority, Community and Conflict*.

Joan Chittister, O.S.B., is the former president of the Leadership Conference of Women Religious and presently chairperson of the International Conference of Benedictine Women. She is the authoress of six books and more than thirty-five articles, as well as being a regular columnist for *The National Catholic Reporter*.

Remi J. De Roo is the bishop of the Diocese of Victoria, Canada. He is president of the Western Conference of Catholic Bishops in Canada. He is also the former chairperson of the Human Rights Commission of the Province of British Columbia and a founding member of the World Conference of Religions for Peace. His most recent book is *Cries of Victims—Voice of God*.